The Prince and the Infanta

The Prince and the Infanta

The Cultural Politics of the Spanish Match

Glyn Redworth

Yale University Press
New Haven and London

For information about this and other Yale University Press publications, please contact:
U.S. Office: sales.press@yale.edu   yalebooks.com
Europe Office: sales@yaleup.co.uk   www.yalebooks.co.uk

Set in Minion by Northern Phototypesetting Co. Ltd, Bolton
Printed in Great Britain at the University Press, Cambridge

Library of Congress Control Number: 2003113189

ISBN: 0-300-10198-8

A catalogue record for this book is available from the British Library

10 9 8 7 6 5 4 3 2 1

Published with the generous assistance of the Aurelius Trust

For the Countess Russell and Miss Joan Henderson

Contents

Illustrations

Colour plates

Illustrations in the text

Map

Figures

Chronology in Old Style

1603 Accession of James as king of England and Ireland

1604 Peace with Spain

1611 John Digby (later earl of Bristol) first sent to Madrid as ambassador

1612 Marriage of Elizabeth to the Protestant prince, the Elector Frederick

1613 Gondomar arrives in London

1617 Marriage agreement proposed, but dropped because of James's reluctance to grant liberty of conscience

1618 Outbreak of Thirty Years War

1619 Frederick accepts the Bohemian crown

1620 Gondomar returns to London and Catholic forces occupy Rhineland

1621 James calls a parliament, angrily dissolved in December amid anti-Spanish clamour

1622 *c.* May Charles promises to visit Spain incognito

      Sept.   Gondomar signals that Charles should undertake the journey; Porter subsequently sent to confirm situation in Madrid

      26 Oct. Olivares informed by Felipe IV that the marriage is not to take place without Charles's conversion or at least full liberty of conscience

      Nov.   Olivares considers alternative Habsburg marriage for Charles

1623 3 Jan. James and Charles agree to an autonomous Catholic household for the Infanta and promise not to persecute Catholics in their own homes

      17 Jan. Prince and Favourite set out for Spain

      7 Mar. Prince and Favourite reach Bristol's residence in Madrid

      2 Apr. The first 'easy' terms for dispensation dispatched from Rome

      8 Apr. Second 'harder' terms for dispensation dispatched from Rome, but pre-dated as if also 2 April

      31 May Charles first refused permission to return home

13 June James warned by Cottingham of the extent of Spanish demands

14 June James writes to advise acceptance if necessary for Charles's return

7 July   Charles announces his acceptance of Spanish demands

20 July James and Privy Council assent to Spanish demands

25 July Charles exchanges binding promises with King Felipe

28 July News reaches Madrid that James and Privy Council have given their assent on 20 July

5 Aug.   Copy of agreement of 20 July reaches Madrid

31 Aug. Charles leaves Madrid

2 Sept. Charles says goodbye to Felipe at the Escorial and leaves behind powers for proxy marriage

3 Sept. Charles reaches Segovia and revokes powers for the marriage

Oct.   Charles reaches England

1624 Feb. Parliament assembles. War declared on Spain

Acknowledgements

My debts to many people and institutions during the making of this book are enormous. I can mention but few by name. My paramount debt is to the trustees and staff of the Leverhulme Trust. Their generosity and kindness permitted me to complete this manuscript at the Consejo Superior de Investigaciones Científicas in Madrid. I am duly grateful to the University of Manchester for granting me the requisite leave. I am also obliged to the referees from Britain and Spain who supported this project. The readers for Yale University Press were enormously helpful, and one of them proved to be the most astute, as well as the most patient, of critics. Professors Joe Bergin, Brian Pullan and Frank O'Gorman at Manchester as well as Professor Ian Michael have also been helpful and no one more so than Professor Geoffrey Parker. To Regius professors past and present I owe a special obligation for help, advice and encouragement. Much good-humoured tolerance has been displayed by Drs José Manuel Prieto, Alfredo Alvar Ezquerra, Manolo Lucena, Brennan Pursell, and most especially Kathleen G. Cushing. How much I have learnt about the seventeenth century from Conrad Russell and Pauline Croft is impossible to put into words. A particular debt of gratitude for making me think about this topic is owed to Professor Tom Cogswell, and I am grateful to the Aurelius Trust for their generosity in subventing this book. Of the many archives I have worked in, I must single out the staff of the Royal Palace in Madrid and its director, Doña María Luisa Vidriero. At Simancas I am duly beholden to Doña Isabel Aguirre and her colleagues. My thanks must also go to the National Archive, the Foreign Ministry's archive, and the Royal Academy of History, all in Madrid. The Public Record Office in Kew was unfailingly efficient, as were the British Library, the National Library of Scotland, the Library of the Royal Society of Antiquaries, and above all the Biblioteca Nacional in Madrid. I was afforded every courtesy at the Haus-, Hof- und Staatsarchiv in Vienna and in the Oberösterreichisches Landesarchiv in Linz, as well as in the State Archive in Genoa. I am grateful to archivists in Rome, Venice and the National Library of Wales for their assistance, especially when they provided photocopies. Finally, my debt to the librarians of the University of Manchester, especially Deansgate, and all the staff who have worked in Duke Humphrey's and in the other readings rooms of the Bodleian Library, is immeasurable, as anyone who has worked in those places will appreciate.

G.R.
University of Manchester

1. Prologue

At eight o'clock on the night of 7 March 1623, two gentlemen from England arrived in the calle de las Infantas, one of Madrid's darker and narrower streets. Their names were John and Tom Smith. They demanded entrance to the House of the Seven Chimneys, home to the British embassy at the court of the Catholic King. The ambassador, John Digby, heard the commotion from his upper chamber. If he was perturbed, his feelings quickly turned to astonishment. Before him were not two inconsiderate strangers but Charles Stuart, Prince of Wales, and George Villiers, the preferred counsellor of King James I of Great Britain.

With the unsolicited arrival of Prince and Favourite in a foreign capital began one of the most bizarre episodes in British history. For the next half-year the Protestant heir to the Stuart thrones would fight tenaciously to bring home an infanta of Spain as his bride. Even if the visit soon descended into low farce, Charles's arrival was the unforeseen culmination of high-level negotiations stretching back over a decade. King James had long believed that marriages between the leading Protestant and Catholic royal families would help dissolve Europe's century-old division into warring Christian camps. More prosaically, it was hoped Charles's marriage to the Infanta might at the very least pave the way for an honourable solution to the dynastic conflict better known as the Thirty Years War.

The importance of this episode is not simply that it relates to a royal marriage. The visit invites us to take a rounded approach to early modern politicking. It shows how political history and social history are the warp and weft of what we might rightly call 'cultural politics'. Above and beyond the analysis of diplomatic dispatches, we need to explore how the partners in a stately dance could so woefully misinterpret each other's moves and signals. An example of this is Charles's very appearance in Madrid. He failed to appreciate that his Spanish hosts would necessarily interpret his arrival as evidence of a willingness to convert. Their misperception led to weeks of increasingly bitter religious probing by his hosts. The result was that even Spaniards well disposed to the marriage felt let down, while the Prince believed his religious integrity had been questioned.

The Spanish Match cleft political and religious opinion in Britain in two. No thinking person could avoid taking sides. Momentarily, it raised the hopes of Catholics in all of King James's dominions, with the court in particular witnessing a spate of high-profile and hazardous conversions during the Prince's stay at the Catholic Court in Madrid. To those of a more evangelical persuasion, the readiness of the House of Stuart to tolerate Catholicism raised the spectre of civil disobedience. It was a commonplace among opponents of the alliance to point out how an earlier Spanish Match – that of Felipe II and Mary – had led Protestants in England to rebel some seventy years before.

Whether we have in mind the wishful thinking of Catholics or the fatalism of Protestants, the Spanish Match of the seventeenth century is also a timely reminder of the degree of alienation between the House of Stuart and so many of the less tolerant Protestants among its subjects and counsellors. (In similar vein, Charles's visit helps expose the gulfs and tensions which were a part of political life at the Spanish court.) Most of all we need to remain alive to the fact that seventeenth-century politics was never far from being a portentous game. Princes and their sycophants vied for personal satisfaction as much for the aims of religion or party. In the case of Charles Stuart, he set out for Madrid little more than an adolescent, inexperienced in diplomacy, foreign travel and, it seems, affairs of the heart. Passion or rejection, harmony or conflict – these were sadly two sides of the same coin in the seventeenth century.

Conrad Russell once wrote of his relief at not having to explain why the Prince of Wales went to Madrid in 1623.[1] Thomas Cogswell said it was 'one of the most mysterious episodes in early modern English history'.[2] The issue's complexity partly explains why this is the first major study of the Spanish Match since the towering achievements of S.R. Gardiner in the second half of the nineteenth century.[3] Whereas Gardiner made outstanding use principally of the Habsburg state archive in Simancas, I have been fortunate in being able to consult archives that were effectively closed to him. Most notable amongst these is the Royal Library in Madrid, which houses the bulk of the private correspondence of Spain's ambassadors in London. Since Gardiner's time, the thousands of Spanish documents in the British Library have been magnificently catalogued and made accessible to scholars. I have also profited immeasurably from the work by German and Italian scholars on the archives of the Vatican. The rekindled interest in the history of the royal courts of early

1. Juan Pantoja de la Cruz's magnificent depiction of the Somerset House peace talks of 1604 is one of the earliest large-scale group portraits. The Spanish negotiators are seated in front of the tapestry, facing their English counterparts, with Sir Robert Cecil in the bottom right-hand corner. Pantoja never visited England and it is presumed that the painting was based on miniatures or engravings by another hand. The possibility of a Spanish Match was first mooted during these discussions.

2. *Felipe III of Spain*, by Bartolomé González, 1621.

3. *James I of England*, by John de Critz.

4. *Infanta Doña María of Austria*, by Diego Velázquez. This is the only known portrait of doña María of Austria. It was probably painted between 1628 and 1630.

5. *Charles as King*, by Gerrit van Honthurst, *c.* 1628.

6. *Felipe IV*, by Diego Velázquez, *c.* 1624.

modern Europe has enabled me to consider how Charles's room for manoeuvre was constrained by the rigidity and expectations of courtly life. The concomitant appreciation of the politics involved in the giving and receiving of works of art has proved to be of profound importance in divining the intentions of key players.

In addition to new material, this account has been written against the backdrop of revisionist ideas about the Stuart monarchy. Since the 1970s, the tensions between James and Charles and their parliaments have been played down while the political acumen of both princes has been stressed. Though James's stock as king of Great Britain has rightly risen, this account of the Spanish Match firmly sees the Stuarts' commitment to an alliance with the Habsburgs of Madrid as evidence of a desire – and presumably therefore of a need – to find a counterpoise to the belligerent Protestantism of many of their subjects. Charles's foolish miscalculation in presenting himself in person at the Spanish court casts doubt on his judgement rather earlier in his career than is normally the case. His willingness first to assent to public toleration of Catholicism and then to go back on his word almost in a trice is a harbinger of his readiness later in life to make promises he had little intention of keeping.

Most particularly, this study challenges the view that the fate of the Palatinate was uppermost in the minds of Charles and his father. This is highly contentious; as has been said, current revisionist thinking stresses the unity of purpose between the House of Stuart and the political nation. Correspondingly there has been a move towards arguing that the evangelical cause in the Thirty Years War dominated the first two 'British' Stuarts' thinking about the Spanish Match, further confirming the view that on this fundamental issue James and his son shared common ground with their more fervently Protestant subjects. This account places the emphasis differently. While accepting that James and Charles were profoundly concerned about the life in exile of Elizabeth of Bohemia and her children, and fully recognising their wish to see her husband and his family restored to their hereditary territories in the Rhineland, the evidence presented here indicates that the fate of James's son-in-law did not determine Charles's decision to travel to Madrid. For all their undoubted importance, events in the Rhineland played a surprisingly confused as well as secondary role when set against the House of Stuart's longstanding desire for a union with the Habsburgs of Madrid. The most that can be said is that both James and the Prince assumed that, once a marriage was concluded, Spain would immediately intensify its efforts to bring about an honourable peace. After all, Madrid had its own compelling reasons for wanting peace in Germany. The Spaniards rightly wished to concentrate all efforts on their war with the Dutch.

Despite the best attempts of Charles and Buckingham, not all contemporaries accepted their version of history. For instance, Sir Edward Hyde, sometime earl of Clarendon, knew most of the principal players and he never accepted that the Palatinate was the primary cause of the Prince's journey. Clarendon wrote that, since Charles and Buckingham believed that as far as the marriage was concerned 'all substantial matters were agreed upon already', the main aim of the mission was to hasten the Infanta's departure. He recalled that Charles's fear was that Spain's notoriously 'slow progress in all things of ceremony' might otherwise hold her back several months. As for the question of James's son-in-law, Clarendon dealt with this separately and almost as a potential bonus. He conceded that there was not full agreement despite the existence of 'a very friendly deliberation' between the two countries. Therefore it was only 'very probable' that the king of Spain might be so flattered by Charles's appearance that he would agree to whatever King James wanted in the Rhineland.[4] The marriage was a political necessity for the House of Stuart; peace in the Palatinate might have to bide its time.

An element of counterfactualism may help us think afresh about this point. For example, if there had been no occupation of the Palatine lands, and if the Spaniards really did want the marriage to take place, then Charles and Buckingham might still have made a journey to Madrid. There was a vibrant family tradition among the Scottish royal house of venturing abroad to bring back a wife. As for the Rhineland, there is no evidence that the situation there was significantly worse than it had been long before Charles received (as we shall see) what he thought was a signal to present himself in the Spanish capital; news of the fall of the English garrisons at Heidelberg and Mannheim had reached England many months before the Prince left for Spain. Moreover, if Spain had wanted the Infanta María to return home with Charles, then the affairs of Germany were no obstacle. Even without an agreement over the Rhineland, the Prince told his hosts in Madrid he was prepared to marry the Infanta there and then. It would have cost Spain nothing to issue a ringing declaration calling for a just peace between the Elector Palatine and the emperor, and even less for James to hail this as a breakthrough. Whether the House of Stuart would have been able or willing to keep its promises about religious toleration is quite a different matter.

By the time the Prince departed from the Spanish capital, both parties had entered into an apparently binding agreement concerning the date of a wedding by proxy. Despite this settlement, the intensifying mistrust between the two sides, and more than anything else Charles's refusal to convert to Catholicism, meant that the political will needed to realise the marriage was wholly lacking even as the ink was drying on the documents. It is wrong-headed to suggest that the match foundered at the eleventh hour because the king of Spain refused to do King James's bidding in the Rhineland. The earnest matter of the Palatinate had degenerated into not much more than a face-saving formula put about by Buckingham and Charles: it conveniently obscured the fact that Olivares had refused point-blank to hand over the Infanta, regardless of the fact that the Prince of Wales had turned up in person to claim his bride. The Prince and the Favourite were hiding behind the sorrows of Charles's sister, the Winter Queen. The intention was to keep concealed just how catastrophically they had miscalculated what Spain would demand in return for allowing the Prince to leave as a married man. Disgracefully perhaps, this is when the Palatinate finally came into its own for Charles and Buckingham. It became a twisted excuse for a war of vanity.

Turning to Spain, that country's revisionist history – to coin a phrase – has meant that we no longer need rely on studies which concentrate on the institutional or monolithic nature of Spanish government and its plentiful councils. Largely thanks to the work of British, American, and more recently Spanish, historians of the principal figures at court (with John Elliott's studies of Chief Minister Olivares being outstanding)[5] it is now possible to look at the Spanish Match as something more than a bilateral relation between two wholly united governments. There are divisions to be probed even within Spain's ruling elites. Gondomar's ill-judged rivalry with Olivares is one illustration of this. A more important example is just how much of the diplomatic manoeuvring Olivares kept hidden from the Council of State and perhaps from his young master, King Felipe IV.

Since the Spanish Match was of the utmost importance to the honour and renown of both families, it is not surprising that the most intimate evidence comes from the letters which went back and forth between the Prince and his entourage in Madrid and his father's court in and around London. I will call upon these letters as much as possible. It must be stressed at the outset, however, that as the vast majority of these letters were written in the joint names of Charles and Buckingham it is sadly not possible to determine if either of the two held the upper hand at any given moment. All that can be said is that, since the Prince may well have been the driving force behind the decision to travel to Madrid, there is no reason to suppose he was any less single-minded during his time there. For all our talk of cultural misunderstandings, strategic alliances or differing historiographies, these letters to and from Madrid remind us that the story of the Spanish Match revolves around a young man's infatuation, a father's indulgence, and a favourite's determination to carve a position for himself in a new reign.

Spain adopted the new Gregorian calendar in the sixteenth century. England persisted with the older Julian calendar. No solution is perfect. In the hope of allowing the intertwining of events in London and Madrid to be more easily followed I have converted *all* dates to English style (unless indicated otherwise, as with references to letters dated according to the new style, when the corresponding English date is also given). The year has been taken to begin on 1 January. Following the spirit of the age, I am less consistent in the use of names and titles. When referring to James, Charles and Buckingham as King, Prince and Favourite, I have capitalised these titles in order to distinguish them from their homologues in Madrid. With Spanish names, I have tried to avoid anglicisations. It is hoped this will help keep in mind an essential component of this account: that to understand the events surrounding the Spanish Match we must be attentive to the different cultural perceptions and misperceptions of the various actors in the story. Even so, as a historical virtue, consistency is drearily overrated. Whenever I refer to the king of Spain and his family in Madrid, it is as King *Felipe*, the Infanta *María* and so on, but I do not apply this rule to the Habsburgs of Vienna, who play less prominent roles in this account. Olivares is called the count, as he was not yet the count-duke of Olivares. I have tended to use 'British' when referring to the Stuart crown's diplomacy, but at times English has seemed either appropriate or necessary, as when I refer to the parliaments at Westminster, for example. I have also used Irish and British together when emphasising how the Spanish Match had the potential to affect religious life in all of James's dominions. Finally, this account is arranged chronologically as far as possible; however, since I have tried to do justice to the points of view of both London and Madrid, a degree of recapitulation has been unavoidable. This is particularly so for the period from the second half of 1622 to the beginning of 1623, when both Prince Charles and Olivares were engaged in activities not fully understood by King James or by the Spanish Council of State. At the risk of overlap, my priority has been to make each chapter understandable in its own terms.

2. A Spanish Bride

The origins of Charles Stuart's journey to Madrid go back at least to the beginnings of James's reign as king of England. On the death of the last Tudor, Elizabeth I, in 1603, the thirty-seven-year-old king of Scotland succeeded to a kingdom still at war with Spain. The danger to England was not as direct as it had been at the time of the Great Armada of 1588 or any of Spain's later attempts to launch an invasion, but war with Europe's foremost Catholic power still posed a threat to English security. In 1602, just before the old queen died, a Spanish army had to be forcibly dislodged from Kinsale, near Cork on Ireland's south-west coast. The accession of James the following year held out the prospect of an era of peace in Spanish–British relations.

Scotland had never been at war with Spain. Though brought up to be a convinced and utterly committed Calvinist, James was the son of Mary, Queen of Scots, who many believed had died a martyr for her Catholic faith. Rightly or wrongly, it was felt that Elizabeth's successor would be more accommodating to his mother's co-religionists. Some, such as the English-born duchess of Feria, dared imagine that the new King might one day restore the old religion. She wrote to James from her home in Spain praying that God would 'make you as great a saint on earth, as was your blessed mother'.[1] After Elizabeth's death, even James's restless Catholic subjects in Ireland were prepared to acknowledge their new Celtic monarch as their 'true king'. When all this was combined with James's lack of belligerence, it seemed inescapable that he would seek peace with Spain and end a war which had cost England dearly in both money and men. Accordingly, a ceasefire was confirmed and a delegation of Spanish noblemen travelled to James's newly styled kingdom of Great Britain. The Treaty of London, which finally ended all hostilities, was concluded in August 1604.[2]

James's revelled in his title of *rex pacificus*, the Peaceful King. To his credit, he sought not only to bring about peace but to build on it. While still king of Scotland he had demonstrated a profound interest in ecumenical projects

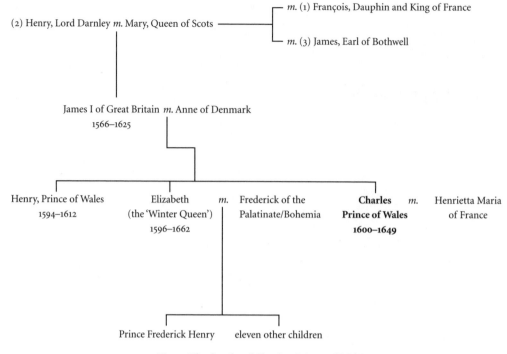

Fig. 1. The family of Charles, Prince of Wales

designed to heal the rifts between Europe's Christians. A scholar of distinction, James could perfectly understand the theological reasons why Christians might not agree among themselves. What he could not admit was that these differences were an excuse for war. Precisely when is unclear, but an idea germinated in James's head that he could lay the foundations of religious peace by a brace of royal marriages between his own family and the leading Catholic and Protestant dynasties of continental Europe. James was in an ideal position to do this. By the time he succeeded Elizabeth to become king of Great Britain and Ireland he was already father to three surviving children. His son and heir was Henry, duke of Rothesay, who became Prince of Wales in 1610. He was born in 1594, a year and a half ahead of James's daughter, Elizabeth. The future Charles I, youngest of the three, was born in Scotland, at Dunfermline Palace in Fife, on 19 November 1600.

When the Constable of Spain came over to sign the peace, hopes of James's conversion were still riding high. The Spaniards were therefore prepared to dangle the prospect of a marriage between the Infanta Ana, Felipe III's elder daughter, and Prince Henry. As a portent of problems that would recur some twenty years later, the Spanish conditions were unambiguous. The Catholic King's subjects, it was claimed, would not countenance a marriage with 'a

1. King James's precocious elder son, Henry, Prince of Wales, was originally
proposed as a potential husband for a Spanish bride.

prince of a different religion, contrary to the ancient custom of this Crown'.[3]
Not only must Prince Henry be brought up in the Spanish capital and convert
to Catholicism, but this condition had to be agreed before negotiations could
proceed further.[4] Spain had no room for manoeuvre. Until Felipe III fathered a
son, Ana was heiress presumptive. Her husband might one day inherit the
crown matrimonial of Spain, just as her grandfather, Felipe, of Armada fame,
had held the crown matrimonial of England while he was married to Queen
Mary Tudor.

How serious was this offer of marriage? In the absence of easy communication and preparatory sessions by minor officials, early modern diplomacy was

largely conducted through a series of direct meetings between councillors and ambassadors. An envoy's diplomatic instructions might indicate a number of reserve positions, but essentially agreement was achieved by a laborious process of attrition. Each side would begin with its list of ideal clauses. Resolution, whether in the form of agreement or in the breaking off of discussions, would be achieved according to how much either side was prepared to concede. In the case of the 1604 offer of marriage the Spaniards probably never expected King James to accept their conditions. In that limited sense, it could be said that the offer was not serious, yet, at the same time, if the stipulations *were* accepted then there would immediately be a basis for more earnest negotiation. There is an essential ambiguity to much of early modern diplomacy. This is rendered even more complicated by the fact that diplomatic negotiations also possessed a semiotic function which barely exists today. To negotiate was an end in itself. In other words, an offer of a royal marriage was an internationally recognised sign of goodwill; whether it would actually lead to a marriage was almost beside the point. In the case of Britain and Spain, the offer of marriage signalled that the House of Stuart was worthy of marrying into the Habsburgs of Madrid, yet, through the conditions which the Spaniards imposed, it broadcast His Catholic Majesty's resolution to defend the Catholic faith.

In 1611 it was the turn of James to make an approach to the Spanish court. He sent John Digby, the future earl of Bristol, on his first embassy to Spain. Digby requested the Infanta Ana's hand in matrimony for Prince Henry. A marriage between the two was now a more realistic prospect. Since the birth in 1605 of a male heir in the form of the Infante don Felipe, Prince of the Asturias and the future Felipe IV, doña Ana was no longer heiress presumptive. She was, though, already betrothed to France's young monarch, Louis XIII. Unwilling to rebuff the king of Great Britain completely, the king of Spain offered Prince Henry his younger daughter, the Infanta María. Again the Spanish assumption was that the Prince of Wales must convert to Catholicism. This was a price that James, as Defender of the Faith, could not countenance. He too turned to France to provide a suitable bride for his heir. It was not unreasonable to expect less demanding requirements from the Most Christian Kings of France. In opposition to the Catholic Kings of Spain, who had always trumpeted their special devotion to the maintenance of Catholicism, French kings were always more willing to make common cause with Protestant princes. They needed to protect themselves from encirclement by the Habsburgs of Spain and their Viennese cousins who reigned over the Holy Roman Empire.

Henry, Prince of Wales, died unexpectedly in November 1612. James substituted one son for another. He looked to France to provide his only remaining son, Charles, with a bride, though a marriage to one of the king of Spain's nieces was also briefly considered.[5] Meanwhile, James continued with the other strand in his plan to unite the dynasties of Christian Europe. In the spring of 1612 he had agreed to marry his daughter Elizabeth to Frederick, the Elector Palatine. Prince Henry died only a few weeks after Frederick had arrived at Gravesend on 16 October 1612 to begin preparations for this, the grandest of Protestant weddings.[6] There was an inevitable delay to the marriage but the Elector Frederick could not be kept waiting long. He was the ruler of the Palatinate, which was centred principally on the Rhineland but also included the lands of the so-called Upper Palatinate, in what is today the northernmost part of Bavaria. The Palsgrave, as he was known in England, ruled over a sophisticated state that boasted, in its capital of Heidelberg, one of the most influential Protestant universities in Europe. Frederick also headed the Protestant Union, a group of German princes who opposed the power, religious as well as dynastic, of the Catholic Habsburgs and their allies. In 1609 Protestants and Catholics had reached the brink of war over whether a Protestant or a Catholic should inherit the duchy of Jülich-Cleves, in north-western Germany.

The marriage between Elizabeth and Frederick was celebrated on St Valentine's Day, 1613. It was of unrivalled sumptuousness. This hid the fact that the Palsgrave was, in the words of an eyewitness, 'much too young and small timbered'.[7] William Shakespeare's play, *The Tempest*, was performed. On the River Thames a mock battle was fought between an English fleet and the Infidel Turks. The extravagance of the nuptials was paralleled only by the cost. James alone was said to be wearing jewellery to the value of £600,000. His wife, Anne of Denmark, was almost as ostentatiously dressed, wearing jewellery valued at £400,000. Even so, she did not look kindly upon her daughter's marriage to the Calvinist Elector. The Queen secretly professed Catholicism. Later, she claimed more than once to Spain's ambassador that the Habsburg blood – a trickle, it must be said – that ran through her veins inclined her towards a Spanish bride for her son.[8]

The gaiety of the festivities could hardly take away James's sense of loss over the death of his son and heir. At least the exuberance of the celebrations underlined the importance that he attached to the joining together of arguably the principal Protestant families of Europe. For the Spaniards such a link was potentially hostile. What for James was the first step in his laudable ambition of reconciling Christians threatened, in Madrid's eyes, the paramountcy of Catholicism. Who was to say that, in time, this marriage of Elizabeth and Frederick might not lead to a revival of the policies of Elizabeth Tudor's reign, when England assumed the mantle of protecting continental

2. Queen Anne, the Danish-born wife of James I, was a crypto-Catholic
who strongly advocated a marriage alliance with her distant kinsfolk, the
Habsburgs.

Protestantism? In fact, Madrid had already responded to the first signs of a
marriage between London and Heidelberg. By June 1612 don Diego
Sarmiento de Acuña, lord of Gondomar, had been named as the new Spanish
ambassador, thereby filling a post which had been left empty for some con-
siderable time.[9] Ambassador Gondomar was understandably reluctant to
exchange the warmth of Spain for the dampness of England. He would have
to suspend his long-cherished hopes of promotion closer to home. In July
1613, he could prevaricate no longer and set sail from the Galician port of
Bayona, *en route* for England.

Gondomar reached London in August 1613.[10] He was to become the most remarkable ambassador ever to have been accredited to the Court of St James's. In all the negotiations and plotting that led up to Prince Charles's astonishing appearance in Madrid in 1623, Gondomar was a key figure. He was born in 1567 in Astorga, in the ancient Spanish kingdom of Leon, where his paternal uncle was bishop; nevertheless he identified himself exclusively with Galicia, where he was brought up, on Spain's north-western Atlantic coast. His family were members of the minor nobility, though distantly related to grander families. Gondomar was an uneasy mix of arms and letters. As commander of the bishop of Tuy's forces he may conceivably have been the Gondomar who helped to defend the Galician coast from attack by Sir Francis Drake's troops in 1589.[11] He also accumulated the largest private library in Spain. This he maintained at his specially converted house in Valladolid, in northern Castile, which he restored to its former glory along with the adjacent chapel of St Benedict, his patron saint. Gondomar was a valetudinarian, and no doubt the opportunity for James to swap tales of illnesses added to his admiration for the deeply learned ambassador. Even so, James had been well disposed towards Spain's new ambassador before he presented his letters of credence.

Gondomar's ship came into harbour at Portsmouth. The captain of the English escort ordered him to lower the flags of Felipe III in salute to those of King James, in accordance with established English custom. The new envoy was told how the king of Spain's own father, Felipe II, had lowered his standard when he came to England in 1554 to marry Mary Tudor. When the ambassador refused to strike his colours, the captain threatened to blow him out of the water. Fortunately James was hunting only a dozen miles away. Gondomar wrote to him outlining his predicament. His motto, he explained, was *Osar morir da la vida* – risking death gives life. He asked to be allowed to return to Spain, 'because I was born of a good and honourable family, and I wish to emulate them; all of which obliges me to die, as I will, to defend my honour and duty, which is that these ships should enter and then return from this kingdom in the state that they left Spain'.[12] James was quite captivated by the swagger of the new ambassador, and an exception was made for his entry into English waters.

The warmth of Gondomar's relationship with James was fortuitous, based as it was on the accident of a near perfect marriage of his talents to the King's needs. To an extent, both were strangers in a foreign land. Many of their conversations were based on exchanging views about England and the English. Foreignness was a characteristic shared by all ambassadors, but Gondomar was better able to play upon this conceit on account of the imagination and boldness which marked him out from other envoys. Above all, his scholarship flattered the King, especially when it was infused with a highly mannered Castilian sense of deference. Both of these attributes the ambassador spiced with an agile wit. A fine example of this combination occurred when Gondomar told the monarch that he, Gondomar, spoke Latin badly, like a king, whereas James spoke Latin well, like a scholar!

Flattery apart, there grew up a sense of common purpose. Gondomar was devout in his religion and James admired this, even in Roman Catholics. They both genuinely wanted peace in Europe, albeit for very different reasons and never at the price of denying the principles of their respective religions. Peace in Christendom would bring for King James the glory that other monarchs achieved by force of arms. For Gondomar, the consolidation of friendship between Britain and Spain would not only surpass all his previous successes, it would also allow him, it must be said, to go home to his library. By the time that Gondomar left England for the first time, in July 1618, he had earned himself the affection, if not always the trust, of many of the leading figures in the land. The greatest nobles vied with each other to feast the departing ambassador. These included the Lord Chancellor, Francis Bacon, with whom he had enjoyed many a philosophical conversation, as well as Thomas Howard, the second earl of Arundel, who had passed on much confidential information to the ambassador in return for an erratic pension. Gondomar's farewell from the King illustrates just how close the relationship was between monarch and envoy. Not only were 'the two Jameses' – Diego and Diego – in tears, but the King granted Gondomar a magnificent concession. The right to take out of England horses, dogs and falcons was a worthy enough tribute to a departing ambassador; more so was the release from prison of the eighty Catholic priests who marched alongside Gondomar as best they could as he left London. But the return of the Spanish artillery, captured by Drake and other English corsairs, was a token of esteem of quite exceptional warmth.

Gondomar was uniquely accepted in royal circles because he became a friend to the King, his Favourite, and eventually to his heir, Prince Charles, when he falteringly emerged from the political shadows. To build up relationships of this degree of intimacy took time, however. Gondomar's first task after his arrival in 1613 was to ensure that Britain's closer links with France and Protestant Germany did not threaten Spain's interests. This he did by trying to smooth over the rough edges of the Treaty of London. For instance, English trade in the New World, even as far north as Virginia and Bermuda, seemed to Spain little more than a continuation of the piracy that had been typical of Elizabeth's reign. Gondomar extracted promises that England would not encroach further on what Spain regarded as her sphere of influence. In return for sterner treatment of the more notorious corsairs of the age, Gondomar was able to reiterate Spain's promise not to interfere in Ireland. Most important of all, the ambassador set the prospect of a Spanish marriage before the King.

Gondomar's opportunity came as early as the failure of the parliament of 1614. James dissolved the so-called 'Addled Parliament' in a fit of self-righteous pique, without the passage of any legislation, not even the granting of taxation. At the opening of the parliament James had explained to his assembled subjects that he had chosen the Elector Palatine for his daughter specifically on the grounds of his religion, even though he could have married her to a far greater prince, but he at least remembered to add that the Palsgrave 'was very noble and a very great lord in his own lands'.[13] However, to James's subsequent annoyance the intensely anti-Catholic House of Commons made clear that it did not relish the prospect of a subsequent marriage between Prince Charles and a Catholic princess of France. MPs also indicated their reluctance to subvent a king whom they regarded as profligate, regardless of whether his greatest expenditure to date had been his daughter's wedding to the foremost Protestant prince in Germany.

In the aftermath of dissolution, Gondomar saw his chance to insinuate that the House of Stuart's political problems might be eased by a Spanish marriage.[14] First he pointed out that the Catholics of England had shown themselves to be the King's most loyal subjects. Then he suggested that, if James were only to stop listening to parliamentary demands to increase the fines for non-attendance at church, he would find that the financial support to be had from the recusants would far exceed anything that MPs would offer him. Though Gondomar seems genuinely to have believed that the Catholics of England were more numerous and more affluent than they were, he was nonetheless pushing at an open door. Even if modern historians do not like the term, James was convinced that 'Puritans' – as we shall see – had seized control of the Commons. This only encouraged the King to believe that the dowry that would follow any marriage to a Spanish princess would provide sufficient money to establish his independence from parliamentary taxation. The threat to parliament did not go unnoticed by opponents of an alliance with Spain. One of the themes of the anti-marriage propaganda was to ask, what might James do if he ever came into possession of more Spanish gold than London could contain, even if its walls were 'built as high as heaven'?[15]

In the discussions between the King and Gondomar about the feasibility of a marriage between the Infanta María and Prince Charles, two sets of misconceptions were in operation right from the start. In combination they allowed the Spanish Match to develop further than perhaps it should have. Gondomar, for his part, did not fully realise that without Charles's prior conversion to

Catholicism a marriage would be extremely unlikely. Instead, the ambassador reasoned – at times at least – that a more tolerant approach from James towards Catholicism might be sufficient for the Spanish king to marry his daughter to a schismatic and for the pope to grant a dispensation to allow a Protestant and a Catholic to marry. Gondomar felt that, in the new religious climate brought in by a Spanish match, the King and his son would quickly realise the advantages of converting to what Gondomar passionately believed was the religion of most people in England. Gondomar's views were discussed on innumerable occasions by the councillors of state in Madrid as well as by committees of theologians. Many shared the view that a more positive attitude towards Catholics (and not Charles's conversion) would be sufficient for Madrid and Rome to consent to the marriage. The possibility of an alliance was still so remote, however, that neither Gondomar nor the Spanish council-lors of state seem to have known about the king of Spain's secret correspon-dence with Pope Paul V. Felipe III had been informed that on no account would the pope issue a dispensation to allow María to be married to Charles without his conversion to Catholicism.[16]

James's misconceptions were even more deep-rooted. They derived from the steady souring of his relations with his subjects, in particular with the Protes-tant landowners who dominated the House of Commons. After the parliament of 1614, the King became ever more fearful that extreme Protestants had seized the initiative, in the lower house at least. As far as he was concerned, their sedi-tion was a form of republicanism, as he chose to describe it. James meant by this that, since they had views on foreign as well as domestic matters, he was in danger of becoming little more than the chief executive of their wishes. As we have seen, the members of the House of Commons had already indicated their lack of enthusiasm for a royal marriage with Catholic France, and as for mat-ters nearer home MPs had manifested their disinclination to grant James suffi-cient funds for the needs of his government and household. Between 1614 and the ultimate failure of his next parliament late in 1621, the King would finally be convinced that only a Spanish alliance would allow him to act with the freedom that belonged to a king. Alliance with the Catholic monarchy would spike the guns of the more intolerant Protestants in the parliament, whereas a generous dowry of half a million pounds, combined with the spontaneous generosity of his own Catholic subjects, would give him the financial independence he craved. Or so James allowed himself to fancy.

All the time the diplomatic merry-go-round continued. Gondomar worked hard to ensure that a draft treaty of marriage was drawn up and by March 1615 a copy was handed over to John Digby, the ambassador in Madrid. A junta of theologians was appointed to ensure that Spain entered into nothing that would be detrimental to Catholicism, even though they too were kept in the dark about Pope Paul's demands for nothing less than a princely conversion in return for a dispensation to marry. By 1617 James was prepared to enter into more formal negotiations. On Sunday, 2 March, James asked his Privy Council to approve his plans. The following month, John Digby, by now an old Madrid hand, was sent back as ambassador to Spain. If James hoped for half a million in sterling, he was to be pleasantly surprised. When Digby returned again to England in 1618 he had talked up the dowry to some £600,000.

James was not to be bought quite that easily, though. Though he was fully prepared to allow the Infanta the exercise of her religion in a private chapel, and even to permit her to bring up any children as Catholics for the first few years of their life, he drew the line at allowing his Catholic subjects liberty of conscience. He would turn a blind eye to their private practice of religion, but nothing more. The negotiations had at least served the purpose of consolidating British–Spanish relations for the time being, as demonstrated by a joint naval operation in the Mediterranean. The pirates of Algiers were a common enemy. They were interfering with Spain's communications with its Balearic and Italian possessions, as well as disrupting England's overseas trade in the 'new draperies', a lighter cloth better suited to a more temperate climate. In October 1620 an English fleet under Sir Robert Mansell set sail for the Barbary Coast. As a further sign of the warmth of relations between the British and Spanish courts, James's principal ambassador in Madrid was elevated to a barony, becoming Lord Digby. Nonetheless, the fact remained that papal insistence on the Prince's conversion meant that, for the king of Spain, an actual marriage was, though never quite impossible, at least a very remote possibility. This was something which James and his son, and indeed all his diplomats, singularly failed to appreciate until it was too late.

The 1617 draft treaty of marriage was to go back and forth between London and Madrid (and Rome) right up to the time of Charles's arrival in Spain, and indeed beyond. New articles were added in 1619 and were brought over by Gondomar when he began his second embassy in 1620.[17] The essential point is that before Charles's journey to Madrid, King James steadfastly refused to allow his Roman Catholic subjects public toleration of their religion. Though James was prepared to show leniency towards the private practice of Catholicism (and various Spanish councillors of state felt that initial leniency would lead to greater rewards), it still held true that both royal courts lacked the political will to go through with the marriage. Neither side saw a need to proceed further with an exceptional marriage between a crown prince of one religion and a princess of another, until, that is, events in central Europe threatened to drag both London and Madrid on to opposite sides in a war that neither of them desired. In 1618, James's son-in-law, Frederick, had begun to take the side of the Bohemian Protestants in their revolt against the Holy Roman Emperor. From then on James was torn between his desire to protect his son-in-law from the full wrath of the Habsburgs of Vienna and his wish to avoid war and keep his distance from more extreme Protestants both at home and abroad. The Habsburgs of Madrid were also being pulled in two directions. Spain wished to concentrate on defending its worldwide empire against the Dutch but was finding it impossible to resist the calls of its Habsburg cousins in Vienna to fight for the Habsburg cause in Bohemia and in the Rhineland. In fact, a marriage between the Infanta María and her Austrian cousin, the Archduke Ferdinand, had already been mooted. For Felipe III, to revive talk of a marriage alliance with the House of Stuart was an all too easy way of maintaining cordial links with Frederick's father-in-law. For James, it once more held out the mouthwatering prospect of preserving his freedom of action at home. James always expected too much from the marriage plans of his children. His daughter's marriage was to prove no exception.

3. Prague

The Electress Elizabeth of the Rhine 'thought of nothing but plays, masquerades, and the reading of romances'.[1] This did not prevent her from playing a role in British history far in excess of her talents, since through her comes the descent of the House of Windsor from the Stuart kings of Scotland. In her lifetime she personified the Protestant cause. Her popularity, and that of her children, was such that at times it seemed to threaten the position of her father and her brother. James was also of the opinion that the Spaniards would go through with the match simply to prevent her from ever inheriting his throne. As he said to Charles, Spain had more reason 'to wish you and yours to succeed unto me than my daughter and her children'.[2] The irony is that Elizabeth's marriage to Frederick, instead of enhancing her father's reputation as a peacemaker, was to have devastating consequences for the reputation of James and his son for sound judgement.[3]

Elizabeth's contribution to the troubles of the 1620s was due largely to a decision taken by her husband, the Elector Frederick. Technically the kingdom of Bohemia was an elective monarchy within the Holy Roman Empire. Its capital city of Prague was already renowned for the beauty of its buildings and its university was one of the great European centres of learning. For almost a century the estates of that realm had obligingly offered the throne to the Catholic Habsburgs. It was a worthy prize. Its ruler, along with the Elector Palatine and five other electoral princes in Germany, shared the privilege of awarding the greatest accolade of all, the title of Holy Roman Emperor. By the early seventeenth century the balance of electoral power still favoured the Catholic princes, but if a Protestant were to be selected as king of Bohemia and control the electorship that went with it, the delicate confessional equilibrium of Germany's constitution would shatter. The armed conflict between the two confessions that had nearly broken out over the succession to the territories of Jülich-Cleves just a few years before might yet engulf central Europe.

In August 1618 the Bohemian estates dethroned the Archduke Ferdinand of Styria on account of his intolerant Catholicism. Prior to that, he had been accepted as their king-designate after the death of the Emperor Matthias. In his place the representatives of Bohemia offered the crown to a Protestant prince, James's son-in-law, the Elector Palatine. The Palsgrave's elevation to the Bohemian kingship took place in August 1619. As it happened, this was just a couple of days before the deposed Ferdinand was elected Holy Roman Emperor, as tradition dictated, in the Römer in Frankfurt. Elizabeth's granddaughter later alleged that the Electress was only consulted by her husband at the last moment. She said Elizabeth's response was that she would answer to God's call.[4] Others claimed she encouraged her husband by saying how she would 'rather eat sauerkraut with a king than roast meat with an elector'. There is little evidence, however, that he needed any encouragement.[5] James's daughter entered Prague in October 1619, and the following month she was crowned queen of Bohemia. Within a year military defeat forced her to abandon her new capital. Hence her sobriquet, the Winter Queen.

Elizabeth's involvement in the affairs of Bohemia drew the House of Stuart into a central European conflict over which it could exercise little direct influence. Those who expected King James to pursue a more Protestant foreign policy now had another Eliza on whom to pin their hopes. The questionable legality of Frederick's acceptance of the Bohemian crown mattered little to those who vied to protest their loyalty to the 'queen of hearts', as she was called.[6] Duke Christian of Brunswick fell platonically in love with her. His battle standard proclaimed that he would venture everything 'for God and for her'.[7] Closer to home, the lawyers of the Middle Temple, in an orgy of self-congratulation, proclaimed their loyalty to Elizabeth so raucously that James woke from his sleep and, fearing a Protestant conspiracy, cried out 'treason, treason'.[8] Elizabeth was the absent darling of the parliament of 1621. In the first session, one Edmund Flood dared to speak disrespectfully of the king and queen of Bohemia. His punishment was to ride a horse backwards through the streets of London and be flogged, fined and sentenced to perpetual imprisonment, all by express order of the overwhelmingly evangelical lower house.

The new king of Bohemia was dismissed by someone who knew him as knowing 'more about gardening than fighting'.[9] He would accompany his troops but he did not command them. James vehemently dissociated himself from his son-in-law's acceptance of the Bohemian crown. He consistently advised Frederick to sue for peace, but his son-in-law was too pig-headed to realise the hopelessness of his plight. Spain was keen that James continue to try to bring about a settlement between elector and emperor, as the crisis in the

Palatinate threatened Spanish preparations for a renewal of hostilities with the United Provinces once the Twelve Years Truce expired. Gondomar was ordered back to London, but by the time he arrived in March 1620 Felipe III had already placed some 7,000 veterans from the Army of Flanders at the emperor's disposal. Led by the brilliant general, Ambrosio Spínola, these veterans quickly seized most of the Lower Palatinate, and by the time Felipe died in March 1621 some 40,000 Spanish troops were ready to be deployed on behalf of his Viennese cousin.[10] As the truce with the Dutch Provinces was set to expire the following month, Spain was particularly keen to show that it was the duty of each branch of the Habsburg family to support the other.

James was caught in an undignified pincer movement brought about by his desire for the Spanish Match seemingly at any cost. If his plans were to prosper, he would have to pursue two very nearly contradictory policies. In order to assuage Madrid, he needed to put pressure on his son-in-law to sue for peace, but at the same time he needed to pacify his Protestant critics by declaring his willingness to take all necessary measures for the defence of the Palatinate. Though James instinctively refused the pleas of his daughter and her husband to intervene directly against the Habsburgs, he did permit Frederick's ambassador, Baron Dohna, to levy troops in his three kingdoms. James was fully aware that what amounted to Protestant public opinion was fiercely in favour of Elizabeth's cause. He knew that large sums of money were being freely donated to the Elector's armies. Later in the year, James felt obliged to appoint a commander, Sir Horace Vere, to take control in his name of the many English troops who had signed up to march across Europe to defend the Rhineland from the expected attack by the Catholic allies.

The Spanish Match was bringing James ever closer to the brink of diplomatic disaster. He persisted in his friendship with the foremost Catholic monarchy despite the fact that a nominally religious war was being waged in Europe. James bore much of the responsibility for this increasingly desperate position. Laudable though it was to try to curry favour with both parts of the religious divide, it left open the possibility that, in a crisis, he might find himself without friends on either side. His predecessors on the English throne had by and large reacted to events. James, however, had made no bones about what his diplomacy was intended to achieve. Since he had so publicly staked his honour and reputation on bringing off a Spanish marriage, he would find himself in an unbearable position if Felipe III's armies were to enter Frederick's patrimonial lands along the Rhine. James could not turn his back on the very alliance that he had so publicly cultivated without branding himself a failure; if he did, the humiliation would be insupportable. He would be conceding that the more radical Protestants among his councillors and subjects had been right all along: that the only way to support his son-in-law was by going to war and abdicating his right to be called the Peaceful King.

On the other hand, it is by no means clear what James could hope to gain from persevering with a Spanish alliance. It was perverse to hope that the Habsburgs of Madrid would desert their cousins in Vienna and hold back from taking the war into the Rhineland. At their first meeting after Gondomar's return to London, James had anxiously raised the question of whether the emperor would invade the Palatine. In a tart reference to Frederick's acceptance of the Bohemian crown, Gondomar's reply was that this was the same as asking him what he would do with someone who had seized London.[11]

When King Felipe's troops finally moved into the Rhineland in August 1620, James could no longer argue that he was standing aloof from the conflict precisely to prevent this from happening. He was acutely aware that he was seen by many of his most vocal subjects as standing idly by, not only in Protestantism's hour of need, but while his grandchildren were deprived of their rightful inheritance.[12] Digby told Gondomar that many people were saying that the King must want his daughter and grandchildren taken prisoner to Spain, since he was doing nothing to help them.[13] One Protestant diarist explained James's apparent indifference by describing him as the queen of Bohemia's 'unnatural father'.[14]

At the time that the Winter Queen was abandoning Prague, James summoned his first English parliament since 1614. Writs went out at the end of 1620, and peers and MPs assembled in Westminster in January 1621. In the speech from the throne, the King indicated the knife edge on which his diplomacy lay. First he indicated his determination to preserve England's peace, then he declared an intention to go to war if necessary. It would tax even a king as wily as James to keep these two almost contradictory aims alive throughout the duration of the parliament. Fortunately, since a parliament had not been called for seven years, MPs were anxious not to vex him. The vast bulk of early modern legislation was not government-inspired but raised at the behest of towns, corporations and private individuals and so MPs had no wish to return to their electorate, as they had done in 1614, with no legislation passed.[15] The parliament readily offered him early on in the session two subsidies, worth about £140,000. Gondomar believed that the earl of Southampton, the leading Puritan and malcontent, as he dubbed him, was behind the parliament's swift offers of taxation. Gondomar was ever quick to spot an ulterior motive. He reasoned that, because the sum was not enough to pay for an army, its real purpose could only be to dissuade the King from an early dissolution by holding out the prospect of even more money later in the session.[16]

3. This stylised depiction of James addressing the parliament from the throne in the House of Lords was reprinted several times during his reign.

Despite the auspicious beginning to the parliament, matters quickly began to get out of hand, and not simply because of the worsening situation in Europe. The problems in the Rhineland had exposed the King's twenty-nine-year-old favourite, George Villiers, marquess of Buckingham, more than ever to the envy of his many enemies. His wife and mother were rightly known to be intimates of the Spanish ambassador. To many, the Favourite's chief aim seemed to be personal enrichment and the advancement of his own placemen. How could he be allowed to advise the King at a time when the very future of the Protestant religion was at stake? A direct attack on the Favourite was almost impossible, not only because of his many clients but because it sailed close to accusing the sovereign of poor judgement. Pressure was brought to bear on Buckingham by attacking his grants of monopolies and other financial privileges to his friends. Sir Giles Mompesson's financial affairs were singled out for investigation because, as everyone knew, he was married to the sister of Buckingham's half-brother. Later in the session, there was talk of declaring Elizabeth and her children the rightful successors to the throne after James and Charles. This was a calculated insult to the Spanish Match's chances of success, or so James believed. He called a halt to further discussion of the matter on the grounds that it was 'neither necessary nor advantageous'.[17] The brittle harmony between King and Protestant subjects in the Commons which had marked the beginning of the session steadily dissipated as news from the Rhineland became ever more menacing. On 4 June 1621, when James had been persuaded to allow the parliament to adjourn over the summer instead of dissolving it outright, the Commons boldly issued a Declaration. If the King's exertions to find a just settlement in the Palatinate failed – and if he asked them – then they were willing to offer him their lives and property. As Gondomar reported back to Madrid, the exuberant generosity of the Declaration was also designed 'to make certain of their reassembly'.[18]

James had been extremely fortunate to have ridden the parliament as well as he did. Despite the many attacks on his Favourite and the obvious distaste for the alliance with Spain, the last-minute Declaration by the Commons actually served James's purpose. It could not be clearer to his friends in Madrid that, if they did not help him to resolve the crisis in the Rhineland, there was an English parliament straining at the leash to declare war on Spain and its empire. James needed an alliance with Spain more than ever to save him from his subjects and a war in the Palatinate. He was prepared to go to amazing lengths to indicate his continued desire to work with Spain. After the parliament was adjourned, he authorised Buckingham to talk with Gondomar about the possibility of a joint British–Spanish initiative to dismember the Protestant United Provinces once the Twelve Years Truce ended. Though the purpose of these exchanges was as much to open up another line of diplomatic communication with Madrid, it is also true that James quietly harboured a deep-seated grudge against the Dutch, despite their common religion. In addition to their attacks on English shipping, he was convinced their agents had incited members of the Commons against him, and the earl of Southampton in particular. Ultimately the dream of a war against the Protestant Dutch may have been a flight of fancy, but it served a purpose all the same. It was a castle in the air to be conjured up whenever relations with Madrid seemed to falter.

What luck James had possessed in the first session of the parliament quickly evaporated over the summer months. Frederick had been ejected from Bohemia in April 1621. His hold on the Palatinate was becoming feebler by the day. Soon only three towns of any significance would remain loyal –

Heidelberg, his hereditary capital, and Frankenthal and Mannheim, which flanked it. Each was in the hands of the expeditionary force serving under General Vere. In Professor Thomas Cogswell's vivid words, these three towns 'held the largest assembly of the prominent younger sons outside the Inns of Court. A parliament-man glancing over the list of Vere's officers, which included last names like Herbert, Sackville, Rich, Holles, Fairfax, Harrington, Wentworth and Devereux, could scarcely fail to find a friend, if not a relative'.[19]

Throughout the summer James intensified his diplomatic efforts for peace. Lord Digby was dispatched on a mission to negotiate with the Archduchess Isabel, who ruled the Southern Netherlands on behalf of the king of Spain. In May 1621 Digby went to Vienna to urge the emperor to accept a ceasefire to which the archduchess had already given her blessing. But the religious and dynastic conflict in Europe was by now so complicated that the emperor could no longer call a unilateral halt to hostilities. The Catholic duke of Bavaria had seized the initiative in the war against Protestantism. Increasingly, he became an independent player in the war. Such was James's admiration for the might of the Habsburgs that he never grasped how little sway Madrid held over Vienna, and much more damaging was his failure to realise that the emperor had already lost control of the ambitious duke of Bavaria. In September the ducal armies occupied the Palsgrave's territories in the Upper Palatinate, on the border with Bavaria. Forces loyal to Frederick, bedraggled and demoralised, retreated to the Lower Palatinate along the Rhine.

After taking time out to procure desperately needed moneys for Vere's soldiers, Digby finally arrived back at court on Wednesday, 31 October 1621. He was received without delay by the King. The next morning, privy councillors were summoned so that they could hear Digby explain (or exaggerate, as Gondomar had it) the meagre esteem in which both the emperor and the duke of Bavaria held the king of Great Britain. Digby confessed that before his mission to Vienna many had taken him for a Spanish pensioner and an enemy to the Palsgrave. Now the exhausted diplomat said he was in favour of massive support for Vere's garrisons and for the 16,000 troops and cavalry from Frederick's army still being held together by General Mansfeld. An immediate injection of £40,000 was necessary. The King's grandchildren were in peril. 'All that mattered now was that they had enough bread to eat.'[20]

These were the greatest secrets of state. That Thursday night, Buckingham paid a nocturnal visit to Ambassador Gondomar's new residence. He dutifully revealed all that Digby had advised. With consummate discretion, Gondomar did not let slip that the Favourite was not his only source of information. Earlier that evening, the ambassador had already penned an account to the archduchess in Brussels of everything that Digby had said at court. Who his prior informant was on that occasion we do not know. As we shall see, it was ever Gondomar's fate to be better informed about the court in London than about what was being planned in Madrid.[21]

Once Digby had delivered his first-hand assessment of the European situation, and explained the desperate need for cash, it was only a matter of time before the parliament was recalled. James acquiesced with the greatest reluctance. He had only just issued a proclamation, a few weeks before on 6 October, stating that his royal pleasure was not to reconvene parliament until February the following year.[22] Now it would reassemble within the month, at the end of November. The efforts of the *rex pacificus* to act as the arbiter of Europe had been exposed as hollow posturing. The question was, would James stand by his friendship with the Catholic king, or use the parliament as an excuse to put an end, once and for all, to the Spanish Match?

4. Westminster

When the count of Gondomar returned to London in March 1620, he was rapturously greeted by James as a long-lost friend.[1] The King and his son rose from their seats and doffed their caps. James attempted a public joke. The envoy, he said, looked like a very good friend of his, the count of Gondomar.[2] Anxious to please, James saw to it that Gondomar was splendidly housed in the bishop of Ely's palace in Hatton Gardens, with the unfortunate incumbent being peremptorily moved on. In deference to the count's objections, James happily agreed to take down some anti-Spanish pictures from the gallery of Whitehall Palace.[3] The King's demonstration of his friendship with Gondomar was not due solely to the rekindling of an old and genuine liking, though; it was also a necessary diplomatic tool. He was relying on Spain to help him defuse the burgeoning crisis in Europe. Gondomar had been ordered back to London in October 1619 in direct response to the moves offering James's son-in-law the crown of Bohemia. The envoy had little wish to return to a city which he, like James, regarded as insalubrious. He delayed his departure for as long as he could, but ultimately he could not shirk his responsibility to help ease the very real danger that Spain and Britain might be drawn into opposite sides of the European war.

This common interest in bringing about peace in central Europe explains why the Spanish ambassador was secretly briefed by Buckingham on James's unpredicted decision to recall parliament in November 1621. The briefing was partly an attempt to deflect the blame on to Digby's empty-handed return from Vienna, as if the hapless envoy were responsible for the crisis in central Europe. James was as insistent as ever that his goal was to avoid war. He was anxious to intimate to Gondomar that the king of Spain had only to throw him a lifeline over the Palatinate for all talk of war to vanish. Accordingly, Buckingham spared no opportunity during his nocturnal visit to the ambassador's residence to pour scorn on Digby. He just wanted to make himself immortal with the

Puritans as the restorer of the Palatinate and the defender of the Protestant religion in Germany. Furthermore, Buckingham gave Gondomar James's word that nothing would be done during the coming parliament without the ambassador's knowledge and approval, since 'the King trusted no one so entirely as him and myself, because he knew that we had no other goal but peace and the common good'.[4] In fact, the King wanted to see Gondomar the following day, Friday, 2 November 1621. If he came at one o'clock, they could speak at leisure.

James was in sombre mood. Leaving the Favourite and Prince Charles to one side, he took Gondomar to a window. There no one could overhear them. James confessed he knew what unspeakable things people were saying about him. If he truly loved his daughter, some said he would declare war. There was speculation that he was not Elizabeth's father nor even Prince Charles's. But they were his children, James protested, and as she was his only daughter he was determined to help her 'recover and hold on to the state that she had married into'. The king of Spain must understand that he was only doing his paternal duty. James then made a point of reminding Gondomar that 'even Digby had spoken to him with notable respect' about Spain's support for a ceasefire. To emphasise the desperate situation he was in, James added that, thank God, Frankenthal, the most threatened of the three towns loyal to his son-in-law, had not been captured. Otherwise he believed 'the people and the Puritans' would surely have turned against him.[5]

The King then uttered some of the most contested words of his reign. He told Gondomar he was not to worry about what he might hear when the parliament reassembled. He would go to Newmarket, taking Buckingham with him. He would leave the Prince behind in Westminster 'with a secret commission . . . and if the parliament wanted to meddle in anything other than aid for the Palatinate, the Prince would dissolve it'. James declared that money for the defence of the Rhineland was the sole reason for recalling the parliament, and he was going to be far away, in order to stop peers and MPs coming to him with their complaints.[6] Buckingham then joined in the conversation, sniggering that they would not even send the money to the Palsgrave but use it against the common enemy. The King laughed, and taking the ambassador by the arm, he said he would be wrong if he thought the common enemy was the Turk. He had the 'stately burghers of Holland' in mind![7] Gondomar was asked to react coldly to the recall of the parliament, so that the King's subjects would believe that a rupture with Spain was a distinct possibility. Digby, whom the King blamed for the recall of parliament, came in for some undignified joshing. Gondomar quaintly asked the King where he would think of placing the images that the Puritans were making of Digby.

This conversation has prompted speculation that James had decided in advance to wreck the coming session. In the words of one scholar, 'King James I sabotaged the parliament of 1621.'[8] At first sight this point of view is tempting. The parliament was indeed acrimoniously dissolved. But in fact the dissolution occurred only after the King, and especially the Prince of Wales, had tried repeatedly to strike a deal with the Commons. That they went to such lengths to make the session a success is unsurprising. A more careful reading of what Gondomar wrote makes it clear that no plot actually existed, nor indeed was a conspiracy even broached by James. First, the King simply said he would end the parliament *if* the Commons misbehaved. It is a commonplace that all monarchs were prepared to dissolve an unhelpful parliament, and such a course of action would only be a repetition of what James had done in 1614. Second and more generally, the *bonhomie* of the discussion is not in itself indicative of a conspiracy. It was an essential part of James's high-risk policy of trying to make Madrid believe that, unless they helped secure peace in the Palatinate, he would have to concede to a warmongering parliament. James was trying to repeat his last-minute success in the first session of the parliament. Then, against all the odds, the lower house had pledged their lives and their property to save the Palatinate, if only the King would issue the call. James was certainly reluctant to recall the parliament, and doubtless he was supported by his Favourite, who had much to fear from a parliamentary investigation into his dealings in Ireland and elsewhere. But the King did not intend to sabotage his parliament. Rather, he calculated that he could take up from where the Commons had left off in June, with their readiness to offer their all to defend the Palatinate. His expectation was that Gondomar would report back to Madrid that only James's goodwill stood between them and open war with a prince whose subjects would lovingly fill his war chest. A Spanish bride would surely be a small price to pay for peace with Great Britain.

Though the King had assured Gondomar that there would be an automatic dissolution if the Commons misbehaved, this is very far from what happened. The increasingly acrimonious set of exchanges between James and MPs was prolonged and public. Even the request for Gondomar to react coldly to the new session went by the board. James soon forgot what he had said, and quickly offered to make an open show of affection for Spain just as the parliament was reassembling. The King asked Gondomar whether he would not prefer to leave London and come and stay with him at Newmarket for the duration.[9] Indeed, in the letter inviting Gondomar to stay with him, the King repeated the assurance he had personally made to the ambassador after

Digby's return that 'he would not get involved in anything that would be dis-
agreeable to' either Spain or the Spanish Netherlands. Gondomar declined the
invitation. He was concerned that the recall of parliament was a Pandora's
Box. Once it was opened, James might be swept up by the anti-Catholic hyste-
ria that would follow.

Gondomar was in a deeply pessimistic mood. With winter approaching, he
was in London without the consolation of either doña Constanza, his beloved
wife, or his books. His health was giving cause for concern. A few days before
Digby's return, he had written to Madrid asking to be relieved of his post. He
even specified the exact day that, some eight years before, in 1613 he had first
set foot in London.[10] Fearing that the House of Commons might grant the
King money *only* if he declared war, Gondomar was concerned that his many
years in England might culminate not in a Spanish marriage but in a return to
war. His anxieties poured out in a letter he sent to the Emperor Ferdinand. He
told him that a war of diversion was possible. (This was a war that did not
involve a direct assault on the Palatinate, but, harking back to the days of
Drake and Hawkins, involved attacking the king of Spain on the high seas or
wherever he was vulnerable.) Gondomar feared that England might yet join
with all the Protestant powers of Europe – the Dutch, the Swedes, the princes
and cities of Germany, even the anti-Spanish Venetians – to force the Habsburgs out of the Palatinate. This was no public playing to the gallery. He
begged the emperor to assure James of his desire for peace by accepting a
ceasefire.[11]

It is hard to imagine any circumstances in which a monarch would plot to
reveal to the world that he was unable to work constructively with his own subjects gathered in a parliament. After all, 'the noisiest weapon in the royal
armoury', as Professor Cogswell put it, was 'a bellicose parliament'.[12] Nonetheless there is no doubting that the second session of 1621 was what today would
be called a 'public relations disaster' for the House of Stuart. As the King confided to Gondomar early in 1622, shortly after his testy dissolution of the parliament, 'those Puritans and malcontents would have [me] die a miserable
death'.[13]

The session had begun, however, with the clearest indications (or so it
seemed to James) that it was his royal intention to work with his subjects and
seize upon the Declaration and other positive aspects of the first session. His
ministers called for a liberal sum to be granted in taxation. The books were
opened and MPs were informed that the entire year's revenue had already been
spent. Pointedly, there was no ministerial talk of war against Spain. All that was
mentioned was a general call for the defence of the Palatinate. The first speaker

was Lord Keeper Williams. On Wednesday, 21 November, he stipulated both what James wanted and did *not* want from the parliament. No new laws were to be passed. All legislation was to wait until after Christmas, as the sole business of peers and MPs was money for the Rhineland. James would make the necessary preparations for its defence, while at the same time he promised to keep up efforts for a peaceful solution. In Williams's vivid words, since 'the breach is now grown so desperate as that it cannot otherwise be repaired, than, as Zorobabel did the walls of Jerusalem, with a sword in the one hand and a treaty in the other'.[14] Cultivating an image for plain speaking, Digby spoke next, in blunter fashion: 'the King must either abandon his children and the Palatinate or declare himself for war'.[15] Though Digby let slip that six Spanish armies were in the field, he avoided naming the king of Spain as the enemy. Gondomar was nonetheless alarmed. At eleven o'clock that night he wrote to warn the Archduchess Isabel of the trouble that lay ahead for James and the Spanish Match. The 'resolve of most people in the Parliament today is not to concede the King anything, but declare war on Spain'.[16]

The depth of hostility towards Spain was evident from the moment backbenchers rose to speak in the so-called 'Foreign Policy Debate'. It began that Friday and demonstrated how the events of the summer, and especially the plight of the Winter Queen and her growing brood of children, had hardened many hearts against the Habsburgs. Quite simply, enough members were eager to tear up the script provided by ministers and replace it with a call for a worldwide religious war against the Spanish Empire. On the very first day, Edward Alford made the uncomfortable link between the invitation to debate 'state matters' with freedom of speech and other constitutional concerns. According to one version of his speech, he claimed that 'We are not a fit Parliament to treat of these great matters for the Palatinate and the rest are matters of state'.[17] This lack of fitness was an ironic reference to the recent proclamation that forbade discussion of such matters. The Secretary of State, Sir George Calvert, tried to argue that the decree was only meant to apply to alehouses. Alford's line of argument is clearer from another version of his speech. 'We are no fit Parliament yet to enter into anything, we are pinioned yet; let's be at liberty till we enter into the debate. Proclamations restrain us from Bohemia speaking, etc.'[18] Debate was resumed the following Monday, 26 November. Again, there was no reluctance to speak out, and precious little reticence. Sir Dudley Digges blurted out that the 'king of Spain aimeth at war, our King at peace'.[19] Sir Robert Phelips blithely discussed what type of war against the Spanish king was most feasible, the very king whose sister was being sought in marriage for the Prince of Wales.[20] Thomas Crew actually mentioned

Charles's marriage, hoping that the King 'would match the Prince with one of the same religion'. At least he had the good sense to add, 'but this is not fit for me to enter into'.[21]

On each subsequent day of the debate, the calls for a worldwide 'war of diversion' against Spain became more heated. The House of Commons was building up a momentum that the absentee King could do little to check. The debate became so free that on the third and final day, John Wilde, the MP for Droitwich in the West Midlands, was so pointed in his attack on the Habsburgs that he was ordered to resume his seat by 'the dislike of the House'.[22]

The muzzling of John Wilde has been seized upon by revisionist historians as a sign of the Commons' reluctance to take up matters of state. They believe it is easy to exaggerate, even invent, conflict between MPs and King. Instead, they prefer to emphasise short-term misunderstandings which had little or nothing to do with the discontent that led to the outbreak of a civil war some twenty years later. The most influential of the revisionists, Professor the Earl Russell, argued that the most salient feature of the foreign policy debate was the Commons' reluctance to dictate to the King what he should do regarding the Spanish Match. He suggested that even the King's command that they debate the state of Europe

> had not encouraged them to attempt to direct, or even collectively advise on, the King's foreign policy. That this was the general mood of the House was confirmed the next morning, 27 November. One single member, Serjeant Wilde, asked that the Commons should name Spain as the enemy, but he 'was quickly stopped by the dislike of the House'.[23]

The quotation is from Pym's Diary.[24] Pym's brief entry does not begin to tell the whole story, though. All that Pym records is that Wilde 'began to speak too liberally of the House of Austria'. From another account, it is clear that Wilde had ample time to deliver a stinging analysis of Spain's role in Europe and to call upon his fellow MPs to be 'suitors to His Majesty to set down who is the Common enemy'.[25] The house may have objected, but by no means as rapidly as Pym's account implies.

To be fair, revisionists are not alone in underestimating the depth of feeling in the parliament. The King himself had grievously underestimated how far events over the summer had aggravated the situation. MPs were no longer prepared to curb their antipathy towards Spain, towards the marriage, or even towards what they saw as James's dithering in the face of Catholic militarism. Just as remarkable is the extent to which the parliament was indulged both by

James and by his son, his personal representative at Westminster. Finally created Prince of Wales, Charles was, according to a Venetian observer, still exceptionally taciturn, though becoming less so.[26] Every evening, it seems, the Prince and privy councillors met to review the day's proceedings and then he reported back to Newmarket.[27] Buckingham also had his own sources of information. His client, Sir George Goring, was an assiduous reporter. What is notable is that both the Prince and Goring were relaying back to the King at Newmarket that there was still every sign that this session of parliament would turn out in the end to be as successful as the previous one. For instance, at three o'clock on Tuesday the 27th – the same day as Sergeant Wilde's outburst – Goring filed another of his reports to Buckingham. From nine o'clock the following morning there would be a committee of the whole house. MPs would first grant supply to maintain Vere's garrisons in the Rhineland and then draw up a petition for the King about religion and for the passing of at least some legislation. Perhaps because of the way the house earlier in the day had dealt with Wilde, Goring was confident that James would be approached with all due constitutional respect, or as he put it,

> in all the humble manner that may be. The house is now in much better order and temper than yesterday it was, and I doubt not but now having evaporated themselves they will every day more & more let his Majesty see that it was nothing but their zeal that first transported them . . . and no way to cross upon his prerogative or direct him in his counsels.[28]

This optimistic tone was echoed in the Prince's dispatch of the following day. Admittedly his letter betrays his growing impatience with the way his future subjects were freely discussing his own marriage. More importantly, he confirmed that a subsidy had been agreed to in principle, but added that MPs expected something in return. For instance, they wanted to be home for Christmas and to have something to show their constituents. His view was

> that this that they have done is not so great a matter that the King need to be indulgent over them for it; yet, on the other side (for his reputation abroad at this time), I would not wholly discontent them; therefore my opinion is, that the King should grant them a session at this time, but withal I should have him command them not to speak any more of Spain, whether it be of that war or my marriage.

Charles's conclusion was that 'this, in my opinion, does neither suffer them to encroach upon the King's authority, nor give them just cause of discontentment'.[29]

The House of Commons had at long last come round to discussing taxation, which was the sole reason why the parliament had been recalled. This led to the most talked about intervention of the session. Goring, Buckingham's agent in the Commons, proposed a motion calling for a declaration of war against the king of Spain, if he declined to help restore the Palatinate to James's son-in-law. We have the account of his actions which Goring wrote to Buckingham only a few hours after he spoke. The motion was cast hypothetically: *if* the king of Spain did not either procure 'a general cessation of arms from the emperor in the Palatinate' or 'withdraw his forces from [the emperor] in case he refuse', then the House of Commons should petition King James for war. There is little doubt that Goring had been provided with the precise wording for the motion. Not only had he delivered it 'with all the care and diligence I possibly could', he had also employed the 'very words' required of him.

Goring admitted that many in the chamber 'think that I have undone myself at court'. But the court knew precisely what it was doing. James had caught the whiff of taxation as far away as Newmarket. It was decided to offer the Commons a concession to encourage them to dig deep into their pockets and end their tiresome debates. The decision to employ a backbench MP, an avowed client of the Favourite but no privy councillor, was intended to mollify the Commons. It would allow them to feel that they were not responding to a ministerial demand. In other words, James was permitting himself to be petitioned over a declaration of war, but only in the most provisional and circumspect of ways. Hence the care with which Buckingham had worded the proposal.[30]

The King and his Favourite had fundamentally miscalculated the mood of the house. The petition the Commons drew up outlined a complete programme of government which, if carried out, would have left James with nothing to do except execute the wishes of the Commons. The best that can be said for James's misreading of the situation is that it was a collective misjudgement. The Prince of Wales had also accepted Goring's motion as the best means of guiding the Commons into drafting a petition consonant with the King's honour as well as that of the Spanish king. For instance, on the day after Goring spoke, the Prince was still urging patience so that the subsidy could be passed. His view was that, although the lower house 'this day has been a little unruly', he still hoped it would 'turn to the best'. Charles was prepared to contemplate further measures to speed up the passage of a finance bill, but self-evidently these did not include a sudden end to their proceedings. What Charles had in mind was to be allowed to make an example of some 'seditious

7. *The Prince of Wales in his Presence Chamber*, by Hendrick van Steenwijk the Younger, *c.* 1620.

8. Though heavily restored and enlarged, the House of the Seven Chimneys stands in Madrid's calle de las Infantas.

9. *The Alcázar and the Bridge of Segovia, Madrid.* The *alcázar* or royal palace stands on a rocky outcrop above the river Manzanares.

10. Juan de la Corte's painting of a fiesta held in the Plaza Mayor in the Prince of Wales's honour early in August 1623.

11. *Venus of El Pardo*, by Titian. Titian was Charles's favourite painter, and his Venus of El Pardo was given to him by King Felipe early in June 1623.

12. *George Villiers, 1st Duke of Buckingham*, Studio of Daniel Mytens. This magnificent portrait was painted only a few years after the visit to Madrid and captures Buckingham's ostentatious manner. The pearls were a gift from King James.

fellows'. Even then, he was prepared to be indulgent until the following Monday:

> and till then I would let them alone. It will be seen whether they mean to do good, or to persist in their follies; so that the King needs to be patient but a little while.[31]

As Professor Cogswell has already pointed out, Goring's motion was essentially 'a modification of the earlier Declaration' of the previous June.[32] Then they had promised their lives and property. James would now be satisfied just with their money.[33]

The King was not to receive a penny from this sitting of parliament. Nor was the Commons' petition in the end couched in the provisional language that had been at the heart of Goring's motion. MPs felt emboldened to include a list of well over a dozen reasons why Catholicism was increasing nationwide, at the very time the King was proposing a Catholic marriage for his son. To add insult to injury they added ten remedies. These ranged from joining a revived Protestant Union in Germany to the increased persecution of Catholics at home. As for a war, they wanted a full-scale conflict which was not confined to the Palatinate. True, they did not name the king of Spain, but he was referred to as the one 'whose armies and treasures have first diverted and since maintained the war in the Palatinate'. Unsurprisingly, MPs called for an end to the Spanish Match. Using a phrase that had already been uttered during the three days of debate, James was asked to marry his heir 'to one of our own religion'.[34] Both domestically and in terms of foreign policy the Commons were now offering the King a complete governmental programme.

Whether James would have been prepared to accept the bigotry and cant contained in the petition for just one grant of money is an open question. We shall never know. His hand was forced, and not least by Ambassador Gondomar's reaction to the petition. If we think back to the swagger of his refusal to lower his master's flag when he first entered English waters in 1613, then it takes no leap of imagination to understand how Gondomar could not stand aside as a foreign parliament railed against both Spain and the pope. As the Commons put it, the former was 'aiming at as large a temporal monarchy as the other at a spiritual supremacy'. Gondomar threatened to leave England without waiting for his cherished recall. James must act on the assurances that had been made to him before the parliament began. In the words of S.R. Gardiner, 'the like of [Gondomar's letter to James] had never before been placed in the hands of an English sovereign':

if I were not so certain of the King's word and his goodness that he would punish and set things right with the speed and the severity that was called for, I would have left his Kingdom without waiting a third day.

Gondomar added that if only he had an army with him, he would punish those responsible himself.[35] This letter must have wounded his friend the King to the quick.

Gondomar's threats were not feigned. So frightened was he that the King would be unable to resist the clamour for war that he took it upon himself to write to the duke of Alburquerque, the Spanish ambassador in Rome. No further action should be taken regarding a papal dispensation for Charles's marriage until it was clear what James would do, warned Gondomar. The King of Great Britain had a stark choice, to go either with Spain or with his parliament, and since James was not in London Gondomar could not be sure which path he would take.[36] Gondomar's temerity in sending not merely information but instructions to a fellow ambassador required him to write separately to his king, to justify his outlandish behaviour.[37]

The Prince of Wales's patience snapped when he saw the petition. He sent a copy to his father, angrily exclaiming 'that his marriage was so much prostituted in the House'.[38] (Later it was claimed that the petition shown to the King had not included the formal protestations regarding respect for James's prerogatives.[39]) At ten o'clock on the morning of Tuesday, 4 December, an angry letter was passed to the Speaker of the House of Commons.[40] The King reprimanded members for their interference in 'matters far above their reach and capacity'. His command was 'that none therein shall presume henceforth to meddle with anything concerning our government'.[41] The following evening, Buckingham wrote to Gondomar. He enclosed a copy of the King's letter to the Speaker to reassure him that James remained committed to friendship with Spain. The King was, he said, resolute – *constantissimo* – and he hoped to be able to give him further news within a couple of days.[42] In fact, James continued to look for ways to persuade the Commons to grant the subsidy. The Commons found both time and temerity to draw up a *second* petition. Even so, according to Secretary Calvert, Prince Charles's anger abated enough for him to work hard at mediating between his father and the Commons.[43] No further message was to come from Buckingham for almost a fortnight while every effort was made to salvage the parliament. All Gondomar could do was cling to the belief that at least the King's Favourite was agitating for James to have done with the parliament.

On 18 December 1621, the day after a final plea from the King about the need to grant a subsidy, the House of Commons made their Protestation. In a public rebuke to the King for his friendship with Spain, members registered their absolute right to petition him as they saw fit regarding 'arduous and urgent affairs concerning the King, state and defence of the realm, and of the Church of England, and the maintenance and making of laws, and redress of mischiefs and grievances which daily happen within this realm'. This James tore out with his own hands from the official Journal of the House of Commons. Gondomar may have liked to claim that the King had finally done as he had promised and ended an impertinent parliament, but the damage to James's reputation – and to the king of Spain's – was already done.[44] Copies of the Protestation had been made and distributed throughout the kingdom, to be cherished as if they were precious heirlooms.

What happened in parliament at the end of 1621 has implications for how we look at early Stuart history in general and not just the Spanish Match. To suggest that the disaster arose out of a misunderstanding (let alone sabotage) is to deny that there was constitutional conflict between MPs and the crown. Conrad Russell has pointed out that the petition was one of grace, not of right; that is, the House of Commons was merely asking the King to end the Spanish Match and persecute Catholics, not claiming the authority to dictate to the monarch. From a revisionist point of view, the breaking up of the parliament represents little more than a political blunder. The misapprehension may have been bitter, but it was transitory. It did not reflect ongoing tensions concerning the crown's prerogatives. Yet this distinction between political and constitutional issues is wholly artificial. James felt that the religious aspirations of some parliament-men had led them to claim rights which struck at his vision of a king's liberty to exercise his office. In a word – in *James's* word – their demands were 'anti-monarchical'.[45]

By the end of 1621, a vociferous cluster of MPs had come to identify their own salvation with an active defence of continental Protestantism. In particular they identified with the cause of the Palsgrave Frederick and his wife, Elizabeth Stuart. If we can judge by the lower house, then divisions ran so deep that there are signs that English society was dangerously split over whether to take up arms against Catholicism. Though the King and the Commons both earnestly desired a conclusion to the problem of the Rhineland, they had fundamentally different views on how to achieve this. James wished to bring it about as part of his ecumenical vision for Europe, whereas for the Commons the war in the Palatinate was in itself a diversion – the real aim being an evangelical crusade.

If the constitution did not in the first place divide King and Commons, then politics did. Yet all disputed political issues in the end revolve around who is taking the decisions, and that makes for a constitutional issue.

James's prestige had been dealt a withering blow by the dissolution. Echoing the King's own words that he had summoned it expecting gratitude only to be accused of poor government, the Venetian ambassador added that the Spaniards might well use the acrimony in the parliament as an excuse for not going through with the marriage.[46] Gondomar had been even less sanguine. He feared that the King might choose to throw in his lot with the parliament. Instead, the calamitous end to the session convinced the House of Stuart that it needed the Spanish Match more than ever.

5. Father, Son and Favourite

Charles Stuart had only just finished celebrating his twenty-first birthday when the stormy final session of the parliament of 1621 began. Already he was of an age 'more than full ripe' for a bachelor prince.[1] The interminable negotiations over the Spanish Match were not the sole reason why the Prince was unmarried. James had been zealous in his determination to preserve the life and health of his only remaining son. For many years Charles had been kept firmly in the background. He was shy and loath to speak; even a friendly source made excuses for the fact that 'our Prince Charles' was 'of such mildness, and indeed [had] such very sweetness of manners'.[2] He was also liable to fits of temper that arose out of frustration. In his early years, he had been overshadowed by his larger-than-life brother, Henry. Later, his sister's effervescence was to cast a long, often political, shadow over her younger sibling. Nonetheless, Charles cut an elegant figure. He was well proportioned, with fine features of an unmistakably aristocratic mien. He was also extremely short, probably being only about five feet tall. For all his qualities, including an inherited love of learning, he had to struggle to capture his father's attention.

It was no consolation that King James was prone to infatuation. The untimely death of Charles's elder brother, Prince Henry, had increased his capacity to fall prey to the attractions of a series of handsome young men. A pattern emerged. To become his favourite, they had to be approved by his wife, Queen Anne, originally a princess of Denmark. James had sailed across the North Sea to escort her back to Scotland. At the Queen's invitation, the most enduring of the King's favourites, the twenty-two-year-old George Villiers, was appointed a groom of the bedchamber.[3] Though privately inclined towards Catholicism, the Queen had joined forces with Archbishop Abbott of Canterbury to promote Villiers as a rival to another of the King's favourites. Eight years older than Charles, Villiers was all that the Prince was not. Tall, charming and dashingly handsome, he was also something of a ladies' man. His rise was steady, though not at first dramatic. He was knighted the day after his induction into the King's bedchamber. He became a viscount in 1616, then an earl and finally, on 1 January 1619, he was created marquess of Buckingham. This last elevation prompted one of those civilised remarks that so endeared Ambassador Gondomar to James's court. He had himself been made a count, the Spanish equivalent of an earl, in June 1617. Until 1619, he and Buckingham shared the same rank. When the Favourite was elevated to the dignity of a marquess, Gondomar said he congratulated him most genuinely, in spite of his pain on seeing him leave the rank of count.[4]

Much ink has been spilt over what sort of homoerotic relationship James shared with Buckingham, mostly with little or no appreciation of the sexual and moral constraints of early modern life.[5] But the strangest relationship at James's court was not the bond between the King and Buckingham. The affection between the Prince and Buckingham is harder to fathom. Where one might have expected to find jealousy, the Prince looked to the Favourite as the best means of attracting his father's interest. He was profoundly grateful for all of Buckingham's efforts to bring them closer together. In turn, the Favourite was well aware that his future in the next reign depended on obtaining the trust of the son in the present. Either way, Charles and Buckingham's comradeship was profound. Strangely, the turbulent half-year they spent away in Madrid only made it deeper. Charles's subsequent marriage to Henrietta Maria proved no obstacle to a loving friendship that ended only with the assassination of the King's Favourite – *Charles's* Favourite – in 1628.

Into this triangular relationship of father, son and favourite stepped Gondomar. He had established ties of affection with the King and Buckingham before Charles appeared at court. From the early 1620s he won the confidence of the Prince of Wales, conversing with him in French, albeit haltingly.[6] The ambassador was welcomed jointly into their company, talking and drinking with all three when diplomatic business was over. He would share with them some of the wines and produce he proudly imported from his beloved Galicia. But Gondomar also had a distinct relationship with each of them: they could go to him for support, or even to reinforce their relationship with one another. For instance, the King could pour out his heart to Gondomar about the disloyalty of his subjects. The Favourite might ask Gondomar for his help against a rival at court, as when he asked him in the spring of 1622 to remonstrate with the King about his enemy the earl of Oxford.[7] Charles was later playfully to call the ambassador his procurer. Gondomar's easy relationship with all three was helpful particularly on account of the intensity of the King's relationship with Buckingham. Not only had the envoy enjoyed the confidence of Queen Anne, he had also come to enjoy excellent relations with the Favourite's mother and later his wife.[8] Once, after he had decided to ask Buckingham's mother to intervene with her son, he remarked that England might be turning Catholic. People were praying more to the mother than to the son![9] The analogy was by no means inapt. James told his councillors that, as Christ had his John, he had his George. Simply by being so familiar with the Favourite's family and with the Prince, Gondomar was in a position to smooth over the singularity of James's infatuation with George Villiers.

As a foreigner, Ambassador Gondomar's friendship with King James vaulted the hurdles which normally obstructed relations between monarch and subject. That he was openly Roman Catholic had the perverse effect of making conversation easier: they did not share a common faith, so there was no point wasting time pretending they did. Paradoxically it was this very exclusion from the interlace of religious and dynastic networks within James's kingdoms, his very foreignness, that made the erudite count so trustworthy a companion. There was no one he could betray the King and his family to, not even in Spain. As James wrote to Felipe IV on first hearing of Gondomar's recall in 1622, 'I can truthfully say that, on account of his desire for universal Christian peace and our friendship and that of our realms, I have never treated with another prince's ambassador with greater love'.[10] This is unsurprising. After the fiasco of the parliament of 1621, James looked with increasing desperation to Madrid and the Spanish Match to help restore his authority at home and abroad.

King Henry VIII said that a king's majesty was never greater than when he sat in parliament. There was no more powerful sign of effective rulership than when Lords and Commons agreed to offer their sovereign the money required to put royal armies into the field. James had committed himself to restoring the Palatinate when he was barely able to maintain the three garrisons that looked to him for support. If he was not to capitulate to the will of a parliament that equated his ecumenical vision with religious infidelity, he needed more than ever to secure a Spanish bride. James's options had narrowed considerably after the dissolution of the 1621 parliament. The breach with the House of Commons meant that he could no longer credibly threaten war on land and sea even if Madrid reneged on the wedding. James's only remaining option was to plead for Spain to come to his aid with a marriage, a dowry and – so he prayed – with help in settling the Rhineland.

James did as much as he possibly could to mask his dilemma by pretending that the political initiative still lay with him. Never again, he boasted, would he summon another parliament like the last one. He would reverse the Protestant preponderance by abolishing the oaths which debarred Catholics from public office. Then they would be able to sit in the lower house again, along with his other, more well intentioned, subjects.[11] It is in these moments when James lashes out that we get closest to finding out who he felt his real enemies were. He was, of course, indulging in wishful thinking if he felt he could reconstitute the membership of the lower house. According to an act of parliament of Elizabeth's reign, all MPs were required to swear an oath acknowledging the monarch as the Supreme Governor of the English Church. James had no power to repeal that or any other statute without first calling another parliament. In fact, the only way James could display his newly invigorated forbearance of Catholicism was by invoking the royal prerogative to circumvent the need for parliamentary sanction. Two of the Puritan ringleaders, as James would have it, Sir Edward Coke and Sir Robert Phelips, were dismissed from the Privy Council and imprisoned once the parliament was over. The King had intended to single them out in the proclamation finally dissolving the parliament of 1621. Their crime had been to speak disrespectfully of his fellow sovereign and ally, the king of Spain. Gondomar intervened to alter the wording: he felt it would be a humiliation for either of the firebrands, or indeed for King Felipe, to be named. When published, the proclamation's vindication of the dissolution was couched in less specific terms.[12]

As for halting the persecution of Catholics, James attempted to curry favour in Madrid by any means possible. Instructions were sent from London that Scottish Catholics were to be treated leniently, with privy councillors there being warned that the King's clemency proceeded from 'reasons of state, in the deep mystery whereof every man is not to dive or wade'.[13] In England, a large number of Catholic prisoners were released from jail. Shortly after Gondomar was recalled home in the spring of 1622, Buckingham wrote to him claiming that the cells of Catholic priests had now been stocked with Puritan preachers:

> here are all things prepared upon our part priests and recusants all at liberty, all the Roman Catholics well satisfied, and, which will seem a wonder unto you, our prisons are emptied of priests and recusants and filled with jealous ministers for preaching against the Match.[14]

Madrid surely could not fail to see how much more could be accomplished for Catholics, in Ireland as well as in England and Scotland, by agreeing to marry the Infanta María to the heir to the Stuart thrones.

Events inside and outside the parliament had seriously alarmed James. He knew that political terrorism in the form of royal assassinations was a feature of the age, beginning with the murder of William of Orange in 1584. Closer to home, his own father, Lord Darnley, had been brutally killed by political opponents at the Kirk o'Field in the heart of Edinburgh, and his mother, Mary Stuart, an anointed sovereign, was later judicially murdered by her English cousin, Elizabeth I. Most recently, in 1610, Henri IV of France had been stabbed to death in his coach. As king of Scotland, James had faced numerous conspiracies against his rule and, conceivably, his life, and the indiscipline of the English House of Commons heightened his fears that extremists among his anti-Catholic opponents might take matters into their own hands. He was perturbed by the prospect that his daughter and son-in-law might return to London and become a focus of opposition to his rule. Gondomar was asked if he could not provide the necessary papers to permit his son-in-law and his family to leave Holland and pass through Spanish lines to Heidelberg. Of course, this would have the effect of strengthening the Palsgrave's feeble grasp on what was left of his principality, but more to the point James hoped the desperate military situation to be found there would persuade his son-in-law to sue for peace with the emperor. Most important of all, he just wanted them 'away from here'.[15]

To counteract the growing popularity of the electoral family, James made up his mind to let the Prince of Wales emerge from the shadows. He had taken the first steps in the parliament of 1621, and especially during the second session when he left for Newmarket while Charles remained at Westminster. After the collapse of the parliament, James turned his attention to the composition of his son's household. Choosing who would surround the Prince was a means of influencing his son. It also indicated to a wider world what he, the King, was thinking. Thomas Savage was appointed the Prince's main adviser. A Roman Catholic, he approached Gondomar for advice. Savage was warned by his co-religionist not to take any oaths contrary to his faith and to confront the King and the Prince with the fact of his religion. According to Gondomar, Savage's confession inspired the royal reply that they now trusted him more for his honesty.[16] Endymion Porter was taken into the Prince's service as a groom of the bedchamber. He too was no friend to the hotter sort of Protestants. He was related to Buckingham and fluent in Spanish and had once served as a page in the household of the count of Olivares, the new king of Spain's favourite.[17] Towards the end of March 1622, James announced in the Privy Council, with full histrionics, that he was getting old. From now on the Prince of Wales would assist him in government. He praised his son in such terms that many of the councillors felt it appropriate to shed tears. Soon after, another Catholic

4. Sir Francis Cottington was Charles's secretary. Fluent in Spanish, he was
called a 'hispaniolised Englishman' on account of his pro-Catholic
sympathies.

sympathiser, Francis Cottington, was recalled from Madrid to become the
Prince's secretary,[18] although negotiations for the marriage meant that this
'hispaniolised Englishman' remained in Madrid a further half-year.[19]

The governor of the Spanish Netherlands, the imperious Archduchess Isabel,
was fond of reminding Gondomar whenever he reported James's promises of
leniency towards his Catholic subjects that all this had been said before. He
needed to give lasting proof of a change of heart. Gondomar knew full well that
words came easily to James. He later expressed himself bluntly on the topic.
James, like all heretic kings, would say anything to please. Spain could not

afford to be 'taken in by his words'. Only deeds mattered, as far as the ambassador was concerned. Admittedly he wrote this while trying to avoid being sent back to London, but it was all part of a constant message he had fed back to his masters in Spain while he was ambassador in London. For all his liking for James, Gondomar, as a Galician, was acutely aware that England and her merchants were becoming wealthier largely at the expense of Spain and her empire. If Madrid and London did not reach a lasting accommodation, then a war of religion and commerce was only a matter of time.[20] Whether James's indulgence towards Catholicism in the aftermath of the 1621 parliament would persuade Spain to go through with the marriage would be left to Digby's negotiating skills. As soon as the worst of the winter weather was over, James sent him back to 'perfect the Match' once and for all.[21] The previous November, Lord Keeper Williams had said in the House of Lords that James would pursue peace in the Rhineland with a 'sword in the one hand and a treaty in the other'. The sword had since fallen from James's grasp. As for the treaty, that was now in the hands of the king of Spain.

The importance of Digby's embassy was signalled by his elevation, shortly after his return to Madrid, within the ranks of the peerage. He became earl of Bristol, a city which had longstanding trading links with Spain. In an exchange of courtesies, Gondomar was prevailed upon to take the patent back with him when he returned to Madrid.[22] A further indication of the good relations between the two countries was the inventive financial deal which Digby struck with Gondomar. He agreed to hand over 20,000 *ducados* in London in return for the payment of a similar amount on his arrival in Madrid. This way both ambassadors would avoid losing out to exchange rates and commission.[23] This mattered, since for all the importance of the London embassy, Gondomar rarely had enough money to pay his expenses and meet all the pensions he had liberally distributed to leading courtiers.[24] A singular example of the 'special relationship' which James was trying to foster with Spain occurred when begging letters arrived from Mansfeld, the Protestant general in the Rhineland. They also contained a threat. If money was not forthcoming Mansfeld would take his army, and the war, into Imperial Bohemia. Gondomar was invited to inspect Mansfeld's letters. On at least one occasion a copy was made for him as he looked on.[25]

Gondomar left London for Madrid on 16 May 1622. He had been recalled naturally enough to partner Bristol in the negotiations for the marriage.[26] He travelled by the overland route, through Paris, as the threat from Dutch men-o'-war was said to be too great to ignore. He arrived to find Bristol fulfilling his instructions by indicating to the Spaniards what they might gain from closer amity with James. In return for a Spanish bride and everything this would do to promote a settlement in the Palatinate, the English navy would not only take action against the Dutch but would again help sweep the Mediterranean clean of Muslim pirates.[27] As for the marriage, the draft of 1618 still served as the basis for a treaty. The conditions agreed were consonant with James's role as supreme governor of the Church of England and protector of the Kirk in Scotland. The Infanta and her servants would be allowed to worship freely in her own chapel, but his subjects would only be allowed to attend when and if he granted individual licences. The King had also accepted that the children of the marriage should spend their early years with the Infanta, and he had even gone so far as to accept that they would not lose their rights to the throne if they professed their mother's religion.[28] As for his Catholic subjects at large, James stood by a letter he had written to Felipe III in April 1620. He was not in a position to repeal the penal laws, but he gave his word as a king not to enforce them, and certainly not as far as the death penalty. James's concessions may not have changed, but events in Europe had. With the war in Germany, and the expiry of Spain's eleven-year truce with its rebellious 'subjects' in the United Provinces, it appeared to London that Madrid might yet find a marriage on these terms an acceptable proposition.

The dilemma for King Felipe IV and his advisers was whether the benefits to Catholicism were sufficient to excuse his sister's marriage to a Protestant. The question had been the same in his father's reign. For some, notably the Jesuits, the presence of a Catholic queen in the British Isles would prove sufficient reward. Unlike James's wife, Queen Anne, she would exercise her religion publicly and bring up her children as she saw fit. The Infanta's court would be a beacon of Catholicism, guaranteeing that her Catholic subjects would not be persecuted. For others, marriage to an infanta of Spain was a prize requiring far more of James. Either his son must convert to Rome or there must be a full parliamentary repeal of all laws persecuting Roman Catholics. As one of the committee quipped, if a mere woman, Elizabeth I, could in nine months overturn all the good laws which Queen Mary Tudor had struggled to introduce, what was stopping James from repealing bad ones?[29]

Bristol's mission in the second half of 1622 was critical. If it failed, the preference of James and his Favourite for governing without benefit of parliament would collapse and Prince Charles would be humiliated into spurning the bride he had so vociferously championed during the clashes with MPs. The Prince instructed Bristol to report at once whether the marriage would go through, as he had no desire to risk the loss of his friends nor the love of all his people.[30] Anxious for news, now Buckingham let slip to Gondomar that the only leverage they had over the Spaniards was the fear of an aggressively Protestant succession in England:

> it only rests now that, as we have put the ball to your foot, you take a good and speedy resolution there to hasten a happy conclusion of this match. The Prince is now two and twenty years of age and a year more than full ripe for such a business. The King our master longs to see an issue proceed from his loins, and I am sure you have reason to expect more friendship from the posterity that shall proceed from him and that little angel your Infanta than from his majesty's daughter's children.[31]

Less given to such posturing, King James was more conventional in his diplomacy than either his son or his Favourite would prove to be. He was content to let the negotiations rest in the experienced hands of the new earl of Bristol.

Bristol arrived in Madrid on 29 May. Despite a cordial welcome it was made abundantly clear that James would have to offer further religious concessions as well as intensify pressure on his son-in-law before the marriage could take place.[32] In typically Galician fashion, Gondomar had warned Madrid that both 'sail and oar' were needed to reach a satisfactory agreement.[33] King Felipe set up another committee or *junta* to scrutinise every exchange in the formal negotiations. The new committee still included his confessor, fray Antonio Sotomayor, who was later to head the Inquisition. It met almost daily in the convento de Santo Domingo, to the north of the royal palace, not far from Olivares's town house and, more importantly, where the confessor had his cell. The newly returned count of Gondomar also attended. At the same time as these meetings were taking place, a tribunal of cardinals reconvened in Rome. When it pronounced on the marriage in July 1622 the negotiations entered uncharted waters. The cardinals' emendations set a course whereby the *bonum publicum* – the common good of all Catholics – and no longer the personal liberty of the Infanta or her children was the only acceptable destination. James should indicate precisely the concessions he would grant his Catholic subjects. (There was giddy talk of a Catholic church in every town.) The Infanta's chapel ought to be freely open to all. Other expectations chipped away the Anglican Church's pretensions to be the one national church. The Infanta's clergy needed to be under a Catholic bishop, as well as exempt from all secular authority. Female children might remain with the mother until they were twelve, but male children were not to leave their mother until they were fourteen.[34]

James the scholar had a point when he railed against the new conditions which his unofficial ambassador, the Catholic George Gage, brought back from Rome. The King correctly told Bristol that the exemption of the clergy did not even apply in countries which acknowledged the papacy. James conceded that any children of the marriage could stay with their mother until they were seven (longer if they were ill), but as for his Catholic subjects' liberty of worship he could not go beyond his letter of two years earlier and his promise not to enforce the laws against them.[35] Buckingham and Charles were also incensed. The Prince complained to Gondomar that 'ye ever promised that the King my father should be no further pressed in matters of religion'.[36] In the light of his own concessions when he was in Madrid, Charles's statement of principle rings hollow indeed. His petulant threats were interspersed with the pathetic. Spain should consider 'what *malum publicum* must of necessity ensue upon our Roman Catholics' if the match fell through. Charles could bluster as much as he liked, but the reality was that he had prefaced his warning with an opportunistic appeal for Spain 'to look back & consider how much we have already granted'. He continued to plead his devotion to the Infanta:

> But if you wonder how I can love before I see, the truth is, I have both seen her picture and heard the report of her virtues by a number whom I trust, as her idea is engraven in my heart.

During the summer and autumn of 1622, the courier from London seemed only ever to bring further examples of the House of Stuart's diplomatic importunity. For all the talk of a crusade against the Dutch, they had virtually nothing to bargain with.

With Ambassador Bristol eager to make headway, a few of the papacy's more sensible emendations were admittedly taken on board.[37] Though he confessed he had no authority to do so, the ambassador agreed that James would make promises about the 'public good' of Catholics in a private letter, separate from the main treaty, since Gondomar had assured him that James had repeatedly expressed his willingness to do that.[38] By the end of November 1622, John Stone, one of Secretary Cottington's informants, announced that the 'general voice runs through Madrid that the match with England is concluded'.[39] He was right. Within a matter of days the religious articles were apparently concluded. To the optimistic, it seemed as if the basis for the marriage had been agreed, although the absence of an agreement on diplomatic or military matters should have rung warning bells. King Felipe – for reasons we have yet to consider – encouraged Bristol by telling him that his sister might be handed over by the spring.[40] The religious articles were handed to the earl. On Friday, 13 December, the earl passed on the 'good and gladsome tidings' to Endymion Porter, who had been sent by James to speak directly to Olivares, his former master. Little did Bristol know that Charles's servant had also been given another very secret mission by the Prince of Wales.[41]

Mr Porter arrived back in London on Thursday, 2 January 1623.[42] The 'pleasing news' about the conclusion of the religious negotiations left the King 'very merry and jocund'.[43] As the Venetian envoy, Alvise Valaresso, put it the very next day, the marriage was 'an accomplished fact'.[44] Porter had brought with him not only what appeared to be Spain's final religious demands but also King Felipe's irresistible suggestion that the Infanta could be in England before the summer, if only the pope were willing.[45] King and Prince hurried to confirm all that was asked of them. An order was given to prepare ten ships to fetch the Infanta, and Buckingham bragged openly about taking the fleet to Spain.[46] Confirmation of the agreement was rushed to Spain by Simon Digby, who had only recently returned from a diplomatic mission to the emperor's court. He reached Madrid on 25 January, just three weeks before Charles himself was to set out for Spain.[47]

The January accord comprised the official articles of religion and one secret letter addressed to the king of Spain.[48] Each element was subscribed by James and his son. The Infanta's household and servants would be under the ecclesiastical authority of a Catholic bishop, outside the reach of English law. Her church would be for the use of her servants only. Any children of the match would remain with their mother at least until the age of nine. Her servants would not be obliged to swear an oath of loyalty to the crown which was contrary to their religion, and she would have her own bishop. Most momentous of all was a private concession devised to get round the impossibility of a parliamentary repeal of the recusancy laws. The King gave his word he would not interfere with his Catholic subjects' freedom of worship as long as this was confined to their own homes. With only the slightest exaggeration, the Spaniards could pretend that James had 'in effect conceded a toleration'.[49]

For the British monarch, the marriage appeared to herald, if not a solution to the problems of his son-in-law, then at least proof sufficient that he was doing as much as he reasonably could to broker a peace in the Rhineland. Between them, Britain and Spain united would surely be able to arrange some kind of accommodation between his son-in-law and the emperor. A weary James turned his thoughts to the general articles of friendship with Madrid. With singular disdain, Bristol was ordered to proceed with that 'other unfortunate, knotty affair of the Palatinate'.[50] Just as he had gone further in granting freedom of worship than he had ever expected to, James would have to steel himself to accept meagre diplomatic pickings from Spain. The earl of Bristol had already warned London that Madrid was never going to turn against the emperor, for that was 'a thing of hard digestion'.[51] If James were lucky, Spain might proclaim its wish to see the Palatinate restored to the Infanta's prospective sister-in-law and her family.

Two centuries after this agreement, the great nineteenth-century historian
S.R. Gardiner struck a sour note when he contemplated what the King and the
Prince had assented to. In his estimation, the articles meant that 'James and his
son were thus signing away the independence of the English monarchy'.[52] The
worst fears of the parliament of 1621 had come true. It was one thing to ignore
the wishes expressed in the petitions of the House of Commons. To ignore its
fundamental right to repeal legislation was quite another. No one denied that
the monarch had the right, from time to time, to suspend various laws, but the
abrogation of the penal statutes against Catholicism struck at the heart of the
Anglican state. Since Henry VIII's break with Rome, the English commonwealth had been built upon the understanding, even under the Catholic Queen,
Mary Tudor, that crown and parliament jointly decided both temporal and
spiritual matters.

More positively, the agreement of January 1623 marked a potential turning
point in the history of James's three kingdoms. It seemed to hold out the
prospect of a degree of religious toleration that would not materialise for
another two hundred years. According to an insider in the embassy in Madrid,
with 'the articles reflecting both upon the Church and State being capitulated',
and with agreement on both sides, 'there wanted nothing to consummate all
things'.[53] The pope could surely not refuse to sanction the match now that both
royal families were in agreement on religion. But, for Charles Stuart, Endymion
Porter's return with the draft of a marriage treaty was a signal that the time was
fast approaching to take Madrid – and his bride – by storm.

6. Post Haste!

'Talk of the Spanish Match', wrote Sir Simonds D'Ewes, 'lay somewhat dead' until Endymion Porter returned to London at the start of 1623.[1] While the religious conditions for a formal treaty of marriage were hurriedly assented to the day after his arrival, no one, probably not even King James, was aware that Charles and Buckingham had been nurturing their own secret contacts with Madrid. During the previous twelve months, through exchanges of intimacies, the dispatch of highly charged letters, and by half-occluded missions, the Prince of Wales came to the conclusion he knew better than his father's diplomats how to bring home a Spanish bride.

In the wake of the disastrous last parliament, Charles had decided it was high time to learn a little Spanish. He had his first lesson on Tuesday, 19 January 1622, and his second the very next day, almost exactly one year before Porter returned with the marriage agreement. We know this because Buckingham, writing from the King's great house at Newmarket, was carefully feeding Ambassador Gondomar with every detail, giving out for good measure that he too was learning the language. Gondomar received more substantial news a few months later, as he was preparing to leave England for the very last time, in May 1622. The Prince of Wales took him to one side. Charles then made an astounding promise. He offered to travel in disguise to Madrid if this was what was needed for the assent of the king of Spain to the marriage. The Prince had already sketched out the details in his head. With just two servants in attendance, he would 'place himself in the hands' of His Catholic Majesty.[2] Gondomar need only send the word.

The Prince of Wales's declaration meant only one thing to Gondomar. The heir to the British throne was signalling a willingness to convert to Roman Catholicism. To be at the Spanish court meant to be a Catholic. Throughout the palaces of Europe, court life was imbued with religiosity. It was almost unheard of for a prince of one religion to pay an official visit to a prince of a different

confession, at least outside the Holy Roman Empire. The hazards of incorpo-
rating them into the ceremonial life of the court were too great, and nowhere
were royal pomp and ecclesiastical devotion more intertwined than at the court
of the Catholic king. That is why James's ambassadors, unlike those of France
and Venice or other Catholic regimes, were deliberately excluded from the great
religious ceremonies of the court. Indeed, religion still managed to entangle a
diplomat as experienced in the sensibilities of the Spanish court as John Digby.
Shortly after his return to Madrid, he caused great offence when it was noted
that he and Lady Bristol failed to stand for the sacrament of the altar as it passed
by his window during the festival of Corpus Christi. A highly charged denun-
ciation was compiled for King Felipe's ministers.[3]

Gondomar was by no means alone in assuming that if the Prince ever went
to Madrid it would be to convert to the religion of his bride. When Charles
revealed himself at the House of the Seven Chimneys, even Bristol took it for
granted that he was about to convert. In fact, Gondomar had long fancied that
England was ripe for conversion. He maintained that the failure of the parliament of 1621 was one of the most momentous events to have happened in England since the time of Luther and Henry VIII. An end to the schism between the
British Isles and Rome appeared to be just over the horizon. Quite on what
basis is unclear, but Gondomar had always held that at least half of James's subjects were either Catholic or prepared to follow the lead of a Catholic monarch.
Charles's offer to go secretly to Madrid seemed to indicate that the Prince of
Wales might be willing to give that lead.[4]

Prince Charles had made the first of a series of grave miscalculations. He had
overestimated Gondomar's importance as a policy-maker. The count was in no
position to know whether the appearance of the Prince of Wales in Madrid
would be welcomed by King Felipe and his principal advisers. King James may
have looked upon Gondomar as a member of his Privy Council, as well as his
'inner cabinet', but, as far as the grandees of Spanish courtly life were concerned, he was no more than an influential, and often irritating, functionary.[5]
He may have been a consummate ambassador (and grudgingly recognised as
such even by his political enemies in Madrid), but this minor noble from an
outlying province was never a member of the king of Spain's inner circle. King
Felipe III's chief minister, the duke of Lerma, had dispatched Gondomar to
London to be rid of an irksome suitor. Felipe IV's great favourite, Olivares, also
had little time for Gondomar. Dripping sarcasm, he later pointed out that he
simply did not believe that England was as 'omnipotential' as Gondomar would
have him believe. Though Gondomar was included on his return from London
in the meetings of the committee in Santo Domingo that monitored negotia-

tions for the marriage, he was only grudgingly allowed into the *consejo de estado* – the Privy Council – and even then strictly on account of the Prince of Wales's astonishing arrival in Madrid. Effortlessly giving out in London the impression that he had the ear of the king of Spain, Gondomar was adept at self-promotion, and when the Prince finally arrived in Madrid, it was Gondomar who extensively briefed the newsletter writers of the time. In return he was ascribed a key role in their melodramatic accounts of the visit, at first often overshadowing Olivares.[6] During his first year as ambassador to King James, he had written over a hundred letters to his king (not including those to the duke of Lerma). No one in London could be expected to know that don Diego's 'longwindedness' was the subject of both amusement and frustration in Madrid.[7]

The Prince of Wales had rashly invested Gondomar with a political secret far beyond the count's standing at the Spanish court. If Charles wanted the king of Spain to know he was prepared to travel to Madrid, he should have transmitted this information directly to King Felipe or to his most favoured minister. Instead, the Prince's promise went to Gondomar's head, and he appears to have used it in the hope of advancing his career at the Spanish court as much as to further the cause of Catholicism in the three kingdoms. Once he was back in Madrid and sitting on the steering committee that met in Santo Domingo, Gondomar was fully aware, at the end of the summer of 1622, that another committee in Rome was vociferously demanding far more significant concessions over religion before they could recommend that a papal dispensation be granted. Perhaps don Diego feared that these new demands would raise the stakes so high that James might be obliged to call off the match. This would destroy all he had worked for during his long years in London and rob him of the higher title of nobility which he felt was commensurate with his bloodline. Gondomar decided the time had come to activate Charles's promise to turn up in Madrid. He calculated that if the Prince of Wales were willing to place himself in the hands of the Catholic king, then his obvious goodwill towards Catholicism would make a papal dispensation either unnecessary or impossible to refuse. A marriage without a dispensation might have been a discourtesy towards papal authority, but hardly anyone believed it invalidated a Christian marriage.[8] Indeed, a spell at Europe's most Catholic court would very likely secure Charles's conversion.

In the first half of September 1622 Gondomar dispatched an extraordinary trio of letters. They are the key to unravelling how Charles convinced himself that he should travel to Madrid. The first letter was written to King James on 1 September. The new king of Spain was strongly in favour of the Spanish Match, Gondomar told James. So much so that Felipe would ensure that the

pope was satisfied about the questions of religion in order 'that not only would
he be able to grant the dispensation which we desire, but that he shall be obliged
to grant it'.[9] With studied playfulness, he reminded James in his own hand that
the only bad deed he had ever done him was to address him in French! At the
same time Gondomar wrote a similar letter to Buckingham. The letter is a perfect composite of his ambassadorial arts, full of solidarity and innuendo. He said
how fondly he remembered walking with the duke in the open gallery next to
his room in his mansion overlooking the Thames. Some matters, he went on,
were better suited to personal communication than to being written down –
least of all in French. He then repeated that King Felipe was determined to go
ahead with his sister's marriage. 'And so I hope to God that we shall see each
other soon in this country here, and embrace each other, as agreed'.[10]

Few letters in the annals of diplomacy match the piquancy of the third letter.
Just over a week after the one written to James, Gondomar wrote once more to
Buckingham, but this letter was composed in a style remarkable for the sexual
imagery that was employed between the ambassador of one monarch and the
Favourite of another. It was written in Spanish. Perhaps Gondomar's excitement was such that he could not concentrate his mind enough to compose a
letter in their shared language of French. More likely the choice of language was
determined by the fact that it was to be handed over – in the utmost secrecy –
by Francis Cottington, the 'hispaniolised Englishmen' who was now the
Prince's secretary and fully at home in the Spanish language. The letter commenced with a few words of erratic English. 'My Lord, My good freind', it
began. Then Gondomar repeated his joke that there was nothing he wanted to
say in French, but in Spanish he wanted to express how envious he was that
Cottington was to have the opportunity of kissing Buckingham's hands. Turning abruptly from courtly exchange to the rougher language of innuendo, he
trumpeted that the marriage had been decided upon. It was time for the Prince
of Wales to 'mount' Spain.[11]

If only for its potent imagery, and for the fact that it has languished unnoticed for over a hundred years in the British Library, this letter would merit
quoting at length:

> I omit a thousand things that I should like to tell you, since the bearer of this
> letter is Francis Cottington, who will give Your Excellency a detailed account
> of it all by word of mouth. I will say only that, as far as we here are concerned,
> the decision has already been made, and with very great enthusiasm, that the
> Prince of Wales should mount Spain. All the others that tried must look
> somewhere else for their relief. Also, the wish here is that the matter should

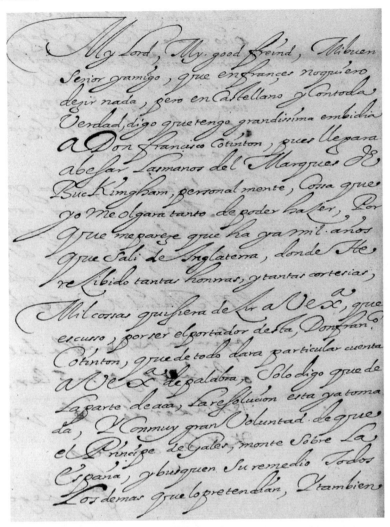

5. Gondomar's handwriting was notoriously bad. A secretary usually wrote out
his letters to which he would add a few lines, as in the case of this letter to
Buckingham. Written from Madrid in the second half of 1622, the letter claimed
the marriage had already been decided and hinted that Charles should turn up
in person to claim his bride.

be dealt with post haste. But, as to the posts of Spain, I cannot make them
move faster than is their wont, but in the end they do arrive with truth and
certainty. Though I am no great postilion I spur hard and may Your Excellency do the same at your end.[12]

Cottington must have handed over this letter on his return to England on
Friday, 4 October 1622.[13] Another member of Charles's household, Endymion

Porter, was about to set out for Madrid. Now Porter would be serving two masters. At one level he was undertaking a diplomatic mission for King James, but secretly he was also on Charles's business. The King could not fail to be perturbed at the deteriorating situation in the Rhineland, and there had been precious little news from Spain over the summer. As Buckingham put it to Sir Walter Aston, one of James's permanent representatives in Madrid, 'we are in great disorder here, with your delays there, but I hope all will at length jerk to the best'.[14] Porter was officially dispatched in order to explain how seriously James took the situation in the Rhineland. 'Those thin garrisons' sent to man the three towns still loyal to his son-in-law had not prevented their being besieged by Catholic troops who, nominally loyal to the emperor, were barely under his control. In fact, news of the fall of Heidelberg reached England just before Porter set out, increasing the sense of desperation with which James called upon Madrid to engineer their restitution or to join forces with England against their Viennese cousins. The King was playing for time. For all his jabber about joint Hispano-British action against the emperor's forces, it has to be conceded that the only remotely realistic request was that the king of Spain should permit any troops in James's pay 'a free and friendly passage through his territories'.

Endymion Porter put these would-be 'peremptory messages'[15] to the count of Olivares, who was steadily taking over from his uncle as King Felipe's chief minister. Though James might once have fancied that the king of Spain might actually turn his own troops against the Imperial forces which were also occupying the Rhineland, the count left his former page in no doubt whatsoever about the absurdity of thinking that one branch of the Habsburg dynasty would take up arms against the other. He was apparently even less than enthusiastic about the marriage.[16] But for all Olivares's plain speaking, King James had no intention of allowing either the match itself or the alliance with Spain to run aground because of an understandable refusal on Madrid's part to wage war against Vienna. James knew that Spain, independently of the marriage, wanted to see an honourable settlement in Germany almost as much as London did. The Spanish genuinely feared that the astonishing successes of the duke of Bavaria at the head of the Catholic League would threaten the paramountcy of the House of Austria.[17] On this occasion, there is no reason to doubt that Felipe meant what he said in two letters he dispatched to Vienna. One was addressed to his uncle, the Emperor Ferdinand, the other to his ambassador at the Aulic Court, Count Oñate. Through his ambassador Felipe passed on the British king's request that a principled solution be found which would restore the Elector Palatine to his ancestral lands. In the letter to his Imperial cousin, King Felipe was unambiguous. He candidly requested that the forces of the Catholic League should not attack the two remaining English garrisons of Frankenthal and Mannheim while negotiations were continuing for a ceasefire.[18] Whether or not this familial pressure was too little (as the insatiable James would have it), it was certainly too late. Colonel Vere surrendered Mannheim on 25 October. James saw no other option but to cling ever more tightly to the belief that once the Infanta María was Princess of Wales – and sister-in-law to the Queen of Hearts – Spain would redouble its efforts to bring about a lasting settlement in the Palatinate.

It is conceivable that James's unremitting attachment to the match may have stemmed from his belief that a marriage alliance with Madrid would by itself lead to peace in the Rhineland. Frankly, he was just as likely to have been mesmerised by the mouthwatering prospect that the Infanta would bring with her a dowry more than enough to prevent his having to go cap in hand again to a Protestant parliament. As for Charles, his wish to be united with her whose 'idea is engraven in my heart' needs no explanation.

Cottington's delivery of Gondomar's batch of letters had added, it must be said, a further, murkier, strand to Endymion Porter's mission. As a member of Charles's household, he was entrusted with the task of sounding out the call for the Prince to turn up in person. Charles needed to be certain. Bristol had warned Cottington in Madrid of the 'inconveniences and difficulties' that would arise if Buckingham, as Lord Admiral, was required to leave court and fetch the Infanta from Madrid.[19] Another reason why Charles needed confirmation was the perplexing fact that Cottington's knapsack had also contained a letter from Olivares. Though it was penned the same day as Gondomar wrote to say that Charles should 'mount Spain', the count's courtesy letter made no allusion at all to the marriage, let alone to a breakthrough in negotiations.

In all likelihood, the ulterior motive behind Porter's mission to Madrid – whether the Prince of Wales should undertake a journey – was never formally discussed with King James and most definitely not with Bristol. (Immediately after Charles's arrival, the plain-speaking earl claimed he was relieved he was 'kept ignorant' of the plan, because had he known he would 'directly have protested against it'.[20]) Nevertheless, Bristol at some stage became convinced that more was being mooted than an official visit by Lord Admiral Buckingham. Four years later, in the parliament of 1626, Bristol revealed that he possessed treacherous correspondence which proved that Buckingham had conspired with Gondomar to deliver the Prince to Madrid as a first step in converting the heir to the throne to papistry. Endymion Porter had been complicit in passing coded messages. Amongst the questions Bristol prepared for Porter was whether he knew of the intended princely visit *prior* to his own mission to

6. Spain's most famous literary *alcahueta*, or procuress,
Celestina, is depicted in this early woodcut. Curiously,
Charles had called Gondomar his *alcahuete*.

Spain. He wanted Porter to confess whether he used 'any words intimating something tending to that effect'. For good measure he insinuated that Porter had not attended Protestant services during his visit to Olivares.[21]

Endymion Porter in every likelihood was also the bearer of a handwritten reply by the Prince to a *fourth* letter from Gondomar, now unfortunately lost. Written in Charles's round, open handwriting, it began:

Gondomar: I do hereby very willingly establish you, according to the desire of your letter, in that honourable office of my principal *Alcahuete*.

Though this word might be used to describe a patron or go-between, by the seventeenth century it was indelibly associated with the eponymous protagonist of Fernando de Rojas's immortal drama of sexual intrigue and licence, the brothel-keeper Celestina. It had come to mean 'pimp' – or, in the case of the crone, 'procuress'. Being the sole Spanish word that Charles employed in this suspiciously brief note, it was of some consequence. In fact, he used it twice, the letter being endorsed, 'To the Count of Gondomar my principal Alcahuete'. To minds as suspicious as Bristol's, the insertion of a single Spanish word might have seemed a pre-arranged signal to indicate that Porter was to be trusted with the Prince's most secret business.[22] By Christmas 1622, Charles Stuart's frustration was overt. Gondomar's replacement in London privately mocked his single-minded belief that all would be well if only he could marry the Infanta. Ambassador Coloma described a meeting with the King where Charles would chime after every word uttered by his father, 'despagne, despagne, dela fauti atendre le remede'. Whether the poor French was the ambassador's or the Prince's hardly matters. Charles's personal frustration is unmistakable.[23] As the earl of Bristol told the Prince, it was evident from his letters that 'the little god hath been somewhat busy with you'.[24]

In spite of all that was expected of him, Endymion Porter only just managed to collect the all-important terms for a marriage agreement. Crossing the Channel on his way to Spain, he had lost most of his papers at sea. One of his servants drowned and he seriously damaged his shoulder, further delaying the start of his mission.[25] When he did finally reappear at court, on 2 January 1623, he was greeted euphorically, with Secretary Calvert writing that he 'was long looked for, and a welcome man'.[26] All this despite the fact that he had brought back with him a crystal-clear message about the situation in Germany: nothing could be expected from Spain other than diplomatic assistance in the Rhineland. The memorandum containing the religious articles made this plain in an unusually obvious way. The very next sentence after the one which raised the prospect of the Infanta's impending departure dealt with the Rhineland; though Bristol had dutifully rung all the changes in the hope of extracting categorical assurances, the fact remained that the Palatinate was not even mentioned by name. The memorandum comprised fine-sounding but empty words about the 'reality and seriousness' of Spain's commitment to peace.[27] Bristol prepared London to expect no more over the Palatinate than 'reasonable satisfaction'.[28] But all this did not matter. There was talk that the Infanta could be in England by the summer.

Despite the general rejoicing at Endymion Porter's return, what Secretary Calvert could not know was that the Prince had his own secret reasons for welcoming back his exhausted servant. He was impatient to know whether Gondomar was to be trusted. Porter's reappearance with the basis of a marriage treaty meant for Charles something highly personal, above and beyond the relentless grinding of his father's diplomatic machine. Spain was anxious to release his bride. Only a dispensation from Rome stood in the way. Gondomar had been right all along. Once Porter had rested, it would indeed be time for the Prince of Wales to mount Spain – post haste!

7. Wind, Metaphysics and the Court of Spain

Spain was ruled over by the young King Felipe IV, who ascended the throne at the age of very nearly sixteen on the death of his father in March 1621. Lanky, still shy of being seen in public, with light-coloured eyes and hair which betrayed his family's origins outside Spain, he was utterly inexperienced in most matters other than the chasing of wild animals. Fortunately the numerous ministerial councils that surrounded him were possessed of a life of their own. They were more than capable of running an empire that was used to being governed by the pen as much as by the sword. The volatile young monarch instantly warmed to the idea of accepting a favourite to relieve him of the more tedious tasks of kingship. At first, the most powerful minister remained a grizzled old warrior, don Baltasar de Zúñiga. His time as ambassador in Vienna, as well as in Paris and Brussels, had confirmed his belief that Spain should have as little truck with heretics as possible. Zúñiga's position was steadily taken over by his nephew, the conde de Olivares, who had been the young king's childhood companion. Though more and more power fell into the count's hands, his grip on the reins of government was never total. The conciliar nature of Spanish government made it impossible to monitor all decisions, and Felipe demonstrated occasional flashes of a budding sense of what was expected of the king of Spain. The king's wishes could never be ignored, but at the start of his reign it was still relatively easy for those of greater age and maturity to lead him in a direction of their choosing.[1]

Felipe's empire was the largest the world had seen. Not only did he succeed to the thrones of Castile, Aragon and Portugal, he also inherited their far-flung possessions in Italy, the Spanish Netherlands, Africa, India and the Far East. Most important of all, he controlled the silver-rich lands of Mexico and South America. Felipe could also lay claim to being the single most important member of the House of Austria. On the death of his great-grandfather, the Emperor Karl V – King Carlos I to the Spaniards – the Habsburg dynasty finally

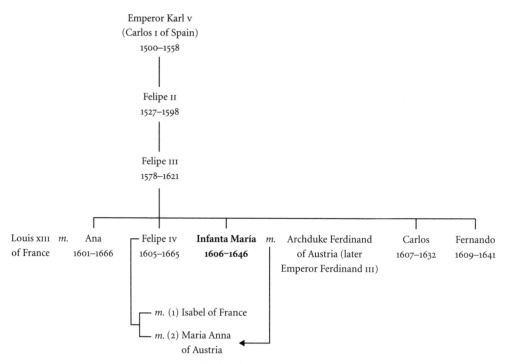

Fig. 2. The family of the Infanta María

split into two.[2] The emperor's brother, Ferdinand, retained control of the old family lands in Austria, exercising rights in Bohemia and parts of Hungary as well. He also inherited the title and position of Holy Roman Emperor. Felipe II, the emperor's son, received Spain and its empire, along with the papal epithet 'His Catholic Majesty', a title granted to his forebears, King Fernando of Aragon and Queen Isabel of Castile, at the end of the fifteenth century.[3] Between them, the two branches of the family formed the paramount Catholic dynasty in the world. As emperor and Catholic King, their collective duty was to champion the Church of Rome.

Felipe IV's possessions were so varied that it was hard for his subjects to think of a single name by which to call them. To label his dominions 'the Spanish Empire' was highly problematic. His Imperial cousins in Vienna claimed to rule the only true empire. Moreover, Felipe ruled in each of his Iberian kingdoms quite separately, rather as did James VI and I in regard to his kingdoms of England, Scotland and Ireland. The solution usually adopted was to refer to this disparate collection simply as *la Monarchía* – 'the Monarchy'. What held it together was little more than the centrality of the royal court and of the reigning family within it. What set it apart from the territories of their Imperial cousins in central Europe was that 'the Monarchy' alone possessed the military power and financial might to defend and augment the power of Roman Catholicism. Spain's sense of mission not only applied to the forced conversion of the subject peoples of the Americas, it also held good in the Old World. The revolt in Bohemia had shown that the Old Faith was not entirely secure, even in the heart of Europe.

Spanish statecraft was genuinely imbued with this sense of mission. If *raison d'état* and the need to break Habsburg encirclement is the key to explaining how France was able to justify its many alliances with Protestants, then *reputación* is crucial for understanding what influenced the policies of Spain and its rulers. Perhaps best translated as renown, the word refers to the strength that Spain gained by fulfilling her duty as the foremost Catholic power. The Spanish king needed always to act in a 'most Catholic' way. In practical terms this might mean that committees of theologians or *juntas* might be called upon to stand in judgement on the morality of the monarch's decisions. No belief system can be self-defeating, however; Spain did not place its religious interests ahead of worldly ones. With so many competing interests, languages and economies, it made good sense to rally such a far-flung empire under the battle-cry of Catholicism.

The religiosity of Spanish political life showed through in the way members of the royal family lived a quasi-liturgical existence.[4] Their daily routine was patterned around religious celebrations. The king and his family were treated with a sense of reverence that bordered on worship. Their most emblematic palace, the Escorial, some miles outside Madrid in the foothills of often snowy mountains, doubled as a monastery. Dedicated to St Lawrence, the complex of buildings was laid out in the shape of the gridiron on which the saint was martyred. At its heart was a cavernous church with a lavishly decorated high altar. The private apartments of the king and queen were designed to overlook the altar so that, from their separate vantage points, they could observe the miracle of the mass. Even in the ancient *alcázar*, the fortress turned royal palace on the western edge of Madrid, the Spanish royal family led a life of seclusion almost as rigid as that of a religious order. When they attended church, the king would be hidden from view behind a curtain. He had become an object of veneration almost as if he were himself a precious relic. His regal presence was always felt but rarely revealed.

Of course, there were times when even the king of Spain was able to break free from the stifling protocol of the court. In August 1622, the archbishop of Granada had heard enough colourful stories about Felipe's amorous adventures to take it upon himself to caution Olivares against the king's night-time excursions from the palace. (Madrid was built largely on a rocky outcrop and was blessed with a multitude of tunnels, some of which notoriously connected the palace to the seedier parts of town just beyond the walls.) Despite being the king's former tutor, the cleric was given short shrift. Only a clergyman, he was told, could have imagined it was possible to curb the king's youthful excesses.[5] As far as we know, Charles was to evince no interest in joining his host in discovering Madrid's lowlife, but at least in his red-blooded desire to hunt the young king found one passion he could share with the far greener Prince of Wales.

Felipe IV inherited the Spanish Match from his father. For both of them the challenges it posed were as much emotional as diplomatic. The new king was exceptionally close to María, considering her 'the most perfect creature I have known'.[6] They had been brought up together, and at the start of his reign he was loath to contemplate the loss of his much-loved younger sibling. He was also adamant that she should have a marriage that befitted her status, and María was regarded as highly attractive, at least for a princess. Just weeks before his arrival, Bristol told the Prince,

> she is of a fair hair and complexion, of a middling stature, being of late well grown. She hath the fairest hands that ever I saw. She is very straight and well bodied, and a likely lady to make you happy, and England with you, by a plentiful issue.[7]

Her Habsburg ancestry was fully evident, as James Howell in the embassy disarmingly revealed:

> she is a very comely lady, rather of a Flemish complexion than Spanish, fair haired and carrieth a most pure mixture of red and white in her face. She is full and big lipped, which is held a beauty rather than a blemish or any excess in the Austrian family, it being a thing incident to that race.[8]

Bristol also mentioned that she possessed a 'more grave and settled manner' than was usual in England. Though a year younger than her brother, the now sixteen-year-old María was already wedded to the rigid protocol that the Habsburgs had adapted from the usage of their ancestors, the dukes of Burgundy. The earl of Carlisle visited Prince Charles in Madrid, and he was naturally curious to see the Infanta at close quarters. When he was finally admitted to an audience, the princess was sitting in a chair of state raised above the ground. Despite 'his complimental motions and approaches', Lord Hay, as he was still known, 'could not draw so much from her as to put out her hand to him when he went to kiss it'. She remained 'as immoveable as the image of the Virgin Mary, when suppliants bow to her on festival days'.[9]

The Infanta was fiercely Catholic. As we shall see, her brother the king acknowledged to Olivares that she did not relish the prospect of being married to a Protestant, regardless of the terms of any settlement. The match would create as many difficulties as it would solve for the Spanish branch of the Habsburgs. When marriage with Protestant England had first been mooted at the start of James's reign, it was still credible to believe that the son of Mary, Queen of Scots, might restore Catholicism in all his realms. Though the marriage took on renewed significance once James's son-in-law had accepted the Bohemian crown, there remained no overwhelming military or political reason why Spain needed an alliance with England. It was not regarded as a major power on land, if in Spain its navy, for very obvious reasons, was believed to have a tremendous capacity to irritate. Merciless English raids on Lisbon and Cadiz were etched into the popular memory, but only a couple of years after Charles's visit to Madrid, Olivares sarcastically reminded Gondomar that if England were as strong as he made out he would seek its friendship, but he simply did not

> believe that she was so formidable as you suggest, because when all was said and done she might be very powerful at sea, but I do not believe it is so ingrained or substantial that she could bring off any real conquests.[10]

It was largely in a negative sense that a marriage alliance with Britain had strategic value. So long as amicable relations were maintained with King James, there was less chance he would assist the rebellious Dutch. If his friendship were lost, then he might place himself at the head of a Protestant coalition comprising the Dutch as well as the Scandinavian powers. If James were to offer his son in marriage to France, then a coalition of all Spain's enemies might be achieved, with conceivably disastrous consequences for an empire that, for all its strength, felt its resources overstretched and its possessions almost too far-flung to be adequately defended.

Though there was always the fear that if the Prince of Wales were to die unmarried the Stuart crown would pass to the Winter Queen and her husband, this was no compelling reason to marry the king of Spain's sister into a country which still harassed Catholics. Friendship with James could be maintained by other means, which, as we shall see, Olivares was to ponder. The damage to the Monarchy's *reputación* would be immeasurable. On top of this, marriage to Charles, who was, when all was said and done, the Elector Palatine's brother-in-law, might lead to an unintended breach with the other branch of the dynasty in Vienna. That was never to be contemplated, as Endymion Porter bore witness after his acrimonious exchange with Olivares.[11] True, relations between the two Habsburg capitals were at times strained.

Spain was opposed to any suggestion that the emperor might offer the electoral rights of the Palatinate to the Catholic duke of Bavaria. Despite being the
Palsgrave's distant relative, he was clamouring for the Palsgrave's electoral dignity to be transferred to him in reward for his victories in Bohemia and the
Palatinate and, as some claimed, in recognition of his superior title.[12] Spain's
view was that to transfer the electoral dignity would make resolution of the
problems of Germany impossible, as well as consolidating the duke's claim to
be the most active Catholic prince in the Empire.[13] But despite the friction
between Madrid and Vienna a breach between the two branches of the family
was inconceivable. A successful outcome to the Spanish Match would doubtless oblige Madrid to try even harder to reach a negotiated settlement in central Europe, but it would be pushing at a door waiting to be unlocked. Vienna
was also not averse to a negotiated settlement of the conflict, but only if
James's son-in-law would show some sign of contrition.

The angry meeting that Porter had endured with Olivares was never to deter
James and Charles. The real business behind his mission was the marriage: all
else could be put to one side, not least because James by now cordially detested
his son-in-law. He regarded him as the principal author of the misfortunes of
his daughter and grandchildren. Porter was under orders to continue negotiations regardless of what was said about the Palatinate. James Howell, from his
vantage point in the embassy, was well aware of the rebuff over the Rhineland,
yet he maintained that the marriage would go through; otherwise, as he put it,
'my cake is dough'.[14] King James, his son and his Favourite had convinced themselves that, once the marriage was concluded, Spain would be eager to persuade
the emperor to arrange for his allies to withdraw from the Palatinate. Precisely
how, they were too restless to contemplate, nor did they need to. The alternative was to summon a parliament, and that would entail capitulating to
demands for an anti-Catholic crusade, which was a humiliation not to be contemplated. The tragedy is that, much as the Prince and the Favourite held fast
to a belief in the saving grace of the Spanish Match, Spain's young king had
already determined to follow in his father's footsteps. He too would not require
his beloved sister to marry a Protestant.

Shortly before he died, Felipe III drew up his last will and testament. He singled out the Infanta María as especially being in need of her brother's protection.[15] Then, in his last remaining mortal hours, the dying king communicated
to his sixteen-year-old son his true feelings about María's marriage. He had all
but abandoned the English match. Perhaps the distant memory of dire warn-
ings came back to haunt the enfeebled king. In November 1613 there had been
talk of marrying another infanta, his niece, the daughter of the duke of Savoy

13. *Count Duke of Olivares,* by Diego Velázquez. Painted about fifteen years after Olivares put pay to the Spanish Match, Velázquez depicts him as a thoughtful statesman.

14. *Frederick V, Elector Palatine and King of Bohemia, the 'Winter King',* by Michiel van Mierevelt and Studio, *c.* 1628. Frederick V, the leading Protestant prince in Germany, accepted the Bohemian Crown in 1619, thereby plunging Europe into the Thirty Years War.

15. *Elizabeth Stuart, Electress Palatine and Queen of Bohemia, the 'Winter Queen',* by Michiel van Mierevelt and Studio, *c.* 1628. The original 'queen of hearts', Elizabeth of Bohemia married Frederick V of the Palatinate in 1613. Neither her father James, nor her brother Charles ever saw her again, and she was only permitted to return to England after her nephew, Charles II, had regained his throne. This portrait was painted during her long years of exile in Holland.

16. *Equestrian Portrait of the Duke of Lerma*, by Peter Paul Rubens. Though Felipe III's favourite apparently supported a Spanish Match, the duke of Lerma was no friend to Ambassador Gondomar, whom he despatched to England in order to be rid of a troublesome suitor.

17. *Archduchess Isabel*, by Peter Paul Rubens. A daughter of Felipe II, the doughty Archduchess Isabel ruled the Southern Netherlands on Spain's behalf. She supplied the bulk of the troops who occupied the Lower Palatinate.

18. *Charles, Prince of Wales,* by Daniel Mytens. This portrait dates from the early 1620s. It may even have been painted shortly after Charles's return from Madrid, if only because he has a small moustache which dates from his time in Spain.

19. *James Hamilton, Earl of Arran and 1st Duke of Hamilton,* by Daniel Mytens. Dated 1623, this portrait was painted shortly after the earl's return from Madrid and clearly reflects the influence of Spanish portraiture.

and his elder half-sister, to the Prince of Wales. A special committee of half a dozen theologians considered the proposal and no fewer than four of the six objected. Their chilling argument was that merely to advocate marriage to a non-Catholic was a mortal sin, *irrespective* of whether a pontiff granted a dispensation for the Prince and his bride. The spiritual threat to the children of the marriage was simply too great. To confirm this, Antonio de Sotomayor recounted an alarming story he had heard from a clergyman who had gone with the great embassy to London at the start of James's reign. At a still tender age, Prince Charles had been taken away from his Catholic mother, Queen Anne, all for fear she would corrupt her son's religion. The theologian's words carried weight: he was confessor to the royal children.[16]

We know of Felipe III's deathbed confession only because of a businesslike letter his son wrote to Olivares. Towards the end of 1622, he passed on what his father had told him a year and a half earlier. Except in the event that a religious capitulation was forthcoming from the House of Stuart, his father had made up his mind that he would not

> marry my sister Dona Maria with the Prince of Wales, which your uncle don Baltazar understood, and so treated this match ever with an intention to delay it, notwithstanding it was so far advanced that considering withal the aversions unto it of the Infanta, it is time to seek some means to divert the treaty, which I would have you find out, and I will make it good whatsoever it be.

The new king at least had a sense of shame concerning his father's duplicity. He instructed Olivares to 'procure the satisfaction of the King of Great Britain, who hath deserved very much'.[17] To break the marriage yet uphold the peace was to be Olivares's herculean task.

King Felipe's letter became one of Europe's best-known secrets. Charles and Buckingham were taunted with a glimpse of its contents during one of the more heated exchanges with Olivares, as the duke recounted in the House of Lords in 1624 during his exculpatory account of his actions in Madrid.[18] Outlandish though its survival and transmission may seem, the authenticity of the young king's letter seems impeccable.

In his last years, Felipe III consistently harboured grave doubts about whether María's marriage to Charles could ever be justified. Did those very fears about mortal sin come back into play in 1618, when he had politely but firmly pointed out to his councillors that he found it hard to conceive of the marriage without the Prince of Wales's prior conversion? If Charles persisted in his religion, the old king scribbled, it would be easy to break any promises of liberty of conscience.[19]

7. This painting depicts the extraordinary efforts taken to ensure that the future Felipe IV's French bride was handed over at the same moment as his sister was entrusted to Louis XIII, at the midway point in the River Bidasoa separating Spain and France. It illustrates the complex protocol which surrounded royal marriages.

In fact, Felipe III took to pursuing a double-edged policy. While publicly endorsing the negotiations, he covertly worked against them. On one occasion he formally ordered his representative in Rome, the duke of Alburquerque, to present the pope with articles agreed by James, while in the same breath he secretly told him that what he really wanted was for the papacy to stall, at least until things improved in England, 'or if there is another way to marry the Prince with less damage to this crown and to Christendom'.[20] He did the same with Gondomar, with only marginally less candour. In August 1620, the king wrote two letters on the same day to his ambassador in London. The first expressed regal pleasure at James's latest concessions. The second told a very different story. He had not the slightest intention of allowing the marriage treaty to come to fruition 'unless they grant liberty of conscience there', and with all necessary guarantees. Because of the danger that 'speaking plainly' would oblige James to break off negotiations, the king instructed Gondomar to drag out the negotiations over the summer.[21] Finally, if further demonstration were necessary of the genuineness of Felipe IV's letter to Olivares, we only have to consider the timing. It was written just a month after the death of his uncle, don Baltasar de Zúñiga, which is the reason that the new favourite needed to be told the secret about the family pact of the kings of Spain.

Why, then, did Olivares permit the religious articles to go forward to London with Endymion Porter only a few weeks later? Though to the British King and his heir the marriage treaty was a first glimpse of the promised land, others felt no end to their wanderings was in sight. One observer of the diplomatic scene in Spain wearily dismissed the flurry of paperwork passing between Rome and the two secular capitals as 'all wind and metaphysics'.[22] The Genoese ambassador had already concluded that the marriage was never going to happen; it was as pointless as a dog chasing its shadow, he said.[23] If at the court of St James the articles were seized upon as a heaven-sent signal to rejoice, it was the result of an old man's desire to avoid war and a young man's impatience for marriage. It was also testimony to the fact that London was blinded to the subtleties of Spanish statecraft.

It may simply be that Olivares was at a loss as to how to halt the diplomatic machine dead in its tracks. He had only been chief minister for a matter of months, if not weeks. His king had anyway entrusted him with a family secret rather than announcing a change of policy. It was a perverse matter of pride that only the young king and his inexperienced favourite should know that, at the highest levels, the match was an uneasy and dishonourable sham. Had the various members of the *junta* of theologians and the Council of State been informed, it would not be possible to keep this secret for long. It was far better for only Felipe and his favourite to know that the marriage was something to be avoided – unless, of course, the House of Stuart astonished itself and the world by turning Catholic.

Since Olivares's task was to break the marriage and appease King James, it is more than likely that he spied a silver lining to Porter's return with the articles. With religion appearing to be safely out of the way, the spotlight would fall on the so-called temporal articles or general articles of friendship between the two royal houses. This would be the moment to confront the question of James's son-in-law, as well as the implications of their mutual antipathy towards the Dutch and the all-important question of the dowry that a Catholic bride might bring with her. Discussion of these general articles would provide Olivares with his one and only chance to break the match and *still* retain the friendship of the king of Great Britain, entirely as his master wished.

In fact, Olivares had begun planning for this eventuality in his reply to King Felipe's terse letter. His response was swift, being delivered within three days. It was also tightly argued. The count fleshed out the reasoning behind the late

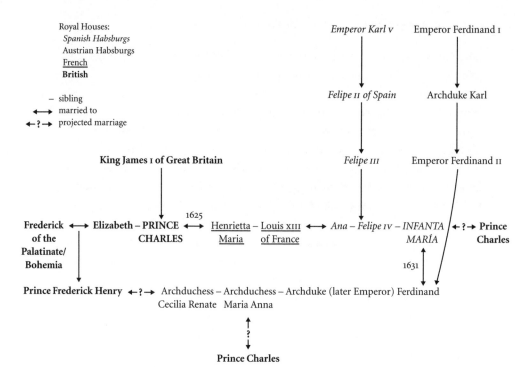

Fig. 3. Olivares's proposed 'dynastic revolution': the Spanish and Austrian marriage plans for Prince Charles and the Infanta María. The baffling interrelationship between the principal European royal families highlights the need to secure prestigious marriages.

king's deathbed declaration. Marriage with England might not only drag Spain into a war with the king's uncle, the Holy Roman Emperor, but there was the absurd danger that Spain might find itself on the opposite side to the Catholic League under Duke Maximilian's leadership. This led on to a flint-like reiteration that concord among the Habsburgs needed to be maintained at all costs. Dynastic and military unity with Vienna was the only way to preserve the honour of his king and the territorial integrity of Spain's empire, not least because the unrest in Germany was interfering with the prosecution of the war against the Dutch rebels. His favoured solution was to take up an idea first aired by Gondomar.[24]

Olivares backed a grand dynastic revolution. James's eldest grandson should be sent to the Imperial court in Vienna. There the nine-year-old Prince Frederick Henry would be brought up a Catholic. This would put him in a position to marry the emperor's younger daughter, the eleven-year-old Archduchess Cecily Renate, and so to inherit his father's lands in the fullness of time. The count's stroke of genius was to see how discussion of the temporal articles would allow him to bid for María's freedom. With religion no longer an obstacle, Olivares could vest himself in the garb of honest broker. He could propose most amicably to his British friends that the best way – the *only* way – of hastening a resolution of the crisis in the Rhineland would be for Charles to marry not the king of Spain's sister but his cousin, the Holy Roman Emperor's elder daughter, the thirteen-year-old Archduchess Maria Anna.[25] The religious articles already agreed might just as easily form the basis for marriage to an archduchess as to an infanta. If Olivares could bring off his plan, he would have bound Vienna, Madrid and London in the bonds of holy matrimony. His master would be the arbiter of Europe.

If there was one thing which this 'mixing up of the marriages' needed it was time.[26] Olivares had first of all to woo the emperor. Though a marriage between María and the Archduke Ferdinand had been been mooted since 1617,[27] the question of a Viennese bride for Charles was novel. The best man for the job was his expert on British affairs. Gondomar braced himself for his first foray into Germany. King Felipe and Olivares worked in conjunction to warn the emperor's ambassador that the suggestion of a trio of Austrian marriages was of the utmost secrecy. In turn, Khevenhüller advised Vienna that Gondomar was the sort of person who 'cared not for fripperies but always got to the heart of the matter'. For good measure, he added that the Spanish favourite disliked Gondomar so much that he might never recall him from Vienna.[28]

As for James, Olivares guessed correctly that he could be persuaded of the benefits of the 'Austrian alternative'. We know this because of a chance remark the British monarch made in choleric letters he dashed off after hearing of the emperor's decision to deprive his son-in-law of his electorship. Towards the end of 1622 Ferdinand had travelled to Regensburg, the traditional meeting place for the emperor and the imperial parliament. In this free city on the banks of the Danube, it was formally announced on 15 February 1623 that Maximilian of Bavaria had been rewarded with the Palatine electorship for the rest of his life.[29] When Charles set out for Madrid two days later, he was completely oblivious to what had been decided in the depths of Germany; James broke the news to him a month later. The King described his feelings of fury and humiliation. He denounced the emperor for having 'now spewed the uttermost of his unquenchable malice' against Frederick.[30] (As the duke of Infantado later admitted in open council, with magisterial understatement, he had 'every right to be angry'.[31]) Four days later there was a break in the clouds when James again took up his pen. He told Charles of 'a whispering' he had heard: Spain was considering a Viennese bride for his grandson. James confessed that, so long as the business of the Palatinate was 'brought to a good end', he no longer cared whether this was through Charles's marriage 'or any other'.[32] The only problem was that the Prince of Wales was by now in Madrid, with only the Infanta on his mind. If Charles's reckless appearance in the Spanish capital did not quite kill stone dead all discussion of the 'Austrian alternative', it dealt it a mortal blow.[33]

When Endymion Porter had arrived back in London in January 1623, it looked to the House of Stuart as if it had snatched victory from the jaws of defeat. Ever since the dissolution of the last parliament the only thing that stood between old King James and involvement in a European war seemed to be the promise of an intimate alliance with Spain. When the Prince realised that his special messenger had brought with him the articles for his marriage, his royal impetuosity can only be imagined.[34] What, he asked himself, could he do to make Spain move more quickly to dispatch his Princess of Wales? John and Thomas Smith now stepped forward with a strategy of their own devising.

8. Dear Venturous Knights

'The Spanish Match cast such a mist before King James's eyes that he could not discern any of the mischievous consequences which attended it'.[1] The new year of 1623 found the King's diplomacy in a parlous state. The catastrophic loss of Heidelberg the previous September had been quickly followed by the collapse of Mannheim at the end of October. The defence of Frankenthal, the last of the three Rhenish towns under the protection of the House of Stuart, could no longer be sustained once the winter was over. James had already begun negotiating its surrender. He could not risk the political pressures which would build up at home as the siege intensified. Almost a month after Charles's arrival in Madrid, the uncomfortable news finally came through that his father had ordered the English garrison to march out. In April, the fortress was finally and ignominiously turned over to the Archduchess Isabel's safe keeping. Though Frankenthal was supposed to return to English hands if peace was not concluded within eighteen months, the submission to the archduchess remained a fate only imperceptibly better than falling to the duke of Bavaria's armies.[2]

According to Professor Thomas Cogswell, Charles's decision to set out for Spain was a rational response to this catalogue of disasters. There was an overwhelming need to discover whether the Spaniards were truly committed to a marriage alliance with Great Britain. In that sense, Cogswell wrote, 'the Spanish journey indeed resembles . . . a bold cavalry charge'.[3] This was the pose struck by Buckingham when he later justified events in the House of Lords. He alleged that, because Porter had come home virtually empty-handed from Spain, 'with a dispatch fraught with generalities, without any one particular or certainty at all', Charles had valiantly decided to go to Madrid to oblige the king of Spain to declare his true intentions.[4]

The rediscovery of the 'pleasing news' about the marriage accord that Porter brought back in January 1623 blows this explanation out of the water.[5] Charles's delight at the news from Spain was without doubt all the greater because of what was happening in Germany, but that does not mean that events there inspired his journey to Madrid. True, there was still no agreement on what Spain would or would not do for James's dispossessed grandchildren. It was simply taken for granted that once the marriage was celebrated Spain would do enough to repair the King's reputation as a concerned grandfather. Most important of all, Porter had brought back with him the king of Spain's promise to press Rome to allow the Infanta to travel to England that spring. Foolhardy rather than intrepid – a silly gallop rather than a cavalry charge – the Prince travelled to Madrid to hasten a marriage he assumed was all but signed and sealed. As Charles's faithful counsellor, the earl of Clarendon put it, the Prince's journey was 'to fetch home his mistress' and 'put an end presently to all those formalities which . . . might yet long retard the Infanta's voyage into England many months'.[6] As no further news came out of Madrid to relieve the winter bleakness, and puffed up with an almost adolescent recklessness, Charles decided upon action. A young and untried heir to the throne would demonstrate to his father and the world how he and his dashing companion-in-arms were 'dear venturous knights, worthy to be put into a new romance'.[7]

How did Charles and Buckingham persuade James to allow 'so dangerous and hazardful a journey'?[8] Clarendon's account is probably the most reliable. He knew nearly all the key players. In particular, he had heard Cottington give his side of the story, so he said, more than once. Clarendon's version of events does not stint on the amount of emotional blackmail and subterfuge needed to obtain the King's consent. This rings true, as *raison d'état* would surely not have persuaded the ageing monarch to part with the two people he loved most in the world.

Charles and Buckingham agreed among themselves that the Prince would go to his father and say to him 'how gallant and how brave a thing it would be . . . to make a journey into Spain'. Only when the King had agreed in principle would it be revealed that they had in mind a 'journey only with two servants'. James had initially been taken with the idea, but once he realised its secretive nature he 'fell into a great passion with tears'. The Prince and the Favourite had cunningly prepared for this eventuality. The next step was to concede that Porter, now rested from his arduous last trip, and the newly married Cottington might go with them. Neither courtier was to be informed that the destination was Spain 'till they were even ready to be embarked'. James argued that they should both be let into the secret, saying they would think of things necessary for the journey 'that they two would never think of'. This gave the King the opportunity of enlisting Secretary Cottington's support against a clandestine journey.

As Cottington related many times, when he heard what James had to say 'he fell into such a trembling that he could hardly speak'. His opinion was that, if Charles appeared in Madrid, the Spaniards would inevitably consider that the accord already reached was no longer binding. They would intensify their demands. Buckingham rounded on Cottington in a manner such as he might treat a member of the House of Commons who was overreaching himself. The Secretary was being asked about the best route to take, not for his opinion on matters of state.[9] This was the beginning of a lifelong feud with the Favourite. All Cottington could do was accept the mission and draw up his will.[10] As for his new wife, he was obliged to abandon 'the poor desolate woman' after only four days, 'without telling her whither where I went'.[11] Given the absolute necessity of secrecy, if only for their safety in France, there is no reason to doubt Clarendon's suggestion (and Cottington's) that James could only have been told about the plans just two or three days before his 'sweet boys' set off on their adventure of a lifetime. As for the King's reaction, he took to his 'naked bed'.[12]

The Prince of Wales had persuaded his father that the time had come, in Gondomar's words, to mount Spain. This is what the King told his privy councillors. When they went down on bended knee to ask if rumours were true about the Prince's departure, they were told that his son had simply wanted to put an end to all further delay by fetching his bride in person, just as Charles's father and great-grandfather had done before him. Odd though it may have seemed in English eyes, this was an established custom in the House of Stuart. King James had sailed to Denmark to bring back Queen Anne, while his grandfather, James V of Scotland, had journeyed to France to woo a bride. This family sentiment probably weighed most heavily with the King. He may even have penned a jingle which was put about to defend Charles's departure.[13]

> Thy grandsire great, thy father too
> Were the examples thus to do
> Whose brave attempts in heat of love
> France and Denmark did approve
>
> So venturous Jack doth nothing new
> If love and fortune he pursue

James could not deny Charles the same freedom to collect his bride as he and his forebears had enjoyed, especially if appearing in Madrid would cast off the need for a dispensation. In Clarendon's view, Charles's 'nature was inclined to adventures'. Even Simonds D'Ewes, no friend to the Spanish Match, could appreciate that the Prince was spurred on 'happy in the imaginary love of her he never saw and perhaps willing to prove famous for this noble venture'.[14]

The elements of high farce in the journey now fall into place. To travel overland to Spain, during the height of winter, unguarded and incognito, is explicable only in terms of immature adventure. It clarifies why Charles was willing to present himself at the most rigid of courts without the pomp and trappings of a state visit.[15] The intention was for a chivalrous knight to capture his princess, *not* for a lone prince to exert pressure on a foreign sovereign to declare for or against a friendship. It explains the secrecy surrounding his arrival. Don Carlos Coloma, Gondomar's replacement as ambassador, was completely in the dark; and the first he knew that something was afoot was when Porter and Cottington left together early one morning. Only later did he get a hint that the Prince and the Favourite were on the move.[16] The element of surprise was essential to the theatricality of the plan. Since all outstanding matters, in Rome as well as in Madrid, were to be resolved by the Prince's declaration of his love for the Infanta, nothing must detract from the wonder of his arrival.

Reaction to the Prince's departure was fervid. The Venetian ambassador described it as

> a monster among decisions, a labyrinth without head or way out. No action more remote from all imagination or belief ever took place, or less founded in likelihood, to say nothing of reason.[17]

D'Ewes confided to his diary that the Prince's departure 'was the doleful day that made every good Protestant sad for'.[18] John Holles, who was close to the English court, was more biting. He remarked mordantly that his old friend Gondomar must be using 'us according to our religion, to depend rather on faith than on good works'.[19]

To others less erudite, the journey seemed plain odd. If the marriage really was agreed, then why not collect the Infanta 'with a navy royal'? A splendid fleet to fetch her had long been talked about.[20] The misgivings of a kingdom deprived of its heir were so great that the members of the Privy Council resolved to attend St Paul's Cathedral in a public display of conciliar loyalty.[21] The King commanded that the visit should not be criticised from the pulpits. As usual at moments of high tension, jokes were told. The story was soon doing the rounds that the bishop of London had ordered his clergy to say no more about the Prince's visit other than to pray for his return. 'An honest plain priest' followed his instructions to the letter, praying 'That God would return our noble Prince home in safety to us, *and no more*, supposing that the words *no more* to be a piece of the prayer'![22]

Was it Charles's or Buckingham's idea to steal away to Madrid? Many have put it all down to the marquess's 'incomparable vanity'.[23] The sense of alarm as news of the departure leaked out points us in a different direction. Of course, it is always possible that neither Buckingham nor Charles could really remember who first proposed the journey amidst the merriment of the Christmas festivities. It was rumoured they had taken advantage of court masques to try on their false beards.[24] Clarendon, who was always keen to protect Charles's reputation whenever he could, put the blame squarely on Buckingham. On the other hand, King James, with his own reasons for not wishing to expose his beloved Favourite to criticism, assured the Privy Council it was entirely the Prince's idea.

The King was probably right. It made no sense whatsoever for Buckingham to propose a secret journey. His absence from the court left him perilously exposed to the malicious tongues of those left behind, even if they both expected to come home with the princess by the end of May. It was simply too dangerous for even a subject as mighty as Buckingham to advise the King's son – the King's only son – to absent himself from his realms. True, Buckingham needed to preserve his relationship with the Prince, as sooner rather than later Charles would succeed his father. Nonetheless, there is no inkling that their friendship was under threat at this time, and it would surely have been obvious to the duke that spending so much time together was as likely to ruin a friendship as to consolidate it. Most significant of all, Buckingham was in love. The tone of the letters he exchanged with his wife during the long summer of 1623 makes it hard to imagine that he would have abandoned her of his own volition, even if his father-in-law jokingly advised him not to woo the ladies of the Spanish court on account that he might be poisoned. He warned him that 'if you desire whores you will be in danger of burning'.[25] For Charles, there was a family tradition to follow. If the Prince proposed the visit, then Buckingham was obliged to go along with the idea for fear of jeopardising his position in the next reign. Like Buckingham, Charles too was in love, but his love was as yet unseen and still in Madrid.

Monday, 17 February 1623 was a day of frenetic activity. At seven o'clock in the morning Cottington and Porter left Holborn for Dover.[26] Their job was not only to act as decoys: they needed to secure a commercial ship to take the Prince's party across the Channel.[27] A few hours later, Charles and Buckingham left Tibolts, in Hertfordshire, for the Favourite's house, Newhall, in Essex, where the Prince was lavishly entertained during his overnight stay.[28] In his excitement, Charles rashly boasted to Phineas Pette, the shipbuilder, that he 'should shortly come to sea in the *Prince*', the ship designated to fetch the

Infanta.[29] The King played his role in the deception by removing his court to Newmarket. Prince Charles's household servants were instructed to assemble there in two days' time.[30] Instead, the next morning, the 18th, Charles and Buckingham slipped out of Newhall for Dover. They were accompanied only by Sir Richard Graham, a Scotsman and the Favourite's master of the horse. At Tilbury they crossed the Thames to Gravesend. After the success of the initial choreography of their departure, the failure to plan ahead now became disconcertingly evident. There, 'for lack of silver, they were fain to give the ferryman a piece of two and twenty shillings'. Guessing from the guinea coin that they might be going abroad to duel, the boatman sent word to the authorities at Rochester. Charles and Buckingham were too quick for the city fathers to intercept them, but as soon as they had passed through Rochester they spied the French ambassador's coach ahead of them. They were forced to take cover 'and teach post-hackneys to leap hedges'.[31]

The mission almost came to an abrupt end when they were successfully detained at Canterbury. The two bearded strangers travelling under such suspiciously plain names were stopped by order of the mayor. He claimed he was acting under the authority of privy councillors and, in particular, the lieutenant of Dover Castle, Sir Henry Mainwaring. 'At all which confused fiction', Buckingham decided that the only thing to do was 'to dismask his beard' and announce that he, as Lord Admiral, was undertaking a surprise inspection of the fleet. Even then a baggage boy who had been at court realised what was afoot, but, in ways we do not know, 'his mouth was easily shut'. The royal party reached Dover around six o'clock in the evening. They met up with Porter and Cottington, who were waiting with two servants, Kirk – another Scotsman – and James Leviston of the Prince's bedchamber. A stormy night prevented them from embarking before five or six o'clock on the Wednesday morning for Boulogne, where they finally arrived by two o'clock that afternoon. Both Prince and Lord Admiral of the Fleet Buckingham were violently sick during the crossing,[32] something which must have brought back to Porter unhappy memories of his recent near-fatal crossing of the Channel. Once they were on French soil, the difficulties of maintaining their masquerade started over again. Two Germans who had travelled in England saw through their disguise but were persuaded by Graham that they must be mistaken,

> Which in truth is no very hard matter, for the very strangeness of the thing itself; and almost the impossibility to conceive so great a Prince and Favourite so suddenly metamorphized into travellers, with no greater train, was enough to make any man living unbelieve his five senses.[33]

Paris threw up the first of the diplomatic dangers that the journey was bound to pose. In an act of gross discourtesy, the king of France had not been notified of the passage of the heir to the British throne through his dominions. Charles and Buckingham had argued they would be out of France before news of their dash to Madrid became public knowledge. James decided that 'the bare stopping of the ports, there being so many blind creeks to pass at', would not contain the news, so he instructed Viscount Doncaster to inform Louis XIII of his son's 'passing unknown through his country'. As he said, he did this 'for fear that, upon the first rumour of your passing, he should take a pretext to stop you'.[34]

There was time for sightseeing. It was in Paris that Charles had his first taste of the grand European style of architecture. He spent a whole day touring the city and went to the court at least twice. Wisely, he and Buckingham took steps to intensify their disguise. Periwigs were purchased, 'somewhat to overshadow their foreheads'. At a rehearsal of a masque, he spied Queen Anne, who was surrounded by her sister-in-law Henrietta Maria and 'as many as made up nineteen fair dancing ladies, amongst which the queen is the handsomest'. The queen of France was the Infanta María's sister. Charles confessed it 'hath wrought in me a greater desire to see her sister'.[35]

On 23 February the two adventurers set out from Paris on the ten-day journey to the Spanish border. It was Lent, so there was little meat to be had.[36] The temptation when they came across a goat and her kids was too great to resist, and Graham was overheard by the Prince boasting that he would sneak up on one of the kids. 'Why Richard', interjected the Prince with Graham's ancestral connections with the south of Scotland in mind, 'do you think you may practise here your old tricks again upon the borders?' While the others pathetically tried to round up a young goat, Charles fired a Scottish pistol he had with him. He shot the kid in the head from horseback. According to Sir Henry Wooton, who was so intrigued by the Prince's journey to Madrid that he found out as much as he could about it, this episode demonstrated that 'His Highness even in such flight and sportful damage had a noble sense of just dealing'.[37] Four days after leaving the French city of Bayonne, the Prince and the Favourite, still in disguise, crossed the border into Spain. They entered by the time-hallowed way, via Irún, where the Pyrenees fall towards the sea.

Unfortunately, neither Charles nor Buckingham left a record of their first impressions of Spain. What we do have is an account by Sir Richard Wynn, a member of a distinguished Welsh family, and one of the gentlemen of the Privy Chamber who sailed at the beginning of April to join Charles. Only through his eyes can we get a flavour of how Spain might have appeared to John and

Thomas Smith.[38] It was evident straight away that the average Spaniard was far poorer than his English counterpart. The king of Spain might be the wealthiest monarch in Christendom but his subjects lived more frugal lives, eking out a living on land that was for the most part rocky and barren. The houses had no glass, something which had become increasingly affordable in England since the second half of the sixteenth century. In what must have been an early form of squash, Sir Richard noted that the men played 'tennis off the house, such as is used in Wales'.[39] Meat was still scarce when Sir Richard arrived, though this doubtless had something to do with the drought which, it was said, auspiciously ended with Charles's arrival. The straightforwardness of Spanish eating habits aroused attention: at times a plank would serve as a table and there were no napkins.

In contrast to the simplicity of living was the swagger of the Spanish male. Many men sported a cape and carried a sword. Male pride was made easier by the fact that women undertook a much larger share of the work, including labouring, than in England. (Perhaps that was why Sir Richard felt that the women were plump and ugly, unless – he remarked inexplicably – they were of English descent!) Though the husbands might display a disdain for money, their wives would not so readily turn up their noses at cash. At least this was the moral of one of Sir Richard's stories. A Spanish don had pointedly refused to take a single penny for his hospitality, leaving it to his wife to extract a very large sum from her guests.

Prince Charles had first-hand experience of the ferocity that might come from the wounded pride of a Spanish nobleman. On his way to Madrid he made the acquaintance of an ambassador's son. He remarked that he knew of an embassy in London where the son was far too ugly for his beautiful wife. It turned out he was talking to that very son. All that prevented a duel was the revelation that the nobleman was threatening the Prince of Wales. Whether or not this story is entirely true, it is an anecdotal reminder of the journey's dangers. Charles might feel that, as long as his sister lived, the king of Spain would do his best to ensure no harm befell him in Madrid; the real perils were to be found along the way.

Diplomatically, at least, we know what Charles and Buckingham felt about their mission as they entered Spain. Their views were expressed in a series of startlingly vivid letters which they sent back to England after their paths crossed with Walsingham Gresley, the earl of Bristol's man, just outside Bayonne. They took him back over the border as they continued into Spain. There they felt they could deliberate and write to James with less fear of disturbance than in France. They gave Gresley letters for the King telling him that they

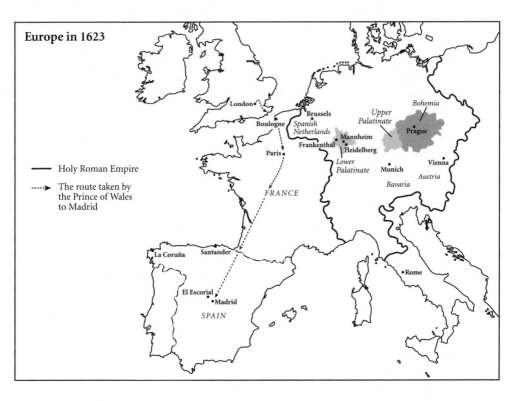

Europe in 1623

— Holy Roman Empire

----▶ The route taken by
the Prince of Wales
to Madrid

remained in the best of health, 'undiscovered by any Monsieur'. As for the earl's dispatches which Gresley was carrying, Charles and Buckingham said they contained nothing which 'hath made us repent our journey'. The need for papal permission was still causing delays, so it was a good thing, they argued, they had set out so soon. They pointed out that still

> the temporal articles are not concluded, nor will not be, till the dispensation comes, which may be God knows when; and when that time shall come, they beg twenty days to conceal it, upon pretext of making preparations [for the Infanta's departure]. This bearer's errand was answered by our journey thither . . .

They could not read the most important parts of Bristol's dispatch, as it had not occurred to them to take a cipher with them. When the King replied to their first letters from Spain, he warned them that on no account must the size of the dowry be reduced.[40]

Madrid resembled Newmarket. This was the bizarre comparison made by Sir Richard Wynn, who said the surrounding countryside was similar, as was the bitter cold blowing off the hills.[41] Prince and Favourite arrived in the capital on Friday, 7 March. They had taken thirteen days to travel from Paris. They arrived with just one servant, having decided at the last minute to ride on ahead of Porter and Cottington. They made their way to the 'Street of the Infantas' on the eastern side of the old city. They reached the earl of Bristol's residence, the House of the Seven Chimneys, at eight o'clock in the evening. The marquess entered the embassy first. His name, he said, was Thomas Smith. He had come to inform the ambassador that Gresley 'had fallen into thieves' hands and had all his letters taken away'. The mysterious guest said he had hurt his leg and so must wait for the ambassador to come down from his room. This was a courtly deception to oblige Bristol to be ready at the door to receive the Prince of Wales. Instead, the earl reported to James how his son

> went to see who it was, and knew my lord of Buckingham but dissembled it
> so well, that . . . he had got him up to his chamber and went presently down
> to the Prince (who stood all this while in the street with his postilion) and
> brought him likewise so handsomely up to his chamber.[42]

One detail stuck in James Howell's mind when he looked back on Buckingham's entry into the embassy. It was the oddity of seeing a royal favourite carrying his own portmanteau. No wonder the ambassador was 'in a kind of astonishment'.[43]

Bristol was right to be shocked at the Prince's 'sudden & unthought of arrival'.[44] The beds and refreshments which would have to be found for his most distinguished guests were the least of his worries. He also needed to think how best to inform the most rigid court in Europe of the presence of the heir to the British throne. Charles's arrival was an aggressive breach of protocol. The safest means of passing on the information was through Gondomar. Though only a member of the Council of War, and not the far more important Council of State, no one could deny his special relationship with England. To allow time for the enormity of the event to sink in, it was planned only to tell him that the marquess of Buckingham had arrived. Gondomar answered the summons to the embassy early the following morning, apparently convinced that the Prince of Wales was already in Madrid. (He claimed he had heard within a couple of hours of Charles's arrival.[45]) Believing his hopes for a royal conversion had been fulfilled, his jubilant comment was from the Nunc Dimittis – Let your servant depart in peace. He then went to Olivares. Seeing Gondomar's state of agitation, the count observed that he must have come to tell him that the king of Great Britain was in Madrid. No, muttered Gondomar, only his son.[46] Around four o'clock that afternoon Olivares sent his coach to fetch Buckingham, along with Gondomar and James's ambassadors. The count was waiting for them in the palace grounds. He and the marquess exchanged pleasantries undisturbed

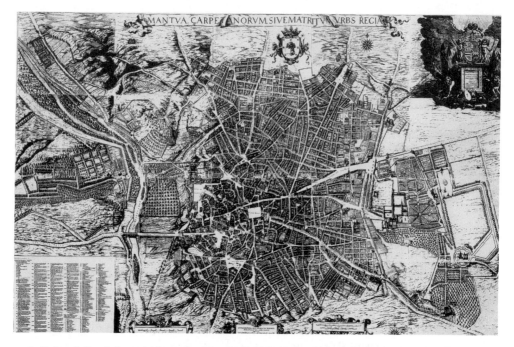

8. Pedro de Texeira's map of 1656 depicts a Madrid that had changed little since Charles's visit. The recently constructed Plaza Mayor is clearly visible in the centre, with the *alcázar* dominating the western limits of the city. The palace which Olivares was to build for Felipe IV in the 1630s is visible on the eastern edge of the city, near the fields where the Prince first glimpsed the Infanta.

in the coach for over an hour before he led them all 'by a back way into the King's private apartments'. Bristol said of Buckingham's private audience with the young Felipe that he behaved 'with so much alacrity and freeness that I never saw the Spanish gravity laid aside before'. Some time that Saturday morning, Gondomar was made a councillor of state. He rushed back to Charles to tell him that an Englishman had been sworn to the council, meaning himself who, he said, 'was an Englishman at heart'.[47] The following day it was arranged for Charles to have a peek at the Spanish royal family.

Earlier, in France, the duke of Epernon, the ancient governor of Guienne, had wanted to entertain the two intriguing young Englishmen. Cottington had prevented this only by saying they were of low standing, 'and formed yet to little courtship'.[48] Though this was untrue, nothing could have prepared Charles for his first experience of the ceremoniousness and rigour of Spanish protocol. On the Sunday, arrangements were made for the king and queen, along with the Infanta María, to take a ride in their respective carriages around the Prado, at that time a park outside the city's eastern limits. The king and his sister would stop to converse, all the while remaining in their carriages. The Prince of Wales was invited to look on, it was said, from an 'invisible coach'.[49]

The Infanta wore 'a blue ribbon about her arm, of purpose that the Prince might distinguish her'.[50]

Endymion Porter had no doubt about the effect the sight of the Infanta had on Charles. He told his wife,

> the Prince hath taken such a liking to his mistress that he now loves her as much for her beauty as he can for being sister to so great a king. She deserves it, for there was never seen a fairer creature.[51]

Another English eyewitness said that Charles 'would have leapt out of the coach to salute the king of Spain, but that Gondomar held him'.[52] Charles had yet to learn that his hot-headedness was not always appreciated in a court where royal protocol was ice-cold. Later in life, when Charles became celebrated for his refusal to play to the gallery, coaches would become a means of concealing himself from his subjects.[53] Perhaps he came to appreciate during his time in Madrid the deference with which Spaniards treated royalty, but on that first Sunday, when news of his arrival had brought the crowds out on to the streets to cheer the gallant Prince, he opted 'to stand up in the coach all the way, to show himself unto them'.[54]

Later that evening, King Felipe could not contain his own excitement. He asked to see the Prince and offered to come to the embassy. Charles could not accept so singular an honour: it would have set up an obligation so great that it would have been almost impossible to repay. Instead, he suggested their meeting should take place in the royal palace. Now it was Felipe's turn to decline, on the grounds that Charles did not yet have with him a sufficiently grand entourage for this to be appropriate. When they eventually met, in the neutral territory of the Prado, the conversation revolved around 'compliments and particular questions of all our journey'. The king of Spain then escorted Charles back to the embassy, but only half-way, and even this was not without incident. 'They were both almost overthrown in brickpits.'[55]

The arrival of the Prince of Wales threw the Spanish court into confusion. Olivares's recent policy of austerity was in ruins. His high-minded intention had been to channel the nation's wealth and energies towards conserving its empire instead of having it wasted on personal display. Within five days of the arrival the recent sumptuary legislation banning the wearing and selling of expensive clothing was reluctantly repealed for the duration of the visit.[56] Instead a committee was formed to plan the festivities and consider in the most minute detail the etiquette appropriate for a Prince of Wales.[57] As for the mounting expense of the visit, it was quipped that Charles had managed to sack the city without an army.[58]

In Spain members of the reigning dynasty played out the role of icons for a religiously inspired empire. If their special status were to be upheld, visiting princes needed to be treated in a corresponding fashion; if not, the uniqueness of royalty would diminish. Similarly, it was incumbent upon a visiting prince to exercise self-denial when accepting the honours offered. Too easy an acceptance might be taken to imply a willingness to capitulate to all that, politically and religiously, might be demanded of him. As John Howell put it, 'among other Grandezas' offered the Prince was the right to receive all petitions of grace in the month after his entry, but Charles was 'wonderful sparing in receiving any, specially from any English, Irish, or Scot'.[59]

The ceremony of Public Entry marked the moment when a royal personage became an iconic figure. Even the wives of the Catholic Kings did not officially become consorts until they had solemnly entered the court.[60] Until his own Public Entry Charles would remain effectively invisible. For instance, on his first Monday in Madrid, the day after he had seen the Infanta and her family in their carriages, the confraternity of the Slaves of Our Lady of the Remedios celebrated the feast of St Joseph. King Felipe commanded all his courtiers to take part in honour of his distinguished guest. In all, seventeen grandees of Spain paraded before the Prince, yet he could only glimpse what was going on from a balcony, being obliged to remain 'hidden behind a shutter on the grounds that he had not made his public entry'.[61]

James had obligingly provided a clue as to how to treat Charles. In the letters of presentation to be passed on to Felipe, James assured his host that Charles was 'the sworn king of Scotland', though what that means is unclear.[62] It was decreed that the Prince would be treated in the same way as the king and other members of the royal family, 'without any exception whatsoever',[63] even though his continuing Protestantism placed firm limits on how in practice he was incorporated into the life of the court. Charles formally entered 'the loyal town and court of Madrid' on Sunday, 16 March. Over 350 prisoners were released, according to the rules for the entry of a king or when the queen gave birth.[64] Charles spent the previous night in the sovereign's apartments of the Royal Monastery of the Jeronimites.[65] On the morning of his entry, he was greeted by the members of the various royal councils, but on this occasion he politely declined the honour of having his hands kissed. On the walls of his receiving chamber were hung pictures of knights and councillors, along with perhaps a less than welcome picture of an English parliament. Charles and Buckingham told James how Felipe 'forced your baby to ride on his right hand' as they travelled in state together. First they left the eastern outskirts of the city, then passed through the Puerta del Sol and the calle Mayor to the old

9. On Sunday, 16 March 1623, the Prince of Wales took up residence in the *alcázar*, Madrid's royal palace. Since it was still presumed that Charles would convert to Catholicism, he was permitted to process along a ceremonial route virtually identical to that followed by a Spanish king after his accession.

Alcázar, on the precipitous western edge of the city that overlooked the River Manzanares.[66] Significantly, the only break in tradition was that the royal procession could not stop at the church of Santa María.

The tedious ceremonies continued even after Charles had formally taken up residence at court. The following day, his second Monday in Madrid, more representatives of Spain's innumerable councils waited upon the Prince between half-past ten and noon. There were fireworks that evening in the palace courtyard. It rained. The next day the nobility turned up to present themselves. The first to kiss hands was the duke of Infantado, 'with all the Mendoza', followed by other great lords along with their followers. It must have been with some relief that on the Thursday and Friday the Prince went hunting, sometimes hawking with the earl of Bristol or accompanying the king to watch courtiers chasing rabbits or hunting partridges on the wing.[67]

Meanwhile, the Prince of Wales was getting used to the household supplied for him. Based on the Burgundian model which had been adapted for use in

Spain in the middle of the sixteenth century, it was of a solemnity unknown in England. The president of the Council of Italy, the count of Monterrey, was named his great chamberlain, and he was assisted by two other counts, including Gondomar. Sixteen of the king's privy gentlemen were assigned to Charles's service, along with many lesser officials. As a kindness, it was said, no bedchamber or personal servants were named. Instead, King Felipe sent eight black and gold keys for the Prince to distribute as he saw fit.[68] Charles gave one to Bristol and another to Buckingham. This caused James to quip that his Favourite – whom he had just raised to the rank of duke – was 'now turned Spanish with his golden key'.[69] The duty of this small army of Spanish courtiers was to interpose themselves on all public occasions between their new master and the mortal world. Whenever Charles dined in public he would first, in an echo of religious purification, dip his hands in water. Then the appointed chamberlain would go down on bended knee to pass him his napkin. The great nobles and the rest of the spectators would observe in absolute reverence, rather as if they were at high mass. Commenting on the excessive flattery involved in Burgundian etiquette, one modern writer has written that when a prince dined in public, his court became a self-contained universe, 'in which all the lesser planets revolved around the sun. The faces of the courtiers became like sunflowers, bent upon following the solar appearance of the prince'.[70]

Cottington had a more down-to-earth approach to court life. With his master already lodged in the royal palace, he told his pining wife that the Prince was now under one roof with his mistress.[71] Be that as it may, Charles would be prevented from speaking to the Infanta for several weeks, and even then only in the most formal and restricted of ways. Charles continued to be blithely optimistic. Casually he placed a wager with one of his servants that he would be home in England – with his bride, it went without saying – 'by the last of June'.[72] What Charles had not realised was that, for all the lavish hospitality and the warmth of the popular reception, his spiritual intentions had yet to be investigated at the court of the Catholic King.

9. Cat and Mouse

Charles would gaze upon the Infanta 'as a cat doth a mouse', said Olivares. He would 'have his eyes immovably fixed upon the Infanta half an hour together in a thoughtful speculative posture, which sure would needs be tedious, unless affection did sweeten it'.[1] She was, Buckingham explained to his wife, 'so delicate a creature and of so sweet a disposition'. She wrote back saying that the King had said how Charles was 'wonderfully taken with her', teasing the duke with the comment that the Prince would 'make a very honest husband, which is the greatest comfort in the world'. When James was told that the Infanta had sent a private message to Charles that he should wear a very large ruff, he took it as a compliment.[2] Katherine Buckingham sent the Prince the best pair of spyglasses she could procure for him, so that he could watch María from afar.[3]

Marriage to a royal princess is never a matter for private affections. There were loftier issues to consider, especially when an infanta of Spain was involved. When Olivares told King Felipe the astonishing news of Charles's arrival, the young king was transfixed by what the occasion might signify. He assumed that the Prince of Wales was about to make a magnificent concession in order 'to overcome the difficulties of religion, without which the marriage could not take effect'. If we are to believe Olivares, Felipe then swore an oath to the crucifix at the head of his bed. By the crucified union of God and man, he promised

> that not only shall the coming of the Prince of Wales not prevail with me in anything touching the holy Catholic religion to go a step beyond that which Thy vicar the Roman Pontiff may resolve, but that I will keep my resolution, even if it were to involve the loss of all the kingdoms.

Olivares said he never heard Felipe IV take a similar oath before or after. The king then instructed his favourite to grant the Prince of Wales everything he asked for that 'is temporal and is mine'.[4]

The impressionable Felipe was not merely forgetting his earlier reservations (and indeed those of his father) about the marriage. He was giving voice to a distinction which had long been a peculiarity of Spanish diplomacy. Any act of state, and in particular the marriage of an infanta, might have spiritual connotations that needed to be assessed independently from the secular or military implications. Most major issues were submitted to a council of theologians, which could advise whether a policy that was politically advantageous was impermissible because of its impact on religion. Similarly, a course of action of little strategic value might become advisable if it furthered the standing of the Catholic faith. In his oath, Felipe noted the great honour the king of Great Britain had done him in surrendering his son, and he also conceded that failure might drive England into an alliance with her enemies. But he was also acknowledging that ultimately he would not be swayed into a relaxation of the religious conditions just because Charles Stuart had paid him the courtesy of a visit and without an intention to convert or at least to grant full liberty of conscience to his Catholic subjects. Five years younger though he may have been, the king of Spain was already showing at least some signs of being a more level-headed politician than the Prince of Wales.

Felipe's reaction needs to be understood against the near-universal assumption in Madrid that the Prince's arrival signified a willingness to change his religion. His evident infatuation with the princess was taken as a proof. Buckingham admitted that the Spaniards were originally hoping for 'a conversion of us both'.[5] This was not just wishful thinking on the part of Charles's hosts, since the earl of Bristol also believed that the Prince was on the point of abandoning the Church of England. He compounded his error by offering to serve loyally after any defection to Rome, as Charles angrily reminded him in 1626.[6] More poignant is that Catholics throughout James's kingdoms rashly assumed it was safe for them to practise their religion openly. One astonished contemporary looked back on this as 'the year the Romish foxes came out of their holes'. Jesuits were spotted on the streets of London. In County Cavan, Irish Catholics were prevented from reoccupying the parish church only by the threat that they would have to sing their mass 'with the sound of musket'.[7]

A contented, even smug, Anglican, Charles never entertained the possibility of conversion. Yet the prospect of a change of religion obliged Felipe and Olivares to fritter away the first weeks of the stay in sounding out the Prince's spiritual intentions. While this was being undertaken, the plans for a Viennese match for Charles's eldest nephew could not be taken any further. As the emperor's ambassador, Count Khevenhüller, remarked, 'the Prince's unforeseen arrival' made it impossible to raise the matter, let alone debate it.[8]

Every inducement was given to lead Charles towards holy water. No one expected the Prince of Wales to humble himself by announcing an on-the-spot conversion. Repentance comes before new life; and it was only Lent. Olivares tried to pave the way in his second audience with Charles; he mentioned the Prince's grandmother, Mary, Queen of Scots and lauded her as a martyr for the Roman Church. Charles politely offered the count a picture of the queen, promising to seek out the newest account of her life.[9] In return, orders went out to prepare to celebrate Easter more splendidly than ever before.

On Palm Sunday, 30 April, the Prince was invited to watch from behind a screen as the royal family processed through the corridors of the palace. The religious and the carnal were marvellously combined, as he had 'a very good view of the lady Infanta, because the procession moved very slowly'.[10] The same day an English Jesuit distributed some £2,000 in alms to various hospitals and religious houses on the Prince's behalf.[11] On Maundy Thursday, Charles looked discreetly on as King Felipe fed the poor and kissed their feet. Good Friday witnessed the most spectacular process of discalced or barefoot friars. The mortification of the penitents was greater than ever, with some covering their face with ashes and wearing chains and crowns of thorns till the blood flowed down their foreheads. Others beat their chests with stones in imitation of St Jerome. All this was done with the specific intention of 'procuring his conversion'.[12]

Belief in the power of intercession remained manifest after Easter, at least as far as King Felipe was concerned. The procession for Corpus Christi early in June also took place with greater solemnity than ever. For the Prince's benefit, all monks were ordered to take part, regardless of any exemptions they might enjoy, along with the three military orders that were formed hundreds of years earlier to wage holy war against the Moors. From a balcony in the palace, he watched from a spiritually safe distance as the mass was celebrated on a specially erected altar. Charles may have been unmoved, but the magnificence of the ceremonies and the presence of the Prince as an 'eyewitness' persuaded one historian to consider it time to begin a life of King Felipe III, in whose reign, he explained, the Spanish Match was first mooted.[13]

Despite requiring Charles's pious observation at all their religious ceremonies, it must be said that the Spaniards only rarely managed to show any respect for the religion of their guests. One example of thoughtfulness occurred early on in the visit, when an especially magnificent banquet was given in honour of the little English court that was gathering at Madrid. Buckingham was treated royally: he and Olivares sat under a canopy while all the other dignitaries had to stand. In particular, the meal consisted entirely of fish in recog-

10. Half monastery, half royal palace, the Escorial was felt to be an inappropriate place for the Prince of Wales to spend Easter in 1623, in case the monks did 'something which might offend' him.

nition of the fact that 'the guests were of a different profession and custom'.[14] Two weeks before Easter, Charles had asked whether he could retire to the Escorial during Holy Week. He was offered the royal hunting lodge of the Pardo instead. Since the royal apartments in the great monastery-palace overlooked the high altar, it was agreed in council that it would be distasteful for a non-Catholic to occupy them, but it was also remarked that the monks might inadvertently 'do something which might offend the Prince'.[15]

Baroque opulence notwithstanding, the most overt attempts to extract a conversion from Charles came with the religious debates that were put on for his benefit. Olivares suggested to Buckingham that it would be discourteous not to listen to the arguments in favour of the Catholic religion. Buckingham obligingly replied he had instructions not to stand in the way of any meetings with clergymen. His only stipulation was that he alone should attend the first session and that it be conducted in secret. It took place in the royal apartments of the monastery where Charles had spent the night before his Public Entry. The meeting was presided over by the king's preacher, fray Francisco de Jesús – the historian of the Spanish Match – with James Wadsworth, an English convert to Catholicism, acting as interpreter. There was a second meeting a week later which Buckingham also attended alone, this time in the palace. It was not to be until 24 April, however, some six weeks after arriving, that the Prince of Wales attended his first and only formal exchange with Catholic divines. All of the king's councils were instructed to pay another formal visit to Charles at the palace in order to distract attention from the meeting.[16] To ensure maximum privacy the encounter took place in the king's apartments. Felipe came out to greet Charles but left him as the discussions began. Charles asked him to stay, but significantly he refused. He would never 'allow himself to listen to a word against the Catholic religion'.

The Prince sat high up in a chair while his interlocutors, the king's confessor and three Capuchins, were seated on benches. Both royal favourites were in attendance. There seems to have been an awkward silence as they waited for their guest to initiate debate or pose a question. When confronted, Charles regally said he knew of nothing they could debate, 'as he felt no scruple whatsoever'. A desultory discussion of the nature of papal supremacy did follow, however. At one stage one of the Capuchins quoted Christ's words to Peter:

> Simon, Simon, Satan hath desired to have you that he may sift you as wheat, but I have prayed for thee that thy faith fail not; and thou, when thou are converted, strengthen thy brethren.

Charles asked for this to be repeated twice in French, claiming that violence was being done to the text. At this Buckingham became so angry that he left the room and trampled on his hat in frustration. It was one thing to discuss the merits of religion in a scholarly debate, but to insinuate that the Prince should convert from a religion that was devil-inspired could not be tolerated. When Olivares tried to arrange another conference, Buckingham refused on the obviously spurious grounds that the Prince was forbidden to discuss religion. Olivares pointed out that this contradicted what he had said earlier, but Buckingham flatly denied ever having said such a thing.

It must be admitted, however, that at the very start of the visit the cause of religion allowed the visit to progress smoothly. The crowd had shouted 'God bless you' whenever the Prince appeared in public, and in return Charles displayed every indulgence towards his hosts' religion, observing their religious ceremonies and processions with appropriate gravity. The princes of the Church he greeted with the utmost respect, his courtesy being arithmetically scrutinised. When Cardinal Espínola called on him, it was calculated that Charles had walked six or seven paces towards the door as he left. He did the same when another cardinal visited him a few days later.[17]

Slowly but surely, differences in religion did more than anything else to sour relations between guest and host. The debate with the Prince had inspired only the first of many increasingly public disagreements between the two favourites.[18]

It was also felt by some that the presence of a Protestant prince in the venerable royal palace was an affront 'to those walls which up to that time had been so pure from this contagion'.[19] The palace was close to a very popular shrine, that of the Virgin of the Almudena, the patroness of Madrid. There, in the eleventh century, a statue of the Virgin had been discovered within the old city walls, to the south of the royal complex, where it had lain hidden since the time of the Moorish invasion 300 years before.

Religious tensions were exacerbated when James took it upon himself to add two chaplains and four assistant clerics to the servants Charles had wanted to follow him to Madrid.[20] James assumed that the Spanish court would be gratified to see for themselves that the Church of England was a true church. He selected two of the Prince's chaplains 'fittest for this purpose', or as D'Ewes put it, 'altogether free from the superstition of being Puritans'. The King chose Dr Leonard Maw and Dr Mathew Wren, both members of an influential circle of high churchmen in the Chapel Royal who were linked to Pembroke College in Cambridge. Their appointment bitterly disappointed more evangelical members of the court.[21] The two chaplains were to take with them all the necessary church ornaments, 'so as their behaviour and service shall', James argued, 'prove decent and agreeable to the purity of the primitive church and yet as near the Roman form as can lawfully be done'.[22] When the King was asked what they should do if they came across the Host being carried through the streets of Madrid, he gave them his usual commonsense advice. If unable to avoid any such encounter, 'they must do as they did there, and so they should give no scandal'.[23] As for Charles's spiritual welfare, it is to be presumed that when James recommended that 'there be one convenient room appointed for prayer', he did not realise that his son had exclusive use of only two rooms in the palace.[24]

Contrary to the hopes of the *rex pacificus*, it was a telling sign of the huge spiritual distance separating London and Madrid that Charles's modest ecclesiastical household merely reminded the Spaniards that they were contemplating a marriage to a heretic. Before the chaplains set sail, Ambassador Coloma warned of the problems Charles would encounter if he tried to hold services in the palace. James anxiously sent a letter overland telling his son to point out that the Infanta was to be allowed 'free exercise of her religion here'. If no compromise was possible, 'my sweet baby, show yourself not to be ashamed of your profession but go sometimes to my ambassador's house'.[25]

As for the two chaplains, Dr Maw's mule saw to it that he never reached Madrid. 'With infinite bounces beyond his resistance', Sir Richard Wynn recorded, the animal tried to teach him to be a good horseman but the wretched

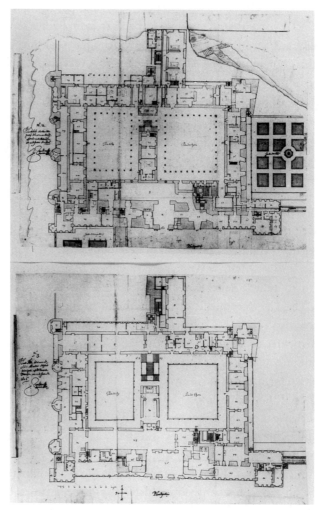

11. Gómez de Mora's plan of the main floor of the royal palace
illustrates the vastness of the *alcázar* but many of its rooms were
used as offices by Spain's many royal councils.

creature only succeeded in making the unfortunate cleric take a tumble, injur-
ing his head and shoulders.[26] Dr Wren at least made it to Madrid, from where
he reported back on the Prince of Wales's Protestant fortitude. Well he might,
as Charles was forbidden from hearing sermons and on no account was he
allowed to make use of the 'best church-plate and vestments' which James had
sent over to impress the Spaniards with the ritual and decorum that attended
communion in the Church of England. Charles had to make do with 'bedchamber prayers'.[27] Olivares had summoned Francis Cottington to remind him

that on no account were the chaplains to try to enter the royal palace, even through the garden. If they did so, all necessary measures would be taken against them. No idle threat: when a German resident in Madrid reported in June that English heretics were practising their religion in their lodgings, the fact that they had come with the Prince did not prevent their being forcibly removed.[28] Hounded as no more than 'ministers of Calvin's sect', Charles's clerics were obliged to take refuge in the embassy.

The chaplains and their assistants had set sail on the *Adventurer*, which lifted anchor on 3 April, arriving in Santander, on Spain's northern coast, five days later.[29] They formed a small fraction of a much grander household that was being sent out to serve the Prince. Before leaving England, Charles had written down in his own hand a list of servants who were 'to follow him by sea into Spain'.[30] Confident his bride would soon be his, he could not afford to be without a princely entourage for long. Heading the Prince's list were two peers, Lords Andover and Compton. Numerous gentlemen were also named, along with a physician, Dr Cragg, as well as a barber and an apothecary. King James decided this was insufficient. He was still worried that Charles and Buckingham would not behave with sufficient gravity or seriousness, which is probably why the elderly Lord Carey was added to the list. At the age of sixty-three, Carey's experience of courtly life stretched back into Elizabeth's reign. James also added Sir Robert Carr and the literary-minded Sir Richard Wynn, along with several other gentlemen and their servants. The resplendent household left the court on 23 March, almost as soon as news reached England of the Prince's safe arrival in Madrid.[31] Its dispatch quickly became an embarrassing mistake. Conscious of his confinement to two rooms, Charles was to order most of his servants back to England as soon as they disembarked. Even those who carried on to Madrid found themselves detained in a rented house outside the city, with orders being given that they 'must not much stir abroad'.[32]

The expense of the visit was escalating alarmingly. James warned Charles that £5,000 had already been spent, and that if 'your tilting stuff' is sent, that 'will come to three more – and God knows how my coffers are already drained'. He instructed him to do his utmost to see that the £150,000 which the Spanish had once promised as an 'advance dowry' was sent to England as soon as possible.[33] The princely flotilla was also conveying out of the country a king's ransom in jewels. During Charles's Public Entry, it had been noted how few gems he boasted. He wrote to his father explaining that the fashion in Spain was to wear 'many jewels'. The ones he had brought with him were simply 'not good enough'. He needed more.[34] Buckingham was at his most playful with the King when he said the jewels would redound not just to James's honour but to the honour of

Charles and the nation. He specifically asked for one or two rich chains for himself, as well as the Portingall diamond for the Prince. In a postscript, the King was coquettishly warned by his Favourite that if Charles did not receive enough jewels, 'I'll stop all other presents. Therefore look to it.'[35]

Lord Compton was entrusted to convey the precious stones rumoured to be worth between £80,000 and £200,000. James made the final selection himself.[36] Though making it clear they were only on loan, he wanted his heir (and indeed his Favourite) to look resplendent. An order was sent to the Tower of London to fetch all the jewels redeemed from Williams the goldsmith. James itemised what he wanted:

> Amongst which was a dressing of pearl. Besides these his majesty would have also sent the fairest head-dressing of pearl, being set with diamonds, it is remembered. And a faire rope of pearl, but not the second or third best. And besides these above, his majesty leaves it to those employed for the jewels to make choice of two or three fine jewels fittest for the wearing of women. A jewel called the Three Brothers, five or six fair jewels that may be worn in men's hats, whereof some to be of 6 or 7 score pounds' value & none under. The fine pendant diamonds that were the queen's, whether they now remain upon a string or be made up upon a feather.[37]

To his future daughter-in-law, the King sent 'an old double cross of Lorraine'. It was an antique, he said, but not without value. James also instructed his son in the art of love-making. Charles was to give the princess a mirror set with his father's picture, telling her that whenever she looked into it she would see the fairest lady in his or her brother's dominions. He also sent her a collar of thirteen rubies, as well as diamonds and pearls, suggesting the Prince should dole them out 'the more sundry times the better'. Charles, he thought, would look good if he wore the diamond known as the 'The Mirror of France' on its own in a hat, set off by a little black feather. As for Buckingham, James seized the opportunity to present him with a table diamond which the Favourite had earlier refused to accept.[38]

The jewels reached Madrid. Most of his servants did not. Around the middle of April Charles sent word that only Sir Richard Wynn and Mr Tyrwhitt were to proceed to the Spanish capital. All in all, eleven gentlemen were ordered to return to England, though apparently several disobeyed.[39] Four or five of the gentlemen arrived back in Dover in the second week of June, disgruntled that they had not come within 120 leagues of the Prince.[40] There were reports that meat and foodstuffs in general were in short supply. A scurrilous ballad circulating in England claimed,

Prince Charles can get no victuals, sufficient for his train
His horses and his trumpeters, are all come back again.[41]

With so little room at his disposal, it was evident that a larger entourage would only prove an embarrassment to the Prince, but to this must be added the likelihood that, once Easter had passed, it was slowly dawning on Charles just what a perilous mistake he had made in assuming the Infanta was his for the taking.

María was herself used as bait to entice Charles towards conversion. Hopes of an early encounter with his beloved had been raised after he was allowed a glimpse of her on his very first Sunday in Madrid. In the weeks following he was persistently rebuffed. On Thursday, 27 March King Felipe wrote to his Council asking for further advice since the Prince had again demanded 'with extraordinary force and more than usual fervour' to be allowed to visit the Infanta.[42] Finally it was decided to allow him to speak to the Infanta on Easter Day, 6 April.[43]

Decked out in diamonds, Charles wore around his neck the insignia of St George, with the garter on his left leg. Some of his clothes were lent him by Olivares, who felt his English attire was unworthy of the solemnity of the occasion. When the king left his chapel, Charles joined him and together they went to greet the queen and the Infanta. The royal ladies came to the door of their chamber and eventually they were all seated in a row, with the king and Prince at each end. The queen was carefully placed between Charles and his beloved. When it was Charles's turn to speak, he rose and first addressed the queen, who stood to receive him. Walking past her, Charles exchanged his first words with the Infanta. He returned to his seat, and after half an hour he and the king processed back the way they had come.[44]

It is interesting to compare the various accounts of their meeting. The official chronicler said that the Infanta María reacted 'with much gravity'. The Venetian ambassador had it that Charles – doubtless following his father's advice – had tried to pass on an affectionate compliment. Such an un-Spanish display of emotion set the courtiers a-whispering. The queen looked on, decidedly unamused. María stared blankly back, forcing Charles to end his speech prematurely. The princess replied with a few stock phrases. Given that she was utterly opposed to the marriage, the Venetian thought her self-control remarkable.[45]

Thanks to a report compiled by Ambassador Bristol, we know what their few words of conversation most likely were. After kissing her hands, Charles said that the friendship between his father and her brother had brought him to Spain 'to make a personal acknowledgment' of that friendship and 'to continue and

12. The 'ladder episode' from an early edition of Fernando de Rojas's *Celestina*, a copy of which Charles purchased in Madrid.

increase' it. The Infanta replied that she greatly valued what he had said. Charles then asked after her health, having heard she had been unwell. She cut him off with the words, '*Que quedava buena, á servicio de su alteza*' – little more than that she was now well, thank you very much – upon which Charles returned to his seat.[46] Yet another observer thought the princess's iron will could be taken for bashfulness. Endymion Porter described the visit in terms of her goodness and her beauty, which gave the Prince 'a just occasion to love her'.[47] Cottington was his usual cruder self. After having spoken to her, Charles was now so attracted, 'as without all doubt she will be with child before she gets into England'.[48]

The Prince of Wales was nothing if not stubborn. He heard that María liked to collect maydew near the Casa del Campo, one of the king's houses in the great park across the river from the palace. Some six weeks after their desultory exchange of compliments, he managed an interception early in the morning of Saturday, 17 May. Only a high wall and a double-bolted gate stood between them, but no one would unlock the gate. With life imitating art, the Prince of Wales climbed the wall 'and sprung down a great height', just as in an episode from *Celestina*, one of the Spanish books he had purchased in Madrid. The Infanta's guardian begged Charles on bended knee to leave at once. The gate was unlocked for him and he departed, crestfallen, having failed to speak to the Infanta. The English claimed at least to have dented Spanish protocol, since when María saw Charles she 'gave a shriek and ran back'. But for the Spaniards, their Infanta 'did not turn her head nor take any notice, but carried on walking'.[49]

This was not the first occasion when the behaviour of Charles's household appeared uncouth. On Garter Day, 23 April, Charles dined in public. Buckingham was placed by his side but seated lower. It was also St George's Day. To honour England's patron saint it was thought appropriate that they be served only by Englishmen. When it came to toasting King James's health, the Spaniards noticed that his loyal subjects did this standing up, and with their hats off![50] Headgear was treated reverentially in Spain; the right to remain 'covered' – that is, not having to take off one's hat in the presence of royalty – was a sought-after privilege. Although Charles's party had acted in accordance with Spanish etiquette, the cavalier manner in which they did so still contravened a fundamental rule of Spanish courtly behaviour. On another occasion, James Howell was embarrassed to report that, although Charles was normally served by the king's own servants, some of his fellow Englishmen would 'jeer at the Spanish fare and use other slighting speech and demeanour'.[51]

The misunderstandings about how to behave at court had a part to play in Charles's failure to secure his bride. Given his refusal to convert, it made it harder to see the Prince as a worthy candidate for the Infanta's hand in marriage. But there was another reason why Charles's stay had turned into an elaborate game of cat and mouse. Olivares quickly saw enough to make up his mind that Charles had not come to Madrid in order to convert. But how to be rid of the Prince? He could not be sent away with a flea in his ear. Spanish courtly life did not allow for such grossness, and anyway it would snap the friendship with King James which Felipe IV felt morally obliged to preserve. The count's near-hopeless task was made harder by the fact that his young sovereign seemed to have become captivated by the idea that the visit might yet bring about the re-establishment of Catholicism in James's dominions. Hoping against hope that the friendship with Great Britain would not unravel, what Olivares had to do over the long summer of 1623 was to find a way to make the Prince of Wales go home of his own accord, preferably with his thoughts turned towards a different Habsburg bride.

10. Dispute, Censures and Conclusions

When Archie the Fool had first heard about the Prince's trip to Spain he put his jester's cap on James's head. The King asked, but what if Charles comes back safely? In that case, cried the Fool, I will put my hat on the king of Spain's head instead.[1] Archie Armstong's name was amongst those added by James to the Prince's list of those who were to follow him to Spain. The King had more than his son's entertainment in mind. Court fools in England and Spain had licence to say what everyone else was too frightened to say.[2] Before the month of April was out, Archie had written to the King, his fellow Scot, informing him that, whereas he had been received by the king of Spain, neither 'men of your own nor your son's men can come near him'. Wearing 'his fool's coat', Archie could come and go as he pleased with the Infanta and her ladies-in-waiting, and it was said he 'keeps a blowing and blubbering amongst them and flurts out [sic] what he lists'. Once, the Infanta delicately indicated her distaste for an English marriage. How strange it was, she remarked, that the Catholic duke of Bavaria should have taken Prague, after a long march, and with much smaller forces than the Protestants. Archie retorted that something stranger had happened in Armada Year.[3] Later, he openly blamed Buckingham for mishandling the negotiations. The duke threatened to have him hanged. Archie replied, 'No one has ever heard of a fool being hanged for talking, but many dukes in England have been beheaded for their insolence'.[4] The king of Spain liked Archie. He gave him a valuable chain to wear and a suit of clothes.[5]

For all Archie's hints about Spanish hesitation, the preparations continued apace in London for the Infanta's imminent arrival. By chance, they had begun the day after Charles arrived in Madrid, when James ordered arrangements to be made for the servants she was likely to bring with her. He was especially concerned for his old friend, Gondomar, who was 'like to come hither'.[6] María's principal residence was to be Denmark House, later Somerset House, on the Strand, where Queen Anne had lived. Her private chapel was to be built near St James's

13. The court jester, Archie Armstrong, was already
famous for his acerbic political comments when, for
whatever reason, James decided to add him to the list
of courtiers whom Charles had chosen to follow him
to Madrid.

Palace. Inigo Jones was commissioned to design, in effect, a small church. Severe
in its classicism from the outside, but more opulently furnished on the inside, it
is now known as the Queen's Chapel, Marlborough Gate.[7] James conveniently
cited the fact that the Infanta might arrive at any minute as an excuse to turn
down Mansfeld's request to supply a further 20,000 men for the war in Germany.[8]

It was the cruellest of ironies that while all these arrangements were being
made Olivares had satisfied himself that there was little or no chance that the
Prince of Wales had come to Madrid to convert. The very instrument which
had led the Prince to Spain in the first place – the papal dispensation – would
now be used to frustrate the match.[9] Charles had reckoned that his presence

would expedite the granting of papal permission. He had even convinced himself that his arrival might make a dispensation unnecessary, just as the Madrid crowds had hoped when they said 'he deserved to have the Infanta thrown into his arms the first night he came'.[10]

On 20 March, the duke of Pastrana had finally set out from the Spanish capital on a long-scheduled mission to Rome. Now one of his duties would be officially to inform the pope of the astonishing news that the Prince of Wales was at the court of the Catholic King.[11] However, news of Charles's arrival was already on its way to Rome, and the pomp of Pastrana's departure only served to mask the fact that other, more secret, signals were being sent to the pontiff. Normally relations between Rome and Madrid were strained on account of the fact that Spain controlled Milan and Naples, to the north and south of the papal states, but the papacy was in triumphalist mood after the defeat of the Protestant cause in Bohemia. In addition to the fact that the papacy had long said the English marriage should only go ahead if the Prince of Wales converted, Pope Gregory XV was more than happy to impose conditions intended to stymie a marriage that might otherwise lead to a compromise over the future of the Palatinate. True, the pope had other reasons to please Olivares if he possibly could. The translation of Frederick's electorship to Duke Maximilian had just been announced, and this the papacy had strongly supported. Rome therefore needed to build bridges with Spain, which had consistently opposed transfering the electoral title on the grounds that it would make peace in central Europe still harder to achieve.[12]

At the outset of Charles's visit, it must be conceded that Olivares had encouraged the papal nuncio in Madrid to press the pope for a speedy dispensation. Bishop Innocenzio de Massimi of Bertinoro duly dispatched letters to Rome on 10 March 1623, the Monday after Charles's arrival, when it was still hoped that a conversion was no more than a matter of time.[13] That very morning the count had said to the Prince 'that, if the pope would not give a dispensation for a wife, they would give the Infanta' to him 'as his wench'.[14] In Rome, the committee of cardinals had reconvened to discuss the dispensation required for the outline treaty signed at the start of January. The matter was in the hands of Cardinal Ludovico Ludovisi, the pope's nephew and Secretary of State. News of Charles's arrival reached Rome on 29 March,[15] which added urgency to their deliberations. On the evening of Wednesday, 2 April a dispensation was sent to De Massimi.[16] The terms of the January agreement were by and large endorsed, even if a number of tedious conditions were added that had to be fulfilled before the dispensation was to be finally handed over.[17] While Rome still accepted that an English parliament would never formally repeal the anti-Catholic legislation, it stipulated that the Infanta should not leave Flanders until there was proof positive that persecution of Catholics had ceased. With a modicum of goodwill these additions were hardly insurmountable, nor were they intended to be.[18] This dispensation reached the papal nuncio in Madrid on 18 April. Rome had dutifully put everything in place for Prince Charles to convert.

Suddenly everything was turned on its head. Before that dispensation arrived in Madrid, another dispatch dated 8 April had arrived in Rome from De Massimi. It brought perplexing news that the count's brief flirtation with the English Match was over. His reluctance to go ahead with the marriage had been rekindled and was burning brighter than ever. Cardinal Ludovisi pretended to receive the rapidly changing news from Madrid 'with the greatest displeasure'.[19] If truth be told, he was more than happy to draw up, there and then, a new and far more demanding set of terms for the handing over of the dispensation. Nevertheless he was obliged to *pre-date* it to 2 April so that it could be exhibited alongside the dispensation that had been sent almost a week before.

With a ready eye for the high moral ground, Ludovisi made as much political capital as he could out of Olivares's change of heart. He accused the count of using Rome to do his dirty business. The first set of terms, he tartly pointed out, had been specifically dispatched in order to demonstrate the pope's goodwill towards Spain. Since even the English agent, Gage, knew that the first dispensation was on its way, all that could be done was 'to draw things out'. To achieve this the cardinal was sending 'the enclosed letters looking as if they were closed on the same date of the [2nd]'. Just in case Charles did decide to convert (or if Olivares was overruled), Ludovisi remitted all matters concerning the handing over of the dispensation to De Massimi's discretion.[20]

Charles and his burgeoning court naïvely awaited the arrival of the pope's blessing. At the start of April Cottington told James of 'the good news we have from Rome'.[21] Charles still hoped to be home by the end of May.[22] The nuncio was known to be opposed to the marriage, but the Prince felt the pope's envoy was being given such 'rude answers' that he would soon fall in line with Spain's apparent determination to celebrate the marriage.[23] One of the reasons why Charles was so comprehensively duped was that at the Spanish court only Olivares and the papal nuncio knew the extent of the skulduggery at Rome. The official Spanish chronicler of the match, Francisco de Jesús, never found out about the pre-dating of the documents. As far as he was concerned, it was the pope who decided to use the (final) dispensation as 'an example to all future ages'.[24] Only later could Olivares safely boast, as he did in 1630, that 'I alone was the minister who undid' the Spanish Match, a claim which was repeated in his defence after he fell from grace precisely twenty years after the princely visit.[25]

The terms engineered by Olivares were a catastrophe for Prince Charles. His ruse was to demand the dismantling of the Anglican state and the humiliation of its monarchy. The informal relaxation of the penal laws which Charles and James had agreed to in January had gone by the board. Now there was a demand for 'the free and public exercise of the Roman Catholic religion and the public liberty of conscience, and that this concession be approved by the council and by parliament'. Since the papacy would not negotiate directly with the schismatic House of Stuart, the king of Spain would have to swear in his name and on behalf of his successors that the king of Great Britain, along with Charles, his Privy Council and the parliament, had accepted Catholic emancipation. King Felipe even had to threaten war in the event that his sister's English family reneged on their promises.[26]

If the parliament of 1621 had demonstrated one thing, it was that the House of Commons would never agree to repeal the penal legislation. True, Rome was being inundated with demands from James's Catholic subjects that the match should be permitted only if there were tangible benefits to Catholicism. For instance, the Irish peer, Viscount Gormanston, was orchestrating a campaign in Madrid on the eve of the Prince's visit to remind the Spanish king that James's Irish subjects must be included in any toleration. During the summer of 1622 Father John Bennett had lobbied the Vatican for the religious freedoms of Catholics in England.[27] But no matter how influential these campaigns were, it was Olivares's volte-face – or rather his definitive return to his original hostility to the match – which alone caused the terms for the dispensation to be so radically increased at Rome. In every previous version of the marriage agreement Madrid had accepted, reluctantly no doubt, that a statutory change to the position of James's Catholic subjects was an impossibility. A royal promise was all that could be hoped for, as Ludovisi had expressly acknowledged in the correctly dated dispensation when he lamented 'the power and the implacable hatred of the Puritans for the Catholic name'.[28] The papal demand that an English parliament sanction liberty of worship in the predated dispensation was intended to have only one outcome – to put paid to the Spanish Match.

There is the delicious possibility that King Felipe was kept firmly in the dark about Olivares's dealings with Rome. Excited by the prospect of a foreign adventure of his own, the young king chirruped time and again how he would 'one day follow [Charles] to London'.[29] He was mesmerised by the prospect of Charles's conversion or, at the very least, by the expectation that his future English nephews and nieces would be raised as Catholics. But just as the late king's enthusiasm for the match had dwindled to almost nothing, Olivares needed to take into account that his own king might at any moment himself conclude that Charles's visit did not presage the triumph of Catholicism over Anglicanism. Olivares was sailing between Scylla and Charybdis. He had to be prepared for a surprise conversion by Charles, no matter how remote that seemed, but at the same time he needed to protect himself in case the negotiations dashed against the rocks. The only safe course to chart was *not* to reveal to his king the shabby details of what he had asked Rome to do. That way, if the unimaginable happened and Charles enthusiastically accepted all Spain's demands, then King Felipe could release his sister confident that his chief minister had all along intended to wring the greatest number of concessions from the Stuart monarchy. Yet, if the Prince of Wales concluded he was being asked to pay too high a price for the Infanta and abandoned his plans for marriage, Olivares's position would still be unimpeachable. No shame could fall on his sovereign if Charles rejected requirements which apparently proceeded from the Holy See, and the count might still be in a position to promote a marriage between James's grandchild and the Habsburgs of Vienna. This was what Olivares ideally wanted: to prevent the marriage and still be in a position to maintain friendship with the king of Great Britain.

Meanwhile, Charles and Buckingham continued blithely in the heady expectation that Spain wanted nothing more in the world than a marriage alliance with Great Britain. At the end of March, they had told James how 'neither in spiritual nor temporal things, there is anything pressed upon us more than is already agreed upon'.[30] So persuaded were they of the power of Olivares's good intentions that they permitted themselves to complain to Pope Gregory about the nuncio's coldness towards them. On the very Wednesday the pre-dated conditions were dispatched from Rome, an envoy arrived at the papal court from the Prince. Ostensibly the mission was to congratulate the pope on his accession, some two years before, but it also asked that De Massimi be ordered to behave *più moderatamente*. The papal response to this naïve appeal was to say that this was how to behave towards heretics. When he converted, he would be treated differently.[31] All the same, Charles felt that the papacy posed no real threat to a match which he believed both London and Madrid wanted. He had the perfect weapon to combat any papal objections.

Bizarrely, the heir to the Stuart thrones was prepared to accept a form of papal supremacy. He had written three days after arriving in Madrid to ask his father 'how far we may engage you in the acknowledgement of the pope's spiritual power'.[32] James unhesitatingly replied, 'I know not what ye mean by my acknowledging the pope's spiritual supremacy'. He let his son down gently but with deliberate firmness. Charles must have misconstrued a passage he had written in his book against Bellarmine, the most eloquent defender of the papacy's power to depose princes,

> where I offer, if the pope would quit his godhead and usurping over kings, to acknowledge him for the chief bishop, to whom all appeals of churchmen ought to lie *en dernier resort*. The very words I send you enclosed, and that is the furthest that my conscience will permit.

To make sure that Charles learnt his lesson, James included a pointed reference to Henri IV, a once-Protestant and much-reviled king of France, who memorably had thought Paris worth a mass. In a hardly less memorable phrase, James pointed out he was no Frenchman 'who can shift his religion as easily as he can shift his shirt when he cometh in from tennis'.[33]

Of course, Charles was not intimating a willingness to convert to Roman Catholicism. He was ineptly enquiring about the possibility of something along the lines of associate membership of a worldwide church, with the pope as honest broker.[34] James must have been astonished at his son's theological and diplomatic naïvety. No pope could welcome an acceptance of only one half of his plenitude of power. If such concessions were necessary for the marriage to go ahead, then Charles and Buckingham had dangerously misjudged the mood in both Madrid and Rome.

The Venetian ambassador had rightly equated the Prince's adventure with a labyrinth from which there was no escape. Even before the terms for the granting of a dispensation were officially made known to Charles, the optimism of the first few weeks in Madrid was beginning to wear thin. James told his boys at the start of April that he would not let the Council know 'any secret in your letters', complaining that Buckingham's rival, James Hamilton, the second marquess, 'would needs peer over my shoulder' to read their letters as they arrived, 'offering ever to help me to read any hard words'.[35] Rumours were flying around. Particularly unnerving, especially for Buckingham, was the threat that a parliament was being called in his absence. Its only purpose would be to undermine the match.[36]

It was only at the end of April that the Prince and Buckingham first got wind of what might (or might not) be in the dispensation. Unknown to them, it frustratingly turned out to be merely the terms of the first dispensation. On 27 April they wrote to James about 'the conditions it is clogged with', ironically the very day that the King was writing a letter to the Infanta addressing her as his daughter.[37] Unperturbed, and using the same image as Venice's ambassador, they announced they were confident they would soon 'get forth of this labyrinth, wherein we have been entangled these many years'. James was to dispatch a fleet as soon as possible to La Coruña to bring Charles and María back to England.[38] The King was told to keep what they thought were the terms of the dispensation a secret at court, otherwise it would 'beget dispute, censures, and conclusions there to our prejudice'.[39] Charles dictated the very words his father was to write back authorising his son to accept the conditions which he expected to receive any minute from Olivares:

> We do hereby promise, by the word of a king,
> that whatsoever you our son shall promise
> in our name, we shall punctually perform.

On 11 May, James sat down at his palace at Greenwich to copy out these words.[40] He had no choice. Buckingham had added a letter of his own, telling the King of his son's 'extraordinary desire to be soon with you again'. James had made no secret of his wish to be reunited with his Favourite, even if that meant leaving Prince Charles alone in Madrid. Perhaps Buckingham thought the King needed to be reminded that one could hardly return without the other.

In contrast to the secrecy enjoined upon King James in his relations with his councillors, Olivares made great show of unburdening himself to the members of the Council of State. Of course he was doing no such thing; but he needed to keep his fellow councillors unaware of the double game he was playing just as much as he needed to keep the Prince of Wales guessing. In early May, Olivares received the revised terms for the dispensation. The councillors of state were invited to give their opinions without ever knowing of Olivares's secret contacts with the papacy. Was it acceptable for Spain to guarantee liberty of conscience in the Stuart dominions? Might the pope be asking too much in calling for a parliamentary repeal of the anti-Catholic laws? In a meeting on 6 May, Gondomar said that to demand statutory repeal of the penal laws might prove too dangerous. No English lord could muster even 500 men against the King but calling a parliament would bring all James's enemies together. Perhaps a royal promise of non-persecution was enough, though he cautiously added that a year's wait would be necessary before the Infanta could be released. Another councillor thought that Charles could marry the Infanta at once, so long as the marriage was not consummated.[41] The challenge for Olivares was to appear in favour of the match, but not too much so.[42] The following day he made a purposefully long speech. For once his loquacity suited his purpose. First he outlined the problems. The business of the marriage was 'without question the most important that has confronted this Monarchy for a very long time'. Yet there was no strategic reason why the marriage should go ahead. He seriously doubted the commitment to toleration. The Prince had only one Catholic councillor, Thomas Savage, and he had not been summoned to Madrid. Olivares artfully concluded his speech by apparently throwing his weight behind the marriage. But the beauty of his argument lay in his conditions. They could hardly have been more severe. If there was not to be unfettered liberty of conscience, then either James or Charles must convert. Even then the Holy See had to be fully satisfied.[43]

As Olivares was speaking up in favour of the English marriage, he was meanwhile quietly putting every administrative obstacle in its way. At the start of May he demanded that all negotiations with Charles and his advisers should henceforth be in writing, partly, it must be said, on account of his worsening relations with Buckingham.[44] He arranged for the papal nuncio to attend a meeting of the Council of State on 12 May so that he could declare that it was not in his power to remit any of the papal conditions.[45] (In fact, he had been granted full discretion in the matter.) A sub-committee of the Council was set up to discuss with Charles what guarantees he could give. Gondomar's inclusion might be taken as a sign of goodwill, but once Charles had appeared in Madrid what influence the count had possessed had dwindled still further. Any suggestion that this committee was designed to expedite matters is crushed by the fact that, later in the month, Olivares increasingly turned to a *junta* of forty theologians for guidance as to whether the Prince's promises were, spiritually speaking, sufficient. This 'junta grande' had been set up shortly after Charles's arrival. It was ordered to convene in the royal palace, in the room reserved for meetings of the *cortes*. Its size – so much larger than the committee of a half-dozen churchmen that had been in semi-continuous session since 1613 – gives a clue to its real purpose, as does its membership. It included the Infanta's confessor, the Franciscan friar, Juan Venido, as well as the queen's religious adviser, the Trinitarian, fray Simon de Rojas. Olivares could turn to it whenever he needed to garner theological objections to the marriage.[46]

At some point early in May, the Prince and the Favourite were informed of the full conditions that were now being demanded in the papacy's name. Without those concessions, they were told, the king of Spain would be unable to guarantee the agreement as Rome demanded. What happened over the next ten days is unclear. This is not just because so many meetings were crowded into such a short space of time. Charles lacked the courage to report back to his father on all the demands that were being placed on him. He hoped that if he reached an accommodation with Olivares he would spare himself the humiliation of having to tell his father that his adventure had turned into a manhunt, with himself as the prey. Three formal meetings took place between Charles's advisers and the Spaniards. Charles asked to attend in person. At the first meeting, all that was

14. The *Spanish Rose* was one of a number of Catholic publications which appeared in 1622. It depicts Christ presiding over the marriage, and optimistically predicted that the union would lead to Catholic emancipation throughout the Stuart dominions.

discussed was the form of words that the king of Spain would use in his sworn guarantees to the pope that James and his son would comply with the agreed terms. At the second meeting, Charles proposed that he and his father should swear on behalf of themselves and their descendants that the laws against Catholics would be suspended, but as for parliamentary corroboration, he could only promise to do his utmost to bring this about. The pope had stipulated that this should be done within the year. When pressed, the Prince agreed 'that it should be within three or six months, or a year, but infallibly within three years'.[47] These words of a king and his heir, Charles ventured, should be sufficient security for the king of Spain to make his promises to the pope.

It was agreed, perhaps after the first conference, that Charles should be asked to put down on paper the most that he was prepared to concede. The offer concerning the toleration of the private practice of Catholicism remained on the table, where it had been since January, but the sticking point was still parliamentary involvement. Even in his second written submission, the most Charles could pledge was that he would personally do all he could to repeal the law. He tried to persuade his hosts 'that it was necessary that the conditions desired for the Catholics should be gradually put in force in order to avoid the undoubted risk of disturbance or sedition'. He did propose two confidence-building measures in the hope of extracting some room for manoeuvre from the Spaniards. They were specifically aimed at reassuring King Felipe, as a faithful son of the Church, that he could in conscience give all the necessary guarantees to the papacy. First, Charles and his father would swear never to attempt to persuade, directly or indirectly, the Infanta to renounce her religion. Second, Charles would promise 'that whenever the Lady Infanta begged him to join Her Highness in listening privately to the conversations and discussions of Catholic theologians he would make no excuse'.[48]

In a singularly ill-judged alternative to the tedious negotiations, Buckingham resorted to bully-boy tactics. With 'extraordinary importunity' he turned up one evening at eleven o'clock at the back door of De Massimi's house. He hectored the nuncio for three hours. Accompanied only by an interpreter, he blustered that unless the marriage went through, things could get much worse for James's Catholic subjects.[49] Just as the duke's relations with Ambassador Bristol had already deteriorated beyond repair, the relationship between Buckingham and Olivares also snapped. It was public knowledge among Charles's courtiers that 'some darkness' had occurred between the two favourites.[50] News of the breach with the Spanish minister also reached London. Buckingham was warned that most people believed the rows between them were 'some sort skinned over, rather than healed'.[51] His worst moment came when, deep in the night, Olivares blurted out that neither Felipe IV nor his father had ever really wanted the marriage anyway.

The Prince's final conference with Gondomar dealt in detail with four of the principal emendations that had come from Rome. Charles argued that it was an insult to Protestants to specify that the wet-nurses for his children must be Catholics, even though in practice the Infanta was free to choose as she saw fit. Equally he found it hard to accept that any children of the marriage must remain with their mother until the age of twelve. It was not the English custom, though again he promised that he would see that in practice this happened. As for allowing his father's Catholic subjects to swear the same oath as the Infanta's servants, this would make it difficult for them to take up public office. Most of all he balked at the pope's suggestion that all Catholics should be free to practise their religion openly in the Infanta's chapel. Quite apart from the inherent dangers of large crowds, this was tantamount to 'a public toleration of the Roman religion', which was something his father had vowed *never* to permit. Was it not enough that they had already promised that Catholics would be allowed the private practice of their religion? Anyway, he reiterated his pledge to suspend all anti-Catholic laws pending their full parliamentary repeal.[52]

On Sunday, 11 May, the day after the Council of State had rejected his last paper, the Prince reluctantly accepted that effective negotiation had stalled. The count promised faithfully to see if the pope would reduce his demands, but he asked Charles in the meantime to dispatch a trusted emissary to London. King James had to be informed of the need for parliamentary action as well as the likelihood that his Catholic subjects would worship openly in the Infanta's chapel.[53] Charles asked that he be allowed to put the case to his father in person. 'His own presence', he explained, 'would be very necessary'.[54] With an eye to his own king's reaction and a need to protect his reputation as a firm negotiator, Olivares could not allow Charles to slip through his fingers before some form of agreement had been reached. Permission was refused. The Prince of Wales was captive in a foreign land.

11. Solely to his Own Courtesy

The Prince of Wales was little more than a hostage at the Catholic Court. Free to explore the city as far as the murderous summer heat would permit, he was not at liberty to return home. At least he had five camels and an elephant to take his mind off his own captivity. Buckingham had 'imprudently begged them for' James, and they were duly offered by King Felipe as a gift to the British monarch. As May progressed, Charles had to pay for their fodder and arrange for an escort to take them to Santander for shipment back to London.[1] They arrived in early July, and though they travelled through the city after midnight they 'could not yet pass unseen' before finally ending up in St James's Park. The gift proved expensive. The elephant was to cost £275 a year to maintain, not to mention the gallon of wine a day that its keeper insisted was needed from September to April.[2]

Charles's detention in Madrid proved to be a once-in-a-lifetime opportunity to acquire works of art in person.[3] Buckingham began almost at once. One of his earliest purchases was a Spanish ebony cabinet that cost him £8.[4] By mid-March, he had spent 12,650 *reales* on an unspecified number of pictures.[5] If two *reales* were worth just over a shilling, then he had already spent something approaching £350. A month later he spent another 10,000 *reales*. This was far in excess of the 2,860 *reales* which Charles paid out for his first batch of pictures.[6] Although it is sometimes forgotten that the Prince was interested in paintings, especially Venetian art, well before he went to Spain, his visit immeasurably broadened his love of pictures. King Felipe had inherited a collection of some 2,000 paintings at a time when the Prince of Wales possessed fewer than two dozen. Realising that art and majesty were inseparable, Charles set about amassing a king's ransom in pictures. No painting was safe, according to the great contemporary art critic, Vicente Carducho.[7] Some pictures he acquired by purchase, others as gifts. Twice he visited the house of don Jerónimo Funes y Muñoz, one of the greatest private collectors in Europe. On the first attempt there was no one to show him round but on his second visit he admired the pictures as well as the collection of swords, guns and crossbows. When the Prince was finally permitted to leave for home, don Jerónimo presented him with three magnificent paintings. Two were by the Venetian artist Titian, and the third by his pupil, Juan Fernández de Navarrete, known as 'El Mudo' or the Mute, for having lost the power of speech in childhood.[8] (Shortly after, as he passed through the former Spanish capital of Valladolid on his way to the coast, Charles took time out to admire paintings by Michelangelo and Raphael in the royal collection there.[9]) Charles also dealt directly with artists. Eugenio Cajés, who was Madrid-born but of Italian descent, received 2,000 *reales*[10] – some £55 – for a *Last Supper*. The work of one 'Alberdua' caught the Prince's eye, and he paid 1,100 *reales* to don Pedro de Mendoza for a depiction of 'Our Lady' by none other than Albrecht Dürer, the visionary German artist of the early sixteenth century.[11] He also acquired copies for next to nothing. He gave Ginés Carbonel 330 *reales* for a copy of Titian's *Christ Bearing the Cross*.[12] Charles also developed his taste for sculpture, acquiring with Baltasar Gerbier's help two ancient marble busts of Marcus Aurelius and Apollo, as well as one of Faustina.[13] Though the dramatist, Lope de Vega, said that Charles was always prepared to pay over the odds for what he wanted, the Prince was sometimes disappointed. Another private collector, Juan de Espina, refused to part at any price with his two books of drawings by Leonardo da Vinci.[14]

A now-lost drawing of the Prince was in all probability undertaken by the greatest artist of the age, Diego Velázquez. Destined to become the archetypal court painter, he was born in Seville in 1599, which would have made him virtually the same age as the Prince. Velázquez was introduced to the court by Olivares, who was fiercely proud of his own Andalusian connections. With Endymion Porter's assistance, Charles paid an unnamed painter a further 1,100 *reales* for 'drawing the Prince's picture'.[15] If we take it that 13 *reales* made one *escudo*, that would amount to almost 85 *escudos*. In his *Art of Painting*, Francisco Pacheco, whose daughter had already married the up-and-coming Velázquez, later recalled that his son-in-law had received 100 *escudos* for the now-lost sketch of the Prince of Wales that he had quickly dashed off.[16]

Charles purchased at least three books of history. He paid 136 *reales* for Herrera's study of the West Indies, which had been the subject of a heated argument between Gondomar and King James about Sir Walter Raleigh's offer to find the legendary El Dorado. Judging by their price, 4 and 33 *reales* respectively, the *Epitome* of the Emperor Karl V and Luis Cabrera de Córdoba's life of Felipe II were second-hand.[17] Charles's reading was not always princely, however. Though his Spanish was never more than rudimentary, he bought two of the bestselling novels of the time, *El Pícaro* and *Celestina*. For all its moralising, the first was a romp through Spain's lowlife. The second was barely more romantic, being the story of star-crossed lovers and their involvement with the scurrilous procuress or *alcahueta* of the title.[18]

Charles's shopping sprees were fitted in between the tedious round of visits and spectacles that continued unabated, despite the growing tension between hosts and guests. On the last day of April Charles watched a procession from a balcony in the Puerta del Sol celebrating the conversion of fifty-two fallen women – presumably one for every week of the year. The Prince witnessed yet another bullfight in the newly created Plaza Mayor, this time with the noble participants on horseback.[19] For the aristocrats who took part in them, it was a welcome opportunity to express both their loyalty and their importance at court, but whether Charles took any pleasure in these time-filling spectacles, we do not know. The great southern magnate, the duke of Medinaceli, was unable to leave Andalusia and come to court. He ensured that his loyalty was noted by sending a particularly ostentatious gift of horses which were paraded through the streets of the capital.[20]

The more cynical amongst Madrid's population were weary of festivities in honour of a visitor who would not, or could not, go away. The satirical poet Francisco de Quevedo, gently mocked the revelries when he entitled one of his poems, 'A bullfight on horseback in honour of the Prince of Wales – with heavy rain'.[21] He satirised a game of *cañas* that took place under the August sun, in which two sides armed with sticks or poles tried to force their way past each other. With bitter innocence he claimed that people only drifted away so that they could return with their voices refreshed:

> The public were watching
> Happy to cheer
> But to moisten their throats
> They left for a beer.

Quevedo proposed that the poetical sunburn he caught while standing in the Plaza Mayor would nonetheless come in handy. True, he had to squander his supper money to get in, but he was consoled by the thought that he had caught more than enough sun to sell to Norway![22]

There is the merest chance that Charles found a fleeting love-interest in addition to the Infanta María. On 31 May, around the time the great-grandson of Montezuma, the last Aztec emperor, was about to make an appearance at court, the Prince and Buckingham slipped out of the palace in a closed carriage. It was ten o'clock at night. Their destination was the house of Vicente Súarez, a musi-

15. This portrait of Francisco de Quevedo, by a follower of Velázquez, appears to capture the intense wit with which the poet so effectively satirised the festivities put on as Charles's visit dragged on through the summer months.

cian of the king's chamber, whose family had been introduced to the Prince by Endymion Porter. They stayed there for over an hour, enthralled by his two daughters' singing. The voice of one of the daughters, Francesca, was said to have 'far more power to give life to all creatures sensitive and vegetative than ever Orpheus's silver-stringed lyre had'. Years later, Porter wrote to the family saying that Charles still remembered his visit with pleasure.[23]

All these diversions could not mask the fact that the heir to the Stuart thrones was being held in Madrid against his better judgement. The request he made to Olivares on 11 May for permission to visit his father had been seriously meant.[24] It formed part of an orchestrated campaign to be allowed to leave. At noon the following day Buckingham asked fray Francisco de Jesús to intercede with Olivares about the Prince's request, since he had been instructed to offer the duke all assistance, as he himself admitted, during his stay. As to be expected, both Prince and Favourite additionally sought the help of their old friend, Gondomar. Charles was forced to put a brave face on the refusal. When confronted by one of his courtiers with the rumour that he would try to leave as mysteriously as he had arrived, he blustered 'that if love brought him thither, it is not fear that shall drive him away'.[25]

Why could Olivares not let Charles go at the first opportunity? When fray Francisco wrote up his history of the Spanish Match, he suggested that Olivares persuaded King Felipe to oblige the Prince to remain in Madrid.[26] There may be an element of truth in this. The unwritten rules of Spanish courtly life still had to be observed: it would not do to allow the Prince to leave in a huff for fear of tarnishing the Catholic King's reputation for hospitality and plain dealing. On the other hand, there remains the intriguing possibility that Olivares may have sensed that he was on the verge of pushing the Prince into accepting perpetual liberty of conscience. This might have made the marriage worthwhile after all. At the very least he would have wrongfooted the House of Stuart into conceding that British and Irish Catholics were being persecuted for no very good reason. Just as likely is that the young king's sensibilities could not be ignored. If Felipe was kept in the dark about the extent of Olivares's double dealings with Rome, and if he accepted that his favourite was genuinely working to achieve the marriage on terms laid down by Pope Gregory, then Olivares could not allow himself to be seen as endorsing Charles's very first request to return to England. It would still be far better for the negotiations to peter out rather than end abruptly. That way, war might yet be avoided. Olivares might even find an opportunity to edge the Prince into realising that an Austrian archduchess might prove more suited to his needs than the Infanta María.

Fray Francisco recorded his personal impressions of the interview when Buckingham came to ask for his help in allowing Charles to return to London. He made a curious but entirely accurate judgement. As the meeting progressed, it dawned on him that Buckingham had arrived in Madrid 'with such confidence in his power of overcoming all the difficulties in the way of the conclusion of the marriage, merely by the help of courtesy'. It was a damning indictment of Buckingham's and Charles's judgement. Politeness alone does not make for treaties. The Prince and Favourite were now hapless guests at a court they wished to leave. This is revealed by the extraordinary circumstances surrounding the choice of who was to tell James of the true state of affairs.

According to fray Francisco, it was the Prince of Wales who nominated Secretary Cottington. In fact, the matter was debated by the Spanish Council of State the day after Charles was refused permission to leave. Olivares toyed with the idea of sending Buckingham, with Gondomar to keep an eye on him, but Gondomar, with his aversion to London life, predictably said that Cottington would be the ideal person to go. In the end, the Spaniards agreed.[27]

Secretary Cottington's departure was delayed until the very end of May.[28] Since Charles still hoped that Olivares really did want the marriage to go ahead, he had asked for the throng of theologians to be consulted over whether there was not any other way of moving the negotiations forward. Their replies were predictably unhelpful, with only the Jesuits, headed by Juan de Montemayor, vociferous in their support for the marriage. He presumably was responsible for arranging for his *voto* or opinion to be rushed into print.[29] At ten o'clock at night on Friday, 23 May Charles was informed that the theologians still maintained that action, not promises, was required. Resolute over the need for a parliamentary settlement, their only concession was that a ceremony of marriage could take place at once, so long as it was not consummated and the princess not handed over for a further twelve months. For Charles, to return without his wife would be dishonourable. It smacked of a lack of trust in his ability to arrange liberty of conscience, as well as leaving the marriage prey to an easy annulment on the grounds of non-consummation. The next day Cottington went to Olivares. In the light of the *junta*'s most recent ruling, he asked that Charles now be allowed to report back to James. Again he was refused. The Secretary then asked for as much documentation as possible about Spain's intentions to be drawn up. Cottington would return to England to prepare James for what he would find in the final draft of the treaty that was to follow on behind him.

Meanwhile, Charles applied himself to overseeing the preparation of a direct submission to King Felipe. He planned to circumvent the theologians' obduracy by appealing to a more worldly set of values, and, he hoped, a more compelling one, namely his host's shared sense of the dignity of royalty. He requested that his word as a prince be regarded as sufficient grounds for the marriage to be consummated. In fray Francisco's words, he was asking that the required guarantees 'should be entrusted solely to his own courtesy'.[30] Charles was pleading with Felipe just as he had done with Olivares. His elderly father, he protested, was 'being weighted down by his years, and with only one son, only looks to see him married'. He put it to Felipe that he was dishonouring his sister by holding her back *en rehenes*, that is, as a hostage. He even said that the delay would allow the enemies inside and outside 'the kingdoms of England' to muster opposition to the settlement. In an equally full reply, the Prince was reminded that King Francis I of France had left Spain without consummating his marriage to the sister of the great Karl V.[31]

The constitutional confabulation of the three Stuart kingdoms was to provide a minor hiccup at the very last moment. A second and third meeting of the 'junta grande' was held in June. Each time it hammered home that the tests which Olivares had prised out of Rome could not be altered. Toleration must be seen to be working before the Infanta María could be released. Charles balked at a last-minute clarification of the oath he was to swear. It was put to him that the members of the Privy Councils in the two smaller Stuart kingdoms would have to swear to end persecution, just as the English privy councillors were required to do. The Privy Councils of Scotland and Ireland were expected to sign up to an agreement specifying that the anti-Catholic laws of Scotland and Ireland would be subject to statutory repeal in the parliaments of Edinburgh and Dublin. The Prince protested that this was asking too much, 'since their laws and way of government were different from England's'.[32] For once, Charles was alive to the different sensibilities that held sway north of the border, and he pointed out that this would be particularly difficult to achieve in Scotland. Needless to say, Olivares endorsed what the theologians were trying to do. Charles was obliged to swear that the 'free and effective exercise of the Catholic religion' did indeed extend to each of the Stuart kingdoms.[33]

On his much-delayed return to London, Cottington carried with him an exhaustive set of instructions.[34] Charles insisted that the King and Council must agree to confirm everything that Spain would demand in the formal treaty that was in the process of being drawn up. Their consent was to be sent back to Charles; he alone would make the final decision whether or not to reveal his father's agreement. Clinging pathetically to the belief that all might yet come right, Charles brazenly asked the King for authority to negotiate an anti-Dutch alliance and discuss the future of the Palatinate. The Prince's bravado could not hide the fact that, on Cottington's arrival, James was at last confronted with the devastating news that his heir might be returning either without a bride or perhaps not at all. Charles shrewdly couched the bad news by way of asking for paternal advice. In the event of a betrothal, should he wait in Spain for María or return empty-handed to England? Taken as a whole, Charles's list of instructions sadly reveals a prince who was thrashing about in search of a solution. At one moment he was demanding that English Catholics petition the king of Spain about the utility of the marriage, then in another he was asking his father to dispatch a 'very peremptory' letter that would threaten to put the recusancy laws into immediate effect.[35]

Charles was fearful. He did not even want his Secretary to know the extent of his anxiety. Cottington was the bearer of a secret letter for Buckingham's crony, Lord Keeper Williams. According to Williams's chaplain and biographer, he was to read out the letter to King James. Then he was to burn it. The contents of the letter testify to the fact that, for all the honour accorded him, Charles knew that his freedom was at stake. He hardened himself to steal away like a thief in the night. If the worst came to the worst, wrote the Prince, he sought his father's permission to escape from Madrid, just 'as secretly as' he had arrived.[36]

12. Stricken Dead

'Sweet boys: your letter by Cottington hath strucken me dead.'[1] James claimed the news from Spain would 'very much shorten my days'. He rushed to countermand an order he had given to a group of nobles headed by the duke of Richmond. Along with Inigo Jones, they were on their way to Southampton to oversee last-minute preparations for the Infanta's arrival.[2] Of considerably greater concern was what to do with the armada of ten ships that was to fetch home Charles and his bride. Though the squadron had been formed on 1 May, for the past fortnight or more it had been kept riding at anchor ready for an immediate departure.[3]

Cottington had reached Dover at two o'clock in the morning of Friday, 13 June. He discovered that the flotilla was about to move into open water, ready to set sail for Spain.[4] As he expected to be with the King by noon to tell him 'the whole wretched story', as S.R. Gardiner put it, Cottington had a difficult decision to make. He took it upon himself to make a suggestion to the admiral, the peppery Francis Manners, earl of Rutland. As deftly as he could, Cottington advised that 'it may be when his majesty hath heard me he will resolve on some longer stay of the fleet'. Buckingham's father-in-law haughtily replied that a letter from a prince's secretary was insufficient authority to disobey a king's command. Fortunately for James, a packet boat was able to intercept the fleet and give the earl orders to repair to the Downs. Had the fleet of ten ships, armed with some three hundred guns, arrived in Santander to find that the Prince of Wales was in no position to return, who knows how the course of history might have been altered?[5]

James had been made to look a foolish old man. Admitting he did not know what to say to his Council, he was nonetheless at his most paternal in his reply to his son. He ordered the Prince to promise anything in his father's name in order to be allowed home. If Spain kept up the demands, he was,

in a word, to come speedily away if ye can get leave and give over all treaty, and this I speak without respect of any security they can offer you, except

16. The brilliant designer and architect, Inigo Jones, was intimately involved in the preparations for the Infanta María's expected arrival in the late spring of 1623.

ye never look to see your old dad again, whom I fear ye shall never see, if ye see him not before Winter. Alas, I now repent me sore that ever I suffered you to go away. I care for match or nothing, so I may once have you in my arms again. God grant it! God grant it! God grant it! Amen, amen, amen. I protest ye shall be as heartily welcome as if ye had done all things ye went for.

With this letter Charles finally had a free hand in the negotiations, as well as the reassurance of a father's affection. S.R. Gardiner, on the other hand, was stirred to further heights of constitutional outrage. 'Never were the evils of personal government presented in a clearer form', he thundered. 'The rights, and it might be the religion, of the country were to be sacrificed for the sake of securing the safe return of a headstrong young man who was really in no danger whatever.'[6]

Was Charles in no danger? While his arch-Protestant sister lived, not to mention 'her numerous issue', there was perhaps no direct threat to his life.[7] A Puritan coup at court in favour of the Winter Queen is surely too fanciful to consider. True, the Prince's health might fail when confronted with the heat of the summer, but the greatest peril was to his political reputation. How could the heir to the throne have been so misguided as to think that a Habsburg bride was his for the taking? As for Buckingham, his position as chief minister was certainly imperilled. In May, his client, Lord Keeper Williams, had warned him that 'you have locked up all things in your own breast and sealed up his majesty's'. Speculation was rife that the mission was heading for disaster. On the day after Cottington's audience with James, Williams again wrote to say it was feared that the marriage was 'at this time in part disjointed'. He begged Buckingham to write to the lords of the council to explain the situation. The marquess of Hamilton, for one, was impatient to make trouble.[8]

While James and his advisers could only brace themselves for the arrival of Spain's final demands, Charles continued in his petulant attempts to wear down Olivares's opposition to his return. He went over the favourite's head, asking King Felipe to overrule his chief minister and to allow him home to negotiate with his father. He begged him to reread James's letters, as 'there you will find peremptory and absolute commands as a king and natural ones as a father'. Unwisely, he complained about 'the unequalness of the conde of Olivares', just as he had done earlier about the papal nuncio, and with equal effect. Forgetting the normal courtesies between princes, he chided his host with how, on his arrival, the count had promised that if the pope would not allow him the Infanta as his wife, he would give him to her as a mistress.[9]

Precisely as Olivares had intended, the *junta* of theologians served to prevent a direct confrontation between Felipe and Charles. Their third and final resolution was relayed by Olivares on 2 July. They had not budged. The princess could not leave until religious toleration had been put into practice. Charles was offered the *junta*'s decision in writing, even though he vehemently protested 'he could not agree to anything [from the *junta*] as his father's orders did not allow him to do so'.[10]

With Prince Charles being buffeted from pillar to post, Olivares at long last felt able to resuscitate the idea of a Viennese marriage. He still could not do this directly. It would be tantamount to revealing that the Spanish Match was already a dead letter. Instead, he asked the Imperial ambassador to air the idea that the Prince of Wales might marry the Holy Roman Emperor's elder daughter. After all, Olivares whispered in the ambassador's ear, the English would never persuade their parliament to agree to the treaty. He even egged the ambassador on by telling him that the Infanta María would never go through with a marriage to Charles anyway.

We shall never know if the 'Austrian Match' had wings. The unwitting Charles Stuart was yet again to catch Olivares off guard and stymie his grand dynastic revolution. He had done so the first time simply by turning up in Madrid. Now he was to astound his hosts by submitting to each and every one of the conditions which had been laid down for the Spanish Match.[11] After almost two decades of negotiation, and after being detained in Madrid for almost four months, the defining moment had finally arrived. Feeling secure in the knowledge of his father's affections, Charles made up his mind to act. He would not even wait for confirmation that the privy councillors back in England had sworn the necessary oaths. On Monday, 7 July he told the earl of Bristol to arrange an immediate meeting with King Felipe. Later that day, the Prince of Wales, accompanied by the now duke of Buckingham, the earl of Bristol and Sir Walter Aston, went to see his host. As Porter reported at once to his wife, Charles 'concluded the business himself with the king'.[12] To the blank astonishment of his father's ambassadors, Charles announced that 'he had seriously made up his mind to accept the proposals made to him with respect to religion, and also to give the securities demanded for their due execution, and that this was the final determination of the king his father'.[13] In token of his earnest, the Prince of Wales gave 50,000 *reales* to be distributed among the lesser officials of the court.[14]

The Spanish court was dumbstruck. Fray Francisco de Jesús had assumed he had come to insist on his departure. How could the Prince change his mind so abruptly, and in under a week?[15] Charles was learning the hard lesson of insincerity. He was a good pupil, with fear and pride contriving to induce him to sign an agreement he had precious little intention of honouring – unless, of course, he and doña María departed together. As he and Buckingham put it to James, whether or not he was contracted to the Infanta, 'marriage there shall be none, without her coming with us'.[16] The new duke began making plans for his return to political life in England. In a wholly unnecessary letter written to Cottington the day after Charles's capitulation, Buckingham put down on paper his excuses for the failure of their adventure. Whereas their letter to James had not mentioned the Palatinate, the duke's letter to Cottington cited the great Protestant cause of the Palatinate – not just the marriage itself – as his excuse for why the visit had gone so badly wrong. Instead of embroiling his father in further negotiations, Buckingham announced that the Prince had chosen to depart at whatever cost, 'making his pretence merely his love unto the Infanta'.[17] The Prince of Wales's double-dealing was equalled by King Felipe's naïvety. As far as we can tell, he remained convinced he had miraculously freed the Catholics of three kingdoms. There was no alternative but to celebrate in the most lavish style possible. For the following three nights there were costly fire-work displays and other festivities and the Infanta was talked of as the 'princess of England'.[18]

Charles had rightly been confident of his father's pledges to stand by whatever he agreed – but only just. Despite James's exclamations on Cottington's arrival, nothing had remotely prepared the King for his first sight of what had been added to the treaty. After three agonising weeks' delay, the final agreement was handed to the King by Peter Killegrew on 7 July, the very day of Charles's capitulation in Madrid.[19] James was flabbergasted. He left his boys in no doubt about his fears. The perpetual abrogation of the penal laws could well result in 'an infinite liberty'. If the Catholics increased in number as a consequence, 'his sovereignty runs a danger'. As for confirmation by a parliament, 'neither did his affection and reason incline to exercise his power that way if it were in his hand'. The requirement that his councillors countersign the treaty was a humiliation, since 'his acts had not need of their fortification', but what 'pinched and per-plexed the most' was that he had no choice in the matter. He had been left with no alternative but to agree to whatever his son had promised.[20]

James summoned a select group of councillors to the royal manor of Wanstead. Since there was an outside chance that they might reject Spain's demands, the morosely Protestant archbishop of Canterbury, George Abbot, was among those not invited. Wisely the King asked for their advice instead of trying to impose his will. He explained his quandary and then left his council-lors to deliberate in private. In the silence that followed, Lord Williams, the Keeper of the Great Seal of England, took the lead. He was Lord Chancellor in all but name and by ancient tradition the office-holder was regarded as the keeper of the royal conscience. Williams asked how could they advise their King unless they knew whether his majesty had conscientious objections to granting liberty of worship. When he came back into the room, James replied that though his conscience was unchanged he was 'willing to hear anything that may move [him] to alter the same'.[21] Williams was as obsequious a client of Buck-ingham's as could be imagined and this was his cue to serve King and Favourite together. Surely our Prince was as good a Protestant as anyone in the world, and so he would not have promised to do anything that was objectionable to our religion? King James had relaxed the laws many times himself, and the French king tolerated Protestantism without being called a heretic, just as the Dutch allowed the Roman religion to be practised in the United Provinces. Williams concluded that Charles had 'admitted nothing in these oaths or articles, either to the prejudice of the true, or the equalising or authorising of the other religion'. Faithful to the Erastian principles of the Church of England, he said it was a matter for the state to decide which laws should be enforced and which should not.

When James called together the remaining members of his Council, the archbishop of Canterbury did indeed raise 'certain grave and moderate questions' but the King was able to retort that the matter had already been settled. All he was being asked was whether or not he would subscribe to the articles.[22] In fact, James was mightily relieved that there had been no greater opposition. All considered, he thought it miraculous that 'our great primate hath behaved himself wonderful well'. Even Buckingham's foe, William Herbert, the evangelical earl of Pembroke, not only declined to make trouble but went 'beyond all the Council in clear and honest dealing'.[23] Nonetheless, at Secretary Calvert's suggestion, the councillors requested they be formally ordered to assent to the articles, under the Great Seal of England.[24] Perhaps it was fortunate that the earl of Southampton, who had caused James so much trouble in the last parliament, chose not to attend these deliberations. Although this was the moment so many of Buckingham's enemies had longed for, Lord Keeper Williams had successfully preserved conciliar harmony. More than anyone else, Williams had stressed the dangers facing the heir to the throne. The overriding need was to bring Charles back 'with speed and safety'.[25]

James's mood was one of resignation. The escalating costs were a grave concern. He had spent £8,000 on Rutland's little armada, and what was happening in Spain was not only dishonourable but threatened 'double charges if I must send two fleets', one for Charles and another for María.[26] As far as the King was concerned, if she was going to come in March the Spaniards could 'send her by their own fleet'. Dismissing in two or three words the fact that he was sending authorisation to discuss a war against both Holland and the Palatinate, the King spelt out to his son that the Spaniards must be made to keep their promises 'anent the portion, otherwise both my baby and I are bankrupts for ever'.[27]

The two Spanish ambassadors, Coloma and the newly arrived marquess of Hinojosa, answered one last enquiry from James about the possibility of immediate marriage. They reiterated that the theologians' insistence upon a non-consummated marriage was irreversible. The earliest that the Infanta could be released was the beginning of March 1624, or 15 April if James were to nominate a specific port. James could prevaricate no longer. Later that day Secretary Calvert sent the envoys a message one-sentence long. They were to appear at court tomorrow to witness the taking of the oaths.[28] The ambassadors dressed themselves in their finest clothes and took with them as large an entourage as they could muster at short notice. They solemnly reported to the Infanta what had been put in place.[29] On Sunday, 20 July, the King and Council publicly swore that no laws would ever be put into effect against Roman Catholics and no new ones would be enacted. In addition, James privately agreed later that day that Catholics would enjoy a perpetual toleration to practise their religion in their own homes. María was also informed by the envoys that she would be completely free to practise her religion and that Charles had himself promised to listen to her theologians. Though it was publicly agreed that her children would remain with her till they were ten, Charles had further promised to ask his father to agree to allow the children to remain with her till the age of twelve, as the pope preferred. If any difficulties arose, Charles said he would put this into effect after his father's death. What the Infanta was not told was that, before he promised a parliamentary revocation of all penal laws within three years at the most, James had explained to the ambassadors 'the impossibilities of the exact performance of' what was expected from a parliament. He had also reserved the right to use the law against Catholics 'in violent cases, according to reason of state'.[30] King James was now emotionally and politically exhausted. If the Prince still could not return after all these concessions, then in the face of destiny, 'there is nothing but a sad submission'.[31] Lord Keeper Williams talked about what had been conceded 'to get your person home again'.[32] On 24 July Rutland was ordered for the last time to set sail for Spain.[33]

Probably no one except the count of Olivares could understand the game that was being played out. The ever wily James may have had an inkling of what his boys were up to. King Felipe, on the other hand, was too busy congratulating himself on a historic achievement. As for those courtiers surrounding Charles and Buckingham, they too seem genuinely to have been taken in. They expected the Infanta to arrive in London some time in 1624. According to Endymion Porter, the Prince was going to contract a form of marriage in Madrid, 'and then he means to go away hence within these three weeks so that we shall all be at home suddenly', with the Infanta following in March. 'God be praised for so great a blessing as we shall all receive by it.'[34] If the Prince's courtiers did harbour any suspicions, they must have realised the danger to their master as well as to themselves if they let slip that a majestic and costly sham was being enacted.

17. The ornate interior of the Queen's Chapel was designed by Inigo Jones to serve as a place of Catholic worship for the Infanta María and her clergy and servants. It was first used by Henrietta Maria.

Charles had one last card left to play before he irrevocably threw in his hand. If he could convince his hosts that he was genuinely prepared to bring to an end the state monopoly of religion in the Stuart dominions, then such a fulsome climb-down might just provoke King Felipe to match his gesture and announce the Infanta's early departure for England. He might even permit the union to be consummated before Charles left. If Felipe declined, then, as far as the Prince was concerned, all bets were off. All that remained would be to achieve a dignified departure, with full courtly honours. Then, as soon as he was safely at arm's length, Charles could renounce the match with impunity.

In a further twist to an already complicated story, news arrived in Madrid on 14 July, while Cottington was still away in England, that Pope Gregory XV had died.[35] This must have been welcome news to both Charles and Olivares. Part of the marriage agreement was that Felipe should promise the pope that he and his successors would take up arms against Great Britain if toleration were not put into effect. With the throne of St Peter vacant, there was no one to whom the king of Spain could make his oath. Given the extra time afforded by the papal interregnum, it would be easier for Charles to break off the match at a moment of his choosing. As for Olivares, Gregory's death provided a breathing space in which he might yet be able to persuade Charles that a Viennese marriage would serve all the better his diplomatic as well as domestic needs. These dark secrets were known only to Olivares, Charles and Buckingham. Papal mortality notwithstanding, Charles's English servants still offered odds of thirty to one that their master would bring off the match.[36]

Instead, Charles was determined to scurry ahead to the end-game. He did not wait for confirmation that there had been no eleventh-hour rebellion by his father's councillors.[37] The solemn exchange of promises between King Felipe and the Prince took place on 25 July 1623, a full eleven days before Secretary Cottington would return, on 5 August, with a certified copy testifying that James and nineteen members of the English Privy Council had accepted Spain's articles.[38] At this late stage, the Prince had for once calculated correctly; unfortunately, the calibration was so fine as to be meaningless. The euphoria which greeted the toleration of Catholicism for the first time in almost a hundred years did indeed lead to a softening of the Spanish position. It was conceded that the ceremony of marriage could take place within ten days of the arrival of a new pope's dispensation, but Charles would still only be permitted to consummate the marriage if he stayed on until Christmas.

There is no way of knowing if this offer of a speedy ceremony of marriage was King Felipe's idea or not. If so, it would run true to form if it were the count of Olivares who insisted that the Prince should stay in Spain while toleration was put into effect. He could always tell his king that this was what the pope demanded. No matter: these concessions were only window dressing. On the sole point that mattered – whether the Infanta could leave for England before the year was out – there was to be little or no adjustment.

On Sunday, 17 August it was announced that the Prince of Wales would leave Madrid at the end of the month. Three days later, Charles finally told his father that the game was all but lost. He confessed he had deliberately avoided writing to him in the fortnight since Cottington's return. He and Buckingham had been trying by 'all means possible . . . to see if we could move them to send the

Infanta before Winter'. This had proved a hopeless task, needless to say. The committee of theologians which Olivares had so cunningly set up simply would not allow their king to alter their original decision.[39] 'To conclude', wrote Charles,

> we have wrought what we can, but since we cannot have her with us that we desired, our next comfort is that we hope shortly to kiss your majesty's hand.

Oblivious to the bluff and counter-bluff being played around her, María obediently copied out a few stilted lines to James expressing her gratitude at the honour being accorded her.[40]

Right up until the end of August Charles continued to throw out empty concessions in the hope that Olivares or his king might relent. A couple of days before he departed Madrid, he joined with Felipe in yet again swearing to all he had promised. This time James's ambassadors and the duke of Buckingham were prevailed upon to add a meaningless promise that they would never carry out any law persecuting Catholics, or allow anyone in their power so to do.[41] For their part, the Spaniards made no further concessions.

The Prince had lost what little patience he had left for his hosts. On the day before he departed from Madrid, he prepared his father for his empty-handed return to London. Charles blamed the pope's illness and death for causing yet another delay regarding 'the capitulations agreed upon'. He complained bitterly that nothing had been done 'to encourage us to rely longer upon uncertainties'. As for the Palatinate, the use of arms had again been ruled out, and Charles had finally been told that the only hope of a solution lay in a new round of negotiations to allow the King's eldest grandson to be brought up in Vienna. Even then the Elector Frederick would be excluded from any settlement.[42] To all practical purposes, it was now too late to hope that an Austrian Match might be conjured up to replace a Spanish Match.

Charles's desperation was increased by the fact that the tail-end of his visit had become bogged down in hypocrisy and tension, and not just at the council board. The much-needed dignified departure was being put at risk by any number of squabbles and misunderstandings which were breaking out. Earlier in August, Endymion Porter had written home to his wife with news of the Prince's return. Teasingly, he asked her to cut their son's hair and not to beat him too much, otherwise he would not grow up to be strong and robust. More sombrely, he added a brief post script. 'Mr. Secretary Cottington is very sick.' A cold had turned into a fever and he had been bled by his doctors, and the Prince's trusted secretary turned to Rome on what he assumed was his deathbed. The commitment to toleration put both Charles and his courtiers to the test. Fray Diego de la Fuente, whom the Secretary knew from the time the friar was in Gondomar's embassy in London, blatantly gave him the last rites. On his recovery, Cottington thought better of what he had done and reneged on his conversion.[43]

The most serious incident of all occurred when Washington, one of the Prince's pages, died of sunstroke. It was a notorious incident which was brought to King Felipe's notice and which provoked at least three anti-Catholic poems. One vicious doggerel-writer claimed that it was pointless asking about 'his disease or pain', since the cause of Washington's death was 'nothing else but Spain'. When an English Jesuit went to administer the last rites he fell into a fight with other members of the Prince's entourage, including Sir Edmund Verney. He returned, this time accompanied by the local equivalent of the police. Eventually Gondomar had to be called to calm a very ugly confrontation with the crowd, and Buckingham was left to remonstrate with Olivares about this violation of a house under Charles's protection. It was by no means the first time Gondomar had prevented Charles's visit ending in a fracas. On one occasion he intervened with the Inquisition in Toledo and Seville. As James Howell said of the count, Charles's servants had much to thank him for during their time in Madrid. In a reference to the count's suffering at the hands of the xenophobic English, he added, this was 'notwithstanding the base affronts he hath often received of the "London boys", as he calls them'.[44]

Charles, on the other hand, was obliged to act during his final weeks in Madrid as the image of propriety. It was far too dangerous to risk revealing he had all but turned his back on the Spanish marriage. He showered the Infanta with jewels, including a priceless diamond brooch in the shape of an anchor. Mostly she received pearls, including a five-carat necklace of 250 pearls – 276 by English reckoning – in recognition of her purity.[45] As no wedding ceremony had taken place it was felt improper for her to receive them, so they were immediately diverted to her brother's Jewel House.[46] She gave Charles a pair of gloves. Felipe received a diamond-encrusted sword that had once belonged to his sister's first English suitor, Prince Henry. Olivares was given the Portingall diamond that had once belonged to King Sebastian. On his last day but one in Madrid, Charles took his public leave of the heavily pregnant Queen Isabel and the Infanta. They were both draped in black to demonstrate sorrow at his departure. Charles reassured María that he would take the Catholics of his kingdoms under his protection. The refusal of the duke of Buckingham to attend was duly noted by the Spaniards, though it seems he was genuinely running a fever.[47]

20. *Don Diego Sarmiento de Acuña, Count of Gondomar,* by Janos Privitzer. Count Gondomar was Spain's greatest ambassador in London. He was a friend to both King James and the Prince of Wales.

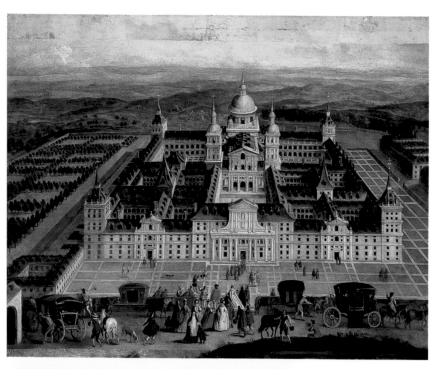

21. *Bird's Eye View of El Escorial*, Spanish School, *c.* 1610. The palace-monastery of the Escorial was built by Felipe II and dedicated to St Lawrence. Its ground plan was said to be based on the grid-iron on which the saint was martyred.

22. *Charles I as Prince of Wales*, by Daniel Mytens, 1624. This portrait of a bearded Charles was painted in 1624, the year in which he brought about his war with Spain.

23. *Karl V with a Hound*, by Titian. Titian's definitive portrait of Emperor Karl V was presented by Felipe IV some time during the Prince of Wales's visit to Madrid. After Charles's execution, it was among the pictures sold by the Commonwealth in 1651, after which it quickly found its way back into the Spanish royal collection.

24. To honour Charles's visit to the Segovia Mint, a 100 escudo gold coin weighing over 300 grams was specially minted.

25. The *columna del adiós,* or 'Farewell Column', was put up to mark the precise spot in the plain below the Escorial where Charles and Felipe said their goodbyes. Within hours, Charles had secretly reneged on his promises.

18. This pencil drawing of Olivares may date from the time of Charles's visit. It is certainly testimony to Velázquez's skill as a draughtsman. From Velázquez's father-in-law we know that he also drew the Prince of Wales at this time, although this work cannot be found.

Charles left Madrid at dawn on Saturday, 30 August 1623. King Felipe and his brothers, don Carlos and don Fernando, accompanied the Prince as far as the Escorial. The following day was spent seeing the sights that the 'Eighth Wonder of the World' had to offer. While at the Escorial, Buckingham had a last private interview with Olivares, the only other person present being his interpreter, Walter Montague. The count was at his most devilish. To make certain once for all that there was not the remotest possibility that the marriage would actually happen, Olivares challenged his homologue to promise to allow the marriage to take its course. He then defied him not to interfere: with another twist of the knife, he announced he would have to make a full report to King James about Buckingham's behaviour. He proved as good as his word. A fortnight later, the Council of State met to decide what to do about the way the duke had treated Olivares 'in public and privately'. To bedevil the marriage one last time, Olivares saw to it that an instruction was given to prepare a dossier outlining the duke's misconduct. Oddly, the order was circulated under a secretary's signature, on the implausible grounds that this was essential to avoid further delay.[48] Since it is unimaginable that Olivares did not already have a charge sheet to hand, could it just be that this rarely invoked procedure was aimed at preventing the young king from finding out what his chief minister was up to? In due course a detailed complaint was sent to the ambassadors in London. James was notified not only of his Favourite's fractiousness, but of how he had been in the habit of coming 'into the Prince's chamber with his clothes half on'. Buckingham even had ridiculous nicknames for the Prince![49]

As for Charles, he had one final and superficially more courteous meeting with Olivares. The affairs of Germany were discussed for the last time during his stay. This is probably when Charles made his final pleas concerning Frederick's restoration to the Palatinate. Earlier he had suggested that his brother-in-law be allowed to administer the Palatinate while his eldest son was brought up in Vienna. His final suggestion was that an eighth electorship be set up, which would at least allow for his nephew to be restored without depriving the duke of Bavaria of his new-found electoral rights.[50]

The Prince's proposal was sensible. At the end of the Thirty Years War an additional electorship would be created to solve the problem of the Palatinate. Even so, we can assume that Olivares had no intention of offering any commitment that might induce the Prince of Wales to persist in asking for the Infanta's hand in marriage. Not only was he unable to make promises there and then on the emperor's behalf, he was in no mood to say anything which might make it easier to stand by the solemn promises he had already made to bring back the Infanta with him. Though Olivares was doubtless circumspect in what he actually said to the Prince during those last days, his mood can be gauged from what he told his fellow councillors. If friendship with James and the emperor could be maintained then 'well and good', but if not, then friendship with England must go, 'even if they had married a hundred Infantas'. As for supporting Frederick's return to the Palatinate, the count's reaction was a brutal *keineswegs* – 'no way'.[51]

The royal party spent Monday, 1 September hunting in the vicinity of the Escorial. The following morning was also taken up with the chase. On the afternoon of Tuesday, the final round of farewells commenced. Originally, King

Felipe planned to escort the Prince as far as the royal lodge at Valsaín. When he learnt that the arrangements had not been completed, he asked Charles to remain one more day. Charles unsurprisingly refused. He said that on account of the heat and the queen's pregnancy, the king should proceed no further than the Escorial. Just before he left the monastery-palace, the Prince signed the powers to allow either King Felipe or the elder of his brothers to act as his proxy in a wedding ceremony with the Infanta. The marriage would take place within ten days of the arrival of a dispensation from the new pope.[52] In the presence of a notary and witnesses, the documents were placed for safe keeping in Lord Bristol's hands.[53]

About five miles beyond the Escorial, before the mountains of the Guadarrama began to rise, Charles and the king of Spain said their goodbyes. Earlier in the day Felipe had written to confirm, by his hand as well as his embraces, that nothing in the world would lead him to break any of the promises he had made.[54] On a small rocky outcrop the prospective brothers-in-law made their last clinches. To mark the spot, the young king caused 'a pillar to be erected as a monument to posterity'.[55]

Despite all his inherited reservations about the marriage, the suspicion lingers that King Felipe had not lost the boyish exuberance he had felt when Charles had astonished the world by appearing in Madrid. There is a solitary piece of evidence which strongly suggests that the Spanish monarch truly believed that Charles would carry out everything he had solemnly sworn to do. It lies in the gift of a single painting. Felipe presented his prospective brother-in-law with the most important dynastic picture in his possession, Titian's definitive portrait of his great-grandfather, the Emperor Karl V, the founder of Habsburg power in Spain.[56] Felipe was utterly convinced that he and his family were fulfilling a providential role. A Spanish princess, Catherine of Aragon, had been the reason why the Reformation had spread to Britain and Ireland. His own grandfather, Felipe II, tried to restore Catholicism with his marriage to Mary Tudor and had almost succeeded. It was only natural for this King Felipe to be captivated by the thought that another Spanish princess would begin to heal the schism that divided the three Stuart kingdoms from Rome. With the final words on the pillar set up by the Spanish monarch were *posteritati sacrum*, and so the monument was optimistically 'dedicated to those who were to follow'.[57] King Felipe can be forgiven for not realising it was the Prince of Wales's intention to spurn the Infanta as soon as he was out of sight.

13. Epilogue – The Codpiece Point?

John Elliott remarked about the Prince of Wales's visit that in the style of negotiating 'the dishonours were ultimately even'.[1] Whether or not Olivares's intrigues with the papacy over the dispensation are to be regarded as deceitful or merely effective diplomacy, the shabbiness of Charles's last ruse plumbed new depths. After he had said his farewells to King Felipe, Charles entered his coach, with Gondomar and Buckingham in attendance. He spent the night in the village of Guadarrama. The following day, after stopping to eat at the king's house at Valsaín, the Prince reached the safety of the royal city of Segovia, which lay some 30 miles beyond the Escorial, on the far side of the Guadarrama mountains.

It was four o'clock in the afternoon of Wednesday, 3 September, when Charles entered the city.[2] A gun salute greeted the Prince from the castle walls as he descended from his coach. He was able to admire the Roman aqueduct, which had already impressed Sir Richard Wynn with its water 'carried upon a wall steeple height'.[3] After touring the *alcázar*, he descended into the valley immediately below the walls of the fortress, since, as was usual with distinguished guests, a visit had been arranged to the royal mint. With its Austrian technology, it was held to be one of the most modern factories in the world. Since precious metals did not normally arrive from the New World till November, the mint was low on supplies. The deputy treasurer was obliged to round up old coins and even purloin gold chains from the notables of the town so that 230 pounds of silver and 15 pounds of gold could be turned into coin before the Prince's very eyes. An ebullient Charles tossed a platter of specially minted silver 50 *real* coins into the air. What caught everyone's eye, however, was the the showpiece production of a *centén*, a bulky gold coin the size of a medallion that weighed 335 grams and had an intrinsic worth many times in excess of its face value of 100 *escudos*.[4]

At one stage during his visit to the castle, Charles's gaze had been directed upwards to where the arms of Castile and England were united in honour of an

19. The Prince of Wales's party rested at the palace of Valsaín after taking their leave from King Felipe.

earlier Spanish Match. King Enrique III of Castile had married a daughter of the English prince, John of Gaunt. Now, some two hundred years later, Segovia was to be the place where a different prince would put an end to his Spanish Match. First, courtesy required Charles to reply to Felipe's letter of the day before, and he wrote to assure him not only of his 'firm and constant resolution to stand by all my father and I have agreed but also to do everything else necessary to confirm their fraternal and sincere friendship'.[5] Then Charles penned a curt note to Bristol. He was commanded 'not to deliver my proxy', which, just the day before, he had solemnly handed over to the earl.[6]

This devastating letter to the earl was entrusted to one of Buckingham's servants, Mr Clarke with the lame arm, as James Howell described him. He was to make his way back over the mountains to the House of the Seven Chimneys and was to act as if he needed to stay behind to put the duke's affairs in order. This at once aroused suspicion. He was one of the Favourite's 'most confidential servants',[7] yet the earl and Buckingham were barely on speaking terms. It was assumed that Edward Clarke had with him something 'to puzzle the business'. When Clarke was told by a suspicious Bristol that the dispensation had probably arrived, he swallowed the bait and handed over his letter.[8] Neither Charles nor Buckingham had wanted their deceitfulness revealed until their stately progress through northern Castile was completed and they were safely aboard an English ship. The reason Charles gave Bristol for reneging on his promises was a concern that the Infanta 'might be forced to go to a monastery', even after the proxy wedding. He had no wish to appear 'a rash-headed fool'. He had come to the conclusion, he told Bristol, that no matter what he said or did, Olivares would find a way to prevent María from ever joining Charles in England, and he was almost certainly right.

Charles set sail for home on Tuesday, 18 September. As soon as Bristol was certain that the Prince was safely out of the country, he trained his fire on Charles's excuses. He loftily said that a rumour had arisen 'from letters of some that accompanied your highness to Santander, as though there might a doubt be made of your highness's affection to the Infanta'. As for talk that María might enter a nunnery, the countess of Olivares had assured him this was risible and even the hard-nosed Infanta was said to be amused at the idea.[9] Bristol was awkwardly placed. King James had instructed him to perform the marriage by proxy no more than ten days after the arrival of the final dispensation. Now his son was countermanding a royal command, at a time when King Felipe could talk of nothing else but combining his sister's marriage with the christening of his first child. María had begun learning English, and Bristol and Aston were refusing to cover their heads in her presence on the grounds that she was to be treated as their princess. No one, it seems, apart from Olivares, had realised that Charles and the much-despised Buckingham had little or no intention of honouring their solemn oaths to tolerate Catholicism.

Fortunately for Ambassador Bristol, James confirmed his son's decision early in October, when he took the extraordinary precaution of dispatching four messengers 'one upon the neck of the other'. These new instructions arrived well before the final dispensation reached Madrid in mid-November. King James endorsed the original canard about María's possible flight to a nunnery but now the fate of the Palatinate was added, thereby pasting a further layer of respectability over Charles's double-dealing. The King repeated how much he desired the match with Spain, but only when his son-in-law was at the same time remarried to the Palatinate. He could not allow his heir to marry yet 'give our only daughter her portion in tears'.[10]

Elizabeth had written a letter to Buckingham which apparently reached him while he was in Segovia. The letter's contents were quickly turned into the stuff of legend. The Winter Queen had invited the duke to be godfather to her current infant; she also sent presents for her prospective sister-in-law, doña María. Almost immediately it was put about that the letter to the duke contained a plea to put a stop to the marriage. Once reminded of her plight, Buckingham miraculously broke the Spanish Match within an hour – or so it was said. As John Hackett wanted to believe, all 'hope of that alliance, and the comfort from it, drowned in the Rhine'.[11] Venice's acid-tongued ambassador in London was not so easily taken in. Dismissing the excuse about the Palatinate as an attempt to salvage the Prince's reputation at home and abroad, Valaresso remarked that, just as Charles went without reason, he was now returning without a bride. Ever bold, the envoy told James to his face that the refusal to hand over the Infanta was an insult and clear evidence that Spain had never been serious about the match.[12]

Curiously, the Palatinate turned out to be much more than a fig leaf to hide behind. By ignoring the fact that near-impossible conditions had been agreed to, and by pretending that they had turned their backs on a marriage that was theirs for the asking, Charles and Buckingham successfully cast themselves in the role of religious heroes. The Prince of Wales was happy to give out that he had rejected his love for the Infanta because his love for the Protestant cause was greater. When Buckingham later spoke about the visit, he depicted the Palatinate as both the reason for the trip as well as the cause of its failure. He claimed they were bound together 'by a reciprocal subordination'. A desperate disease, he said, had needed a desperate remedy. To stress that the Winter Queen's fate was never far from the Prince's mind, he claimed that in one of his blackest moments Charles had penned a letter to his father (never delivered, of course) saying that, if he was ever held prisoner in Spain, James should never 'think upon him any longer as a son, but to reflect with all his royal thoughts upon the good of his sister'.[13]

'How could there be a better pawn for the surrendery of the Palatinate than the Infanta in the Prince's arms?' exclaimed an exasperated Bristol.[14] The Prince and the Favourite were turning matters on their head. To reject the marriage was to brush aside all hope of Spanish help over the Rhineland, as King Felipe was surely not going to stand idly by while María's sister-in-law and her nephews by marriage lived in exile. In fact, Felipe's ministers had already renewed pressure on Vienna to concede a negotiated settlement. In June 1623, Spain enthusiastically signalled her support for a diet in Germany in the hope that it would resolve all outstanding questions.[15] Even Charles testily acknowledged that Olivares had promised 'mediation and courtesy' in restoring the Palatinate, if, he added, little else.[16] Though James may have fancied that the Spaniards might use force to restore the Rhineland, at least ever since Endymion Porter's altercation with Olivares in late 1622 he had accepted that the restitution of the Palatinate 'must now be done by the king of Spain's mediation betwixt the Emperor and me'.[17] James had learnt to be realistic. Just over a week after he had signed away the Protestant Church's claim to universal truth in each of his kingdoms, James wrote, on 31 July, that, *once* a marriage ceremony had taken place, *then* his boys should be seen to do as much as they could about the Palatinate and an offensive war against the Protestant Dutch. 'After the contract', what was crucial, wrote the King, was 'that the world may see ye have thought as well upon the business of Christendom as upon the codpiece point'.[18]

Ironically, the codpiece point had been the overriding reason behind the Prince's chivalric adventure to collect his bride from a foreign land. His subsequent fury at being scorned was in evidence from the moment he returned home. On Sunday, 5 October 1623, after a tempestuous voyage which very nearly cost him his life, the now bearded Charles finally landed in England.[19] Despite having promised to emancipate Catholics only a few weeks earlier, the brideless Prince came home only to be miraculously transformed into a Protestant champion. It is hard to find words to describe the euphoria that greeted Charles. In Cambridge the bells rang for three days running.[20] In London 'there were 335 bonfires or thereabouts' between Whitehall and Temple Bar. The crowd shouted 'we have him, we have him'.[21] God had provided for the safety of Protestantism and the realm once more. Before the princely party had reached London, it was clear to the incredulous Spanish ambassadors that the marriage was a dead letter.[22]

With astonishing foresight, Olivares had foreseen the dangers inherent in the way Charles had confused affairs of the heart with matters of state. On one of the occasions when he had forced the Prince to remain in Madrid, the count asked him to give up any thoughts of going back empty-handed and seeking his revenge, as in Elizabeth's days. He feared that Charles would send 'against us a fleet which may take from us Cadiz, or Lisbon, or Corunna'.[23] Safely back in England, the Prince and Buckingham at once set to work to capitalise on their new status as religious heroes and to prepare for war. Olivares half-heartedly revived his plans to set an Austrian marriage before King James. These were, of course, ignored.[24] Instead, Charles and the Favourite set to work to persuade a reluctant monarch to issue the writs for another parliament. Pathetically, Kings James and Felipe were among the last to accept that the Spanish marriage was never going to take place. The final obstacle to Charles's belligerence was removed on 20 December, when Frederick, whose stubbornness grew with every defeat, rejected out of hand his father-in-law's appeal that he send his eldest son to be married at the emperor's court.[25]

Did Charles's disastrous journey to Madrid matter? Almost exactly a year to the day after he and Charles had set out for Madrid, Buckingham stood up in the House of Lords to give his version of history. He was out to make common cause with his erstwhile political and religious rivals in a grand patriotic and Protestant coalition. No word was spoken about the fact that the Prince had been willing to grant toleration to Roman Catholics as the cost of a Spanish bride. Instead, he and the Prince of Wales asked to be judged according to the standards of the warrior princes who were risking their lives fighting for the Protestant cause in central Europe. Distinct among the clamour for war which greeted the Prince's return were the words of the incomparable propagandist, the evangelical Thomas Scott. He resumed his role as *vox populi* – the people's voice. In the course of 1624 he published nine or ten books which persistently questioned, in varying degrees of directness, the erstwhile attachment of James and Charles to a Catholic alliance.

For all Scott's praise of Charles as a lion among princes, the heir to the throne was portrayed as having been led by the nose by Gondomar. The devilish ambassador had tempted the Prince to go to Madrid where he could place him at the mercy of the king of Spain. At the very least, Scott's double-edged esteem served as a public warning to Charles that he should never allow himself to be led astray again.[26] Indeed, a consequence of the visit was the disturbing thought that Charles might not be quite as steadfast in his Protestantism as he wished to appear. Whether he had ever entertained the idea of abandoning his religion while in Madrid remained a question mark that hovered like a storm cloud whenever people were dissatisfied with Charles and thought back to what had really happened during his six months in Spain. Chaplain Wren discovered this to his dismay when, long after his return, he found himself quizzed by a very high-ranking fellow Anglican about whether Charles had always been true to his religion.[27]

The failure of the visit forced the Prince of Wales to begin looking for a French bride. Despite all his concessions in terms of liberty of religion during the summer of 1623, far less rigorous promises not to persecute Catholics were enough to satisfy France. In 1625, Charles took as his wife Henrietta Maria, the Bourbon princess he had glimpsed two years earlier as he passed through Paris on his way to Spain.[28] The promises he made to the French king about toleration were quickly forgotten, and incredibly he soon found himself at war with France as well as Spain, sending thousands upon thousands to their death. As for Buckingham, he was to reap the whirlwind. In August 1628, the duke was assassinated by an evangelical soldier who had served in a catastrophic assault he had organised on Cadiz.[29] Buckingham had failed to live up to the godly expectations which he had claimed for himself on his return from Spain. The Spanish favourite fared better. The perfidy that he ascribed to the Prince of

Wales confirmed that he had been right all along to prefer a Habsburg marriage. He finally achieved his goal when in 1631, after a long betrothal, María married her Viennese cousin, as he had wanted all along. She died an esteemed Holy Roman Empress in 1646. Three years later, Charles Stuart was beheaded by his Protestant subjects. In the condemned King's last moments, it is perhaps unlikely that he shed a tear for the narcissistic war he had engineered with Spain. Still, it was a shameful price to pay in human misery for a journey that should never have taken place.

Note on Sources

The Spanish Match and in particular the Prince of Wales's visit to Madrid generated an enormous amount of contemporary comment. Almost every great European archive covering this period seems to contain some references to the events described in this study. Unsurprisingly, these references are liberally scattered in letter collections rather than incorporated into specially catalogued anthologies; therefore it is neither feasible, nor would it be particularly valuable, to provide a comprehensive list of sources. Instead, I have described important bodies of evidence as and when they are first cited in the text. This has the great advantage of allowing me to describe the historiographical significance of those sources; nonetheless, a brief overview of the principal sources may be instructive.

The letters of Buckingham and Charles to and from James are at the heart of this study, and the majority have been carefully edited by D.M. Bergeron, *King James & Letters of Homoerotic Desire* (Iowa City, 1999) and G.P.V. Akrigg, *Letters of King James VI & I* (Berkeley, 1984), though these collections must be supplemented by Hardwicke's State Papers (*Miscellaneous State Papers*, London, 1778, ed. by Philip Yorke, earl of Hardwicke) and H. Ellis, *Original Letters*, 1st ser., iii (London, 1829). The following two less well edited works are also important: Godfrey Goodman, *The Court of King James the First* (London, 1839) and Thomas Birch, *The Court and Times of James the First, illustrated by authentic and confidential letters* (2 vols, London, 1848). Unjustifiably neglected is James O. Halliwell's *Letters of the Kings of England now first collected from the Originals* (2 vols, London, 1848).

These royal letters are fruitfully matched by the correspondence of a pair of well-placed writers: James Howell's letters, which in 1623 were written from the British embassy in Madrid, are available in his *Epistolae Ho-Elianae: Familiar*

Letters (London, 1754) and one of the Prince's most trusted servants penned a number of interesting observations on his master's reception in Madrid, for which see the selection made by Dorothea Townshend in her *Life and Letters of Mr. Endymion Porter* (London, 1897).

Much of the backbone for the earlier part of this study was provided by the pioneering work of S.R. Gardiner, and especially his superb knowledge of Count Gondomar's diplomatic correspondence. To that body of material I have added the ambassador's often less formal letters contained in the *Real Biblioteca* in Madrid, which have now been catalogued by the royal library's staff. The British Library preserves a unique selection of Gondomar's letters (e.g. App. 1 below), along with important letters from Olivares and the Spanish kings, as well as S.R. Gardiner's own notebooks of his researches in Spain. Among the Harleian and Additional manuscripts especially, there are to be found innumerable letters or notes from Charles, Buckingham and James (usually but not always in Bergeron or Akrigg), and from leading English and Scottish politicians of the day. Letters from Gondomar are also to be found in the Bodleian Library in Oxford, where the Tanner and Rawlinson collections are a true miscellany not only of letters, but also of drafts of treaties as well as poems and more general comments on how the Prince's visit was viewed back home. The Society of Antiquaries in London also contains letters that were penned from inside the British embassy in Madrid.

The Public Record Office in Kew, as is to be expected, preserves huge quantities of material relating to the official diplomatic correspondence which passed between Madrid and London as well as to official papers generated domestically. Amongst the former are various drafts of memoranda made by Charles and Buckingham during their time in Madrid. In addition to the obvious collections of State Papers Spanish, the naval records at Kew provide details of the fleet which would fetch the royal party back from Santander and they have been most useful in establishing both chronology and intent.

The National Library of Scotland houses a small but intriguing collection of letters dealing with Spanish matters, but of capital importance is their possession of the Prince's account book for 1623 (a less full but still valuable account book for Buckingham survives in the British Library). The magnificent collection of letters relating to the Wynns of Gwydir is preserved in the National Library of Wales, even if I was able to include only a fraction of their many references to the Spanish Match.

Turning to the Spanish archives, they are replete with a frankly giddying number of copies or duplicates of both ambassadorial letters and the discussions which took place in the Council of State. This is as true of the Royal Library as of the *Archivo Histórico Nacional* (which incidentally contains a surprising number of printed news-sheets covering the Prince's visit). As well as much of the formal correspondence which passed between Rome and the king of Spain in the seventeenth century, the archive of the Ministry of Foreign Affairs in Madrid has the collection of documents that provided Francisco de Jesús with the documentary basis for his treatise, *El Hecho de los tratados del matrimonio pretendido por el Príncipe de Gales con la sereníssima Infanta de España, Maria.* (An early twentieth-century copy of these documents was deposited in the Royal Academy of History, also in Madrid, which in its own right houses a vast collection of miscellaneous letters and papers for this period.) The *Biblioteca Nacional* is particularly rich in material dealing with the entertainments provided for Charles while he was in the Spanish capital; and ms. 8717 confirms the details of the marriage settlement sent to England early in 1623 (see below, App. 2).

The great Habsburg dynastic archive in Simancas guards vast amounts of official correspondence, comparable only to the collections held in the Public Record Office. In addition to copies of Gondomar's letters and the diplomatic correspondence with England and Flanders, it should be noted that it now holds the records of the discussions in the Committee of Theologians set up from 1613 onwards to consider the religious implications of the projected marriage in ms. Estado 8341. These documents were only returned to Simancas from Paris during the Second World War and they are vital not least because of the marginal comments made by King Felipe III and his successor.

In Austria, the papers of the emperor's ambassador to the Spanish court, Franz Christoph Khevenhüller, are divided between two state archives: the originals are in Vienna but his own copies are to be found in Linz, having been transferred there from Germany in the mid-1970s. Khevenhüller's published memoirs are largely but not entirely free of *post-hoc* rationalisation, so consultation of both sets of original material is recommended.

The highly secret correspondence between Olivares and Cardinal Ludovisi, most of which resides at the Vatican Archive, forms the crux of this study; and the printed editions by Luigi Arezio and Karl Jaitner jointly provide a safe mode of entry into papal sources. Further work in the Roman archives will undoubtedly add more details to this story. As for the sources available in the Venetian archives, whenever I have compared translations, the material there has been reliably (if artlessly) rendered into English in the *Calendar of State Papers Spanish.* (Most of the nineteenth-century transcripts of the original

Italian are preserved in the PRO.) The records of the ambassadors of Genoa in the city's *Archivio di Stato* contain little important information, apart from confirming how Olivares's clandestine dealings with the papacy remained a closely guarded secret even from one of the Spanish king's closest allies.

Abbreviations

AGS	Archivo General de Simancas
Ambasciatori Genovesi	*Istruzioni e relazioni degli Ambasciatori Genovesi,* ed. Raffaele Ciasca (Istituto Storico Italiano per l'età moderna e contemporanea. Fonti per la storia d'Italia), 7 vols, vol. 2, *Spagna, 1619–1635*
ASG	Archivio di Stato, Genoa
B	followed by a number, refers to letters from Buckingham to James in David M. Bergeron, *King James & Letters of Homoerotic Desire* (Iowa City, 1999)
BL	British Library, London
BNM	Biblioteca Nacional, Madrid
Bod.	Bodleian Library, Oxford
Bristol's *Defence*	'The Earl of Bristol's Defence of his Negotiations in Spain', ed. S.R. Gardiner, in *Camden Miscellany* 6 (Camden Society, 1870)
CD	*Commons Debates 1621,* 7 vols, ed. Wallace Notestein, Frances Helen Relf and Hartley Simpson (New Haven and London, 1935)
Correspondencia oficial	Gondomar, Diego Sarmiento de Acuña, conde de, in *Documentos inéditos para la historia de España*, vol. v in four parts (Madrid, 1936–45)
Gaçeta	Gascón de Torquemada, Gerónimo, *Gaçeta y nuevas de la Corte de España desde el año 1600 en addante*, ed. Alfonso de Ceballas-Escalera y Gil, marqués de la Floresta (Madrid, 1991)
Gardiner	*History of England from the Accession of James I, to the Outbreak of the Civil War*, in 10 vols (London, 1883–84)

Gondomar and Parliaments	*Gondomar and Parliaments, with an Edition of his Unpublished Parliamentary Treatise of 1621*, ed. Glyn Redworth with Jonathan Nelson, Cañada Blanch Monographs, 6 (Manchester: Manchester Spanish & Portuguese Studies, 2002)
HHStA	Haus-, Hof- und Staatsarchiv, Vienna
Howell, *Epistolae*	James Howell, *Epistolae Ho-Elianae: Familiar Letters* (London, 1754)
J	followed by a number, refers to letters from King James in David M. Bergeron, *King James & Letters of Homoerotic Desire* (Iowa City, 1999)
LJ	Buckingham's account of the visit to Spain, given in the Upper House in 1624, *Journals of the House of Lords, beginning anno primo Henrici octavi* (London, 1771? onwards), iii [for 1624], pp. 220–33
MAE	Ministerio de Asuntos Exteriores, Madrid
NLS	National Library of Scotland
OÖLA	Oberösterreichisches Landesarchiv, Linz
PRO	Public Record Office, Kew
RAHM	Real Academia de la Historia, Madrid
RBM	Real Biblioteca, Madrid
Russell	Conrad Russell, *Parliaments and English Politics, 1621–1629* (1st ed. 1979, reprint with corrections, Oxford, 1982)
SRP	*Stuart Royal Proclamations*, i. *Royal Proclamations of King James I, 1603–1625*, ed. James Francis Larkin and Paul L. Hughes (Oxford, 1973)
Tratados	Francisco de Jesús, *El Hecho de los tratados del matrimonio pretendido por el Príncipe de Gales con la sereníssima Infanta de España, Maria*, ed. S.R. Gardiner (Camden Society, 101), 1869
Ven. Cal.	*Calendar of State Papers and Manuscripts relating to English Affairs existing in the Archives and Collections of Venice*, vols xvii, for 1621–23 (London, 1911) and xviii, for 1623–25 (London, 1912), ed. Allen B. Hinds
Wynn	Richard Wynn's account of Spain, in T. Hearne, *Historia vitae et regni Ricardi II* (Oxford, 1729), App. iv, pp. 297–341

Notes

1. Prologue

1 Conrad Russell, *Parliaments and English Politics, 1621–1629* (1st ed. 1979, reprint with corrections, Oxford, 1982), p. 146.

2 Thomas Cogswell, *The Blessed Revolution: English Politics and the Coming of War, 1621–1624* (Cambridge, 1989), p. 12. Professor Cogswell's outstanding work has single-handedly brought the Spanish Match into the framework of revisionist thinking. Though I fully accept that Cogswell's work is more nuanced than any historiographical gloss may suggest, he may be called revisionist when he argues that Charles Stuart's visit to Madrid was a bold and imaginative response to the European diplomatic crisis. It cannot be overlooked, however, that Professor Cogswell has first and foremost been instrumental in refocusing our attention on divisions between the crown and the House of Commons in particular. For a generally revisionist view of early Stuart foreign policy, see the works of Brennan P. Pursell, especially 'Elector Friedrich V and the Question of Influence Revisited', *The Court Historian* 6 (2001), 'James I, Gondomar and the Dissolution of the Parliament of 1621', *History* 85 (2000), and, most important, 'The End of the Spanish Match', *Historical Journal* 45 (2002), pp. 699–726, which trenchantly restates the case for the paramountcy of the Palatinate in the Prince's mind. Though its explanation of the origins of the visit and, most of all, Olivares's attitude towards the marriage is superseded by this account, it nonetheless casts important new light on Frederick's refusal to make peace as well as usefully documenting the descent into war after Charles's return to England. Despite our different views, I am indebted to both colleagues for much friendly advice and encouragement; in many ways Professor Cogswell's study of the revolution of 1624 was the inspiration for this study.

3 Of a lower order than Cogswell's pathbreaking analysis, honourable mention should nonetheless be made of *Carlos de Inglaterra en España: un príncipe de Gales busca novia en Madrid* by Carlos Puyuelo y Salinas (Madrid, 1962). Part of a series entitled 'La historia anecdótica', this account is a delightful foray into the Prince's adventures in Spain. Also valuable for citations is Rafael Rodríguez-Moñino Soriano, *Razón de estado y dogmatismo religioso en la España de XVII: negociaciones hispano-inglesas de 1623* (Barcelona, 1976). Gardiner's principal (and his equally important, if less well known) works are cited in the list of Abbreviations.

4 Clarendon makes the same argument when he reconstructs the Prince's speech to his father. Charles enumerated the 'two points' which the King most wants in the world, the marriage first, with the restoration of the Palatinate second. See Edward Hyde, earl of Clarendon, *The History of the Rebellion and Civil Wars in England begun in the Year 1641*, ed. W. Dunn Macray (6 vols, Oxford, 1988, reissued 1992), i. 14ff., and ch. 7 below.

5 In particular, John Elliott, *The Count-Duke of Olivares: The Statesman in an Age of Decline* (London, 1986); and also John Elliott and Jonathan Brown, *A Palace for a King: The Buen Retiro and the Court of Philip IV* (London, 1980), John Elliott, *Richelieu and Olivares* (London, 1984); and John Elliott and Angel García Sanz (eds), *La España del Conde Duque de Olivares: encuentro internacional sobre la España del conde Duque de Olivares celebrado en Toro los dias 15–18 de septiembre de 1987* (Valladolid, 1990).

2. A Spanish Bride

1 NLS, ms Adv. 33.1.10, no. 4. The duchess was a lady-in-waiting to Mary Tudor (1553–58) before her own Spanish marriage.
2 For the peace negotiations, see Paul C. Allen, *Philip III and the Pax Hispanica 1598–1621* (London, 2000), ch. 6, 'The Policy of Rapprochement', pp. 115–40.
3 *Tratados*, p. 103.
4 From 1601 to 1606, the Spanish capital moved to Valladolid in the north of Castile.
5 See below, ch. 7, n. 16.
6 Roy Strong, *Henry, Prince of Wales and England's Lost Renaissance* (London, 1986), p. 175.
7 See Carola Oman, *The Winter Queen: Elizabeth of Bohemia* (London, 1938, reprinted 2000), p. 84.
8 Bryan Bevan, *King James VI of Scotland & I of England* (London, 1996), p. 133. Dr Jonathan Spangler of New College in Oxford informs me that her nearest Habsburg relations were two princesses in the fifth generation.
9 Carmen Manso Porto, *Don Diego Sarmiento de Acuña, conde de Gondomar (1567–1626): Erudito, mecenas y bibliófilo* (Santiago de Compostela, 1996), p. 19.
10 AGS, Estado Libro 374, fo. 302.
11 Or conceivably an uncle of the same name; see I.D.L. Michael, 'King James VI and I and the Count of Gondomar: Two London Bibliophiles, 1613–18 and 1620–22', pp. 421–36, at 425, in '*Never-ending Adventure': Studies in Medieval and Early Modern Spanish Literature in Honor of Peter N. Dunn*, ed. Edward H. Friedman and Harlan Sturm (Newark, 2002).
12 *Correspondencia oficial*, iii. 71–86, at 75.
13 RAHM, ms N–31, fo. 222.
14 The link between the marriage and the failure of the parliament is explicitly mentioned in the Council of State's debate of 12/2 Aug. 1614, in AGS, Estado 8341, doc. 49. More generally, see Luís Tobío Fernández, *Gondomar y los católicos ingleses* (La Coruña, 1987), p. 260.
15 Cogswell, *Blessed Revolution*, p. 43, his prologue, pp. 6–53, being a brilliant survey of the literary opposition to the marriage.
16 For an overview of Rome's attitude, see *Die Hauptinstruktionen Gregors XV. für die Nuntien und Gesandten an den europäischen Fürstenhöfen: 1621–1623*, ed. K. Jaitner (2 vols, Tübingen 1997), pp. 30–1.
17 The best summary of the history of the drafting of the treaty is to be found in *Tratados*, App. xi, pp. 327–43, but see also below, App. 2.

3. Prague

1 Ludwig Häusser, *Geschichte der rheinischen Pfalz* (Heidelberg, 1856), ii. 311 n. 92, quoting her granddaughter, Elizabeth Charlotte, duchess of Orleans. A more positive and romanticised view is to be found in Oman, *Winter Queen*, pp. 36–7, 51, 60.
2 J10.
3 Elizabeth returned to England after Charles II's restoration, dying in 1662.

4 See above, n. 1.

5 See Pursell, 'Elector Friedrich V and the Question of Influence Revisited', which credits the Palsgrave with more statesmanlike qualities than usual.

6 Howell, *Epistolae*, p. 91.

7 Cited in Pursell, 'Elector Friedrich', p. 138.

8 H. Ellis, *Original Letters*, 1st ser., iii (London, 1829), pp. 118–19. In 1616 it was reported that James believed that in any open war against Catholicism he would probably be assassinated by a Jesuit and for that reason wore protective clothing: Gondomar, *Cinco cartas político literarias*, ed. Pascual de Gayangos y Arce (Madrid, 1869), p. 52.

9 Quoted in G. Parker, *The Thirty Years' War* (London, 1985), p. 52.

10 Ibid., p. 50.

11 This meeting is fully described in B. Pursell's useful and entertaining study, *Gondomar: A Spaniard at King James's Court*, North American Society for Court Studies, Occasional Pamphlets 1, pp. 8–9.

12 Frederick and Elizabeth's first child was born in 1614, the Palatinate being partially restored to her second son, Charles Louis, in 1648.

13 Pursell, *At King James's Court*, p. 9.

14 *The Diary of Sir Simonds D'Ewes (1622–1624)*, ed. E. Bourcier (Paris, 1974), p. 119, for February 1622.

15 For his view of a parliament's functions, see *Gondomar and Parliaments*. The best general introduction is David L. Smith, *The Stuart Parliaments 1603–1689* (London, 1999).

16 *Gondomar and Parliaments*, p. 21.

17 Ibid., p. 15.

18 Ibid., p. 51. Gondomar reported how many believed James was secretly delighted with the Declaration, even if it was passed more to please the Elector Palatine than himself or Charles, AGS, Estado Libro 374, fo. 169.

19 T. Cogswell, 'Phaeton's Chariot: The Parliament-men and the Continental Crisis of 1621', in *The Political World of Thomas Wentworth, Earl of Strafford 1621–1641*, ed. Julia E. Merritt (Cambridge, 1996).

20 Gondomar to Isabel, 18/8 Nov. 1621, AGS, Estado Libro 374, fos 307v–314v, at fo. 307v.

21 Gondomar to Isabel, Thursday, 11/1 Nov. 1621, AGS, Estado 2602, fo. 80 a–d. Thinking war was imminent, Gondomar said he intended to remonstrate with James the following morning, if he was well enough. The envoy normally preferred not to specify who his sources were at any one time, but Thomas Savage and Lord Wooton were particularly close in 1621, the former writing to warn him earlier that year, on the day before Shrove Tuesday, to be on his guard, close all the windows, and not to venture out, on account of English hotheads, AGS, Estado Libro 374, fos 79–80.

22 Victor Treadwell, *Buckingham and Ireland 1616–1628: A Study in Anglo-Irish Politics* (Dublin, 1998), p. 171. The proclamation adjourned the parliament from 14 Nov. until 8 Feb. 1622.

4. Westminster

1 See AGS, Estado Libro 374, fo. 302.

2 Pursell, *At King James's Court*, pp. 8–9.

3 Manso Porto, *Gondomar*, p. 29.

4 AGS, Estado Libro 374, at fo. 308v.

5 Ibid., fo. 311, 'entendia que el pueblo y los puritanos huuieran tomado alguna resolucion desatinada contra el y contra [Gondomar]'. James later surrendered Frankenthal to the archduchess. See below, ch. 8.

6   The text reads in full at AGS, Estado Libro 374, fos 311r–v:

> que lo del parlamento no me diese cuidado, porque el se yria a Nuimarquete, y lle-
> baba consigo al Marques de Boquingan, y dexaba aqui al Principe con una comision
> secreta que solos los tres la sabian, y yo, con que seriamos quatro, y era que si el par-
> lamento se quisiese meter en qualquiera otra cosa mas que en concedelle servicio de
> dinero para socorro del Palatinato, el Principe le disolviese, pues agora no se juntaba
> para mas de solo esto, y que el queria estar lejos, para que se executase antes que pud-
> iesen yr a el con quexas para el remedio

This letter of 18/8 Nov. and one of 6/16 Dec. 1621 have been partially transcribed and translated by Brennan Pursell in *Parliament, Politics and Elections 1604–1648*, ed. Chris R. Kyle (Cambridge, 2001) being Camden Society, 5th ser., vol. 17, pp. 149–78. It supplements Dr Pursell's article, 'Parliament of 1621'. I am grateful to Dr Pursell for reading my account of 1621 and for his constructive advice, even though we differ in our interpretations.

7   'los señores estados de Olanda'.

8   Pursell, 'Parliament of 1621', p. 428.

9   Gondomar to Isabel, 1 Dec./21 Nov. 1621, AGS, Estado 2558, no. 14 a–f, at d. Pursell, 'Parliament of 1621', p. 438, n. 76, concludes that the King was 'content to leave the ambassador to his own devices in London'. Pursell was misled by S.R. Gardiner's faulty reference; see *Gondomar and Parliaments*, p. 12, n. 25.

10   AGS, Estado Libro 374, fo. 302.

11   Gondomar to Ferdinand, 26/16 Nov. 1621, ibid., fos 363–5, at fo. 363v.

12   Cogswell, *Blessed Revolution*, p. 19. The constitutional position of the English parliament was widely understood. Unlike most European countries, neither direct taxation nor legislation could be instituted by the crown without parliamentary approval. Gondomar repeatedly reminded Madrid that parliamentary assent would be required to revoke anti-Catholic legislation. This he did not least because he argued that a request for formal toleration was beyond James's powers and therefore to insist on it would be to scupper any prospect for a marriage alliance with England. As he said in the treatise composed after the end of the first session of the 1621 parliament, the King could neither 'make or unmake laws without Parliament', *Gondomar and Parliaments*, p. 35.

13   'estos puritanos y malcontentos le harian morir miserablemente', RBM, ms II–2108, no. 109, Gondomar to Isabel, 2 Jan./23 Dec. 1622/1.

14   *CD* ii. 434.

15   Ibid., 437.

16   'La Resolucion que oy tiene la mayor parte del parlamento es de no conceder al Rey nada, sino declara la guerra con españa', Gondomar to Isabel, 1 Dec./21 Nov. 1621, AGS, E 2558, no. 14, fol. d.

17   *CD* iii. 434.

18   Ibid.

19   *CD* ii. 445.

20   Ibid., 449. Felipe IV succeeded his father in March 1621.

21   *CD* v. 213. For the way in which the petition was assembled and by whom, see Conrad Russell's masterly essay, 'The Foreign Policy Debate in the House of Commons in 1621', *Historical Journal* 20 (1977), pp. 289–309, at p. 298.

22   Russell, pp. 131–2.

23   Ibid.

24   *CD* iv. 441.

25   *CD* ii. 452; see also, iv. 459.

26 *Ven. Cal.*, xvii. no. 227, p. 168.

27 Treadwell, *Buckingham and Ireland*, p. 179. Treadwell's work is magisterial, but although he shows that the marquess had much to fear from a parliamentary investigation into his Irish landholdings, see notes 30 and 31 below for why I do not accept his evidence for conspiracy.

28 BL, Add. ms 1580, fos 428–9. Following Zaller, Russell misreads the word 'evaporated' as 'disported', which subtly alters the sense of the letter. The point is no longer that MPs have behaved disrespectfully but that they are now prepared to co-operate. For transcripts of these five parliamentary letters, see the Appendix to the Introduction of *Gondomar and Parliaments*.

29 Charles to Buckingham, 28 Nov. 1621, BL, Harleian ms 6987, fos 205–6, also in *Gondomar and Parliaments*, App., Letter 2, pp. 20–1.

30 Treadwell argues that the Favourite proposed the motion without the King's knowledge, to bring an end to the parliamentary investigations into his Irish land dealings. As Goring himself said, it was well known who his master was; therefore I do not see how Buckingham could have expected to have kept this hidden from either King or Prince.

31 Bod., Tanner ms 72, at p. 79. The letter is miswritten as 'Fryday: 3. No: 1621'. The 3rd of the month did not fall on a Friday. In my opinion the date must be amended to the 30th of the month: first, on account of its content, since it refers to the desire for a session and to the King's patience, which I take to refer to his desire for the passage of a finance bill; second, because I see no plausible explanation for the misdating other than the obvious one that the Prince merely omitted a zero. *Pace* Treadwell, who argues for the 23rd, which is extremely unlikely, partly because the Foreign Policy Debate had not yet begun, but also because his suggestion that 'dashing off the letter by candlelight, Charles unobservantly scratched in a dry "2"' is unconvincing. Consultation of the original reveals that there is no space for a preceding letter to have been written in.

32 'Phaeton's Chariot', p. 43.

33 Pursell, 'Parliament of 1621', p. 439 misconstrues parliamentary procedure and perpetrates a logical error when he writes that, once the Commons had fallen into the constitutional trap of accepting Goring's motion, it was only 'a matter of waiting for the passage of the subsidy bill' before parliament could be dissolved. Royal assent to bills usually, though not invariably, occurred at the completion of a session. This would result in there being no opportunity for the punitive dissolution he postulates. Moreover, if a finance bill had been taken through to enactment, the session would *ipso facto* have been a success, and so any dissolution could not be regarded as punitive.

34 J.P. Kenyon, *The Stuart Constitution* (Cambridge, 1966), pp. 43–7. This is the final draft, but the alterations are not significant here.

35 Gondomar to Isabel, 16/6 Dec. 1621, AGS Estado 2558, no. 9, a –n.

36 Gondomar to Alburquerque, 17/7 Dec. 1621, AGS Estado 2558, no. 17 'que es el estado que esto tiene oy con tantas dificultades que aun que la voluntad del Rey es sin duda buena, no se sabe aun lo que eligira por que no esta aqui'.

37 AGS Estado 2558, no. 6.

38 *CD* ii. 518.

39 *CD* v. 237, vi. 228, vi. 482. On 3 Dec., Goring was still predicting that his motion would be adopted in an acceptable manner to James, BL, Add. ms 1580, fos 430–31, also in *Gondomar and Parliaments*, Letter 5, p. 25.

40 See Gondomar to Isabel, 16/6 Dec., AGS Estado 2558 no. 9, a–n.

41 John Rushworth, *Historical Collections* (London, 1659–1701), i. 43.

42 Gondomar to Isabel, 16/6 Dec., AGS Estado 2558 no. 9, postscript.

43 Calvert to Buckingham, 7 Dec. 1621, *CD* vii. at p. 623. The importance of this letter has been overlooked. It further contradicts the notion of a plot to sabotage the parliament by providing explicit evidence of Charles's attempts to salvage something from the parliament. It also reveals that the Prince did indeed possess a 'dormant commission' (as Gondomar claimed to have been told); however, it was not to dissolve the parliament on his own authority but only to adjourn the parliament, *if* the King commanded.

44 Gondomar to Isabel, 1 Jan./22 Dec. 1622/1, BNM, ms II–2108, no. 103, a–f, at a; at c, he reported the fortnight's wait.

45 'we cannot with patience endure our subjects to use such anti-monarchical words to us concerning their liberties', James to Secretary Calvert, Royston, 16 Dec., PRO SP14/124, fol. 43.

46 *Ven. Cal.*, xvii. no. 261, p. 192.

5. *Father, Son and Favourite*

1 Buckingham to Gondomar (undated), BL, Add. ms 1580, fos 353–356v, at 353–4 (undated).

2 'Catholic Clergy of England to the Pope in favour of the Spanish Match', BL, Add. ms 1583, at fo. 294.

3 The standard biography is Roger Lockyer, *Buckingham: The Life and Political Career of George Villiers, First Duke of Buckingham, 1598–1628* (London, 1981). I am grateful for Dr Lockyer's help on a number of points.

4 Quoted in Tobío Fernández, *Gondomar y los católicos ingleses*, p. 206.

5 Given the segregated lives of men and of women, it was likely that there would be heightened friendships between members of the same sex, irrespective of whether there was physical union; and since homosexuality then was conceived primarily in terms of activities (albeit illicit) rather than as an identity, caution should be exercised in labelling the precise nature of James and Buckingham's relationship. James was the first English monarch since 1547 to be married with children.

6 Gondomar to Felipe III, 22/12 May 1620, RBM, ms II–870, fo. 176.

7 The earl of Oxford was disgraced at court for his outspoken support of the Elector. Apparently he accused James of giving all spiritual power to the pope and all temporal power to the king of Spain, Gondomar to Felipe IV, 16/7 May 1622, RBM, ms M, II–2108, no. 64.

8 As for the Queen, on Gondomar's first return to Madrid she wrote in Latin to Felipe III praising him in unusually warm terms, RBM, ms II–2541, fo. 78.

9 J.M. Castroviejo, *El Conde de Gondomar: unazor entre ocasos* (Madrid, 1967), p. 56.

10 Tibolts, dated 21 Feb. 1622, BNM, ms 2394–xv, fos 293–4 (Latin), 294–5 (Spanish). The Latin is 'familiariter', which is translated as 'con mas amor'.

11 Gondomar to Felipe III, 31/21 Jan. 1622, RBM, ms M II–2108, no. 119 a–d, at d, 'podran entrar Chatolicos y bien yntençionados, que vendran en todo lo justo que el Rey quisiere'.

12 Gondomar to Felipe III, 31/21 Jan. 1622, RBM, ms II–2108, no. 119, at fo. a; cf. Russell, p. 143 and *SRP* no. 223, pp. 527–34; cf. p. 531.

13 G.P.V. Akrigg, *Letters of King James VI & I* (Berkeley, 1984), p. 524.

14 See above, n. 1.

15 'para que deseen verlos apartados de aqui y fuera de Holanda', Gondomar to Isabella, 21/11 Jan. 1622, RBM, ms II–2108, no. 115, a–d, at fo. b.

16 Gondomar to Isabel, 31/21 Jan. 1622, RBM, ms II–2108, no. 119, at d. See Gondomar's long dispatch on the state of England compiled in 1616, where he reported that the Prince lacked both a household and supporters, in *Cinco cartas*, p. 52.

17 Gondomar to don Baltasar de Zúñiga, 30/20 Mar. 1622, RBM, ms. II–2108, no. 38; D'Ewes, *Diary*, p. 119. For Savage's religion, see RBM, ms II–2198, nos 21–4.

18 Gondomar to Felipe IV, 1 Apr./22 Mar. 1622. RBM, ms II–2108, no. 48 and postscript.

19 D'Ewes, *Diary*, p. 102; and M.J. Havran, *Caroline Courtier: The Life of Lord Cottington* (London, 1973), p. 67.

20 *Correspondencia oficial*, ii. 228.

21 Howell, *Epistolae*, p. 119.

22 Ibid., p. 131.

23 RBM, ms II–2108, nos 33 and 34; see no. 39 for objections raised by Lord Treasurer Cranfield.

24 Judging by accounts preserved mainly in the RBM, the pensions were paid erratically, rather than not at all, *pace* Charles H. Carter, *The Secret Diplomacy of the Habsburgs, 1598–1625* (New York, 1964).

25 RBM, ms II–2108, nos 30, 31, 40.

26 Ibid., no. 69; he reached Spain on 30 June, BNM, ms 18,430².

27 The earl of Arundel at this time presented Gondomar with a plan to seize the Dutch port of Flushing, RBM, ms II–2108, nos 51, 78; see also Tobío Fernández, *Gondomar y los católicos ingleses* pp. 167–71.

28 See *Tratados*, p. 336.

29 RBM, ms II–2541, fo. 45.

30 Gondomar to Felipe IV, 29 Mar. 1622, 'y si no no quiere abenturarse ni perder a sus amigos, ni el amor de la comunidad de su pueblo', RBM, ms II–2108, no. 37 at fo. a.

31 See above, n. 1.

32 For his arrival, see *Ambasciatori Genovesi*, p. 146; for talks prior to his arrival, see Gondomar to Felipe IV, 29/19 Mar. 1622, RBM, ms II–2108, no. 37.

33 Gondomar to Baltasar de Zúñiga, 30/20 Mar. 1622, RBM, ms II–2108, no. 38.

34 For papal expectations, see *Kardinal Giovanni Francesco Guidi di Bagno: Politik und Religion im Zeitalter Richelieus und Urbans VIII*, ed. George Lutz (Tübingen, 1971), pp. 117–21; and also *Hauptinstruktionen Gregors XV* i. 30–40 (esp. at p. 34), 170. Gordon Albion's *Charles I and the Court of Rome: A Study in 17th Century Diplomacy* (London, 1935), at pp. 21–4, is of some use.

35 The wording of the marriage agreement of 1617, the papal amendments of 1622 and their subsequent incorporation, as well as the final agreement of 1623, can all be found in *Tratados*, App. xi (pp. 60, 327–44); for James's objections to the papal amendments, see pp. 334–8, but cf. below, App. 2.

36 G. Redworth, 'Of Pimps and Princes: Three Unpublished Letters from James I and the Prince of Wales relating to the Spanish Match', *Historical Journal* 37 (1994), pp. 401–9, at 408.

37 For a flavour of the debate, see Bristol to de la Fuente, 22/12 Sept. 1622, PRO, SP94/25, fos 220–230v.

38 Bristol to Calvert, 4 Dec. 1622, PRO, SP94/25, fos 312–315v.

39 John Stone to Cottington, 28 Nov. 1622, Society of Antiquaries, London, ms 203, fos 23r–24r, at 23r.

40 This date was mentioned in the letters of 12/2 Dec. 1622 given to Bristol as well as to the Spanish ambassador in London which went with the articles, see BNM, ms 8719, fos 69v–70.

41 For Porter's date of departure, see PRO, SP94/25, fo. 338; the quotation is from an anonymous letter justifying Bristol's handling of the negotiations, fos 360–1, at 361.

42 D'Ewes, *Diary*, p. 119 and AGS, Estado 8789, no. 15.

43 John Chamberlain, *The Letters of John Chamberlain*, ed. E.M. Thomson (2 vols, Philadelphia, 1939), ii. 471.

44 *Ven. Cal.*, xvii. no. 731, p. 545.

45 For the date of the Infanta's departure, see ibid., no. 754, p. 561, *Tratados*, p. 197, and Bristol to Calvert, 20/30 Dec. 1622, PRO, SP94/25, fos 338–9.

46 Chamberlain, *Letters*, ii. 476 (4 Jan.); *Ven. Cal.*, xvii. p. 564.

47 Bristol's *Defence*, pp. 31–2, and Rodríguez-Moñino, *Razón de estado*, p. 76.

48 For an analysis of the articles, see below, App. 2.

49 'se ha conçedido en sustancia vna toleraçion', AGS, Estado 8341, doc. 69, being a Jan. 1623 copy of a letter which the Council of State asked the king to write to the pope asking for a dispensation. Pursell, 'The End of the Spanish Match', pp. 703–4, provides further details of the conciliar preparations but without realising that these provided Olivares with a smokescreen for his own initiatives, see below, ch. 7, n. 31.

50 For James's ruminations on the agreement, see the letters of the first week of Jan. in Bod.: Tanner ms 73(ii), fos 267, 268, and esp. 271 to Bristol, dated 7 Jan. 1623.

51 Bristol to Calvert, 4 Dec. 1622, PRO, SP94/25, fo. 317.

52 Gardiner, iv. 399.

53 Howell to Sir Thomas Savage, 27 Mar. 1623, Howell, *Epistolae*, p. 132.

6. Post Haste!

1 D'Ewes, *Diary*, p. 119.

2 Charles 'me ha offrezido en much confiança y secreto que, si llegado yo a España le aconsejase que se vaya á poner en las manos de V. Magd. y á su disposicion lo hara y llegara a Madrid yncognito con dos criados'; see Gondomar to Felipe IV, 16 May 1622, RBM, ms II–2108, no. 64 at fo. i. See also *Tratados*, p. 183 and note a, and in Gardiner iv. 369, n. 2, citing a version in Simancas, misdating the letter to 21/31 Jan. 1622.

3 AGS, Estado 8341, doc. 64, 2 June/23 May 1623.

4 See Albion, *Charles I and the Court of Rome*, pp. 12–14.

5 'non seulement de Vre. Conseil d'Estat, mais du Cabinet Interieur', cited below, n. 10.

6 See Henry Ettinghausen, *Prince Charles and the King of Spain's Sister, What the Papers Said. An Inaugural Lecture delivered on 28 February 1985* (University of Southampton, 1985), pp. 4–5.

7 RBM, II–2168, fo. 67r.

8 See Enrique García Hernan, *La acción diplomática de Francisco de Borja al servicio del Pontificado: 1571–72* (Valencia, 2000), *passim*, for an extensive discussion of dispensations and royal marriages.

9 'et que les choses qu'appartiennent à la religion donnent telle satisfaction au Pape qu'il puisse non seulement nous octroyer la dispensation que nous desirons, mais qu'il soit obligé à l'octroyer', Gondomar to James, 10/1 Sept. 1622, Bod., Tanner ms 73(i), fos 192–3. This and the following letter are also printed in Godfrey Goodman, *The Court of King James the First* (London, 1839), i. 234–41. NB: Goodman miscalculates in his conversion to the Julian calendar.

10 'Et ainsy j'espere en dieu que nous nous verrons bien tost en ces pais icy, et embrasserons l'un l'autre, selon l'accordé'; Gondomar to Buckingham, 10/1 Sept., Bod., Tanner ms 73(i), fos 194–5.

11 Gondomar was almost certainly using the strange expression 'mount Spain' to avoid saying 'mount the Infanta'. I am indebted to the members of the Sub-Faculty of Spanish at the University of Oxford for discussion of the language used in this letter.

12 See below, App. 1.

13 Chamberlain, *Letters*, ii. 455.

14 Porter to Aston, 11 Sept. 1622, BL, Add. ms 35,832, fo. 64, with postscript by Buckingham.

15 PRO SP94/25, at fo. 360 (for the document, see ch. 4, n. 40).

16 Dorothea Townshend, *Life and Letters of Mr. Endymion Porter* (London, 1897), p. 38; see also *LJ*, 1624, p. 221. At the end of April 1623, the Genovese ambassador in Madrid expressed his surprise that Olivares was apparently going ahead with the marriage, as he had 'molte uolte' expressed his reluctance: see ASG, Archivio Segreto, vol. 2430, no. 210, a–d, at b. The diplomatic correspondence is contained in vols 2429–1433.

17 *Ambasciatori Genovesi*, p. 71.

18 RBM, ms II–2210, docs 45 and 46, both dated 24/14 Oct. 1622.

19 Charles was reminded of this by Bristol in a letter dated 22 Feb. 1623, PRO SP94/26, fos 38–40, at fo. 40. Though the ambassador doubtless assumed that where Buckingham went Charles was sure to follow, it seems from the earl's statements in 1626 that he assumed that, if Charles did arrive incognito, he would form part of a formally agreed visit by the Lord Admiral and some eighty ships. For references, see below, n. 21.

20 Bristol to James, Madrid, 10 March 1623, NLS, ms Adv. 33.1.10, no. 21, fos a–f, at fo. e.

21 PRO, SP31/8, fos 469–74, being copies of the Sherbourne Papers.

22 For a fuller treatment of Bristol's accusations, see Redworth, 'Of Pimps and Princes'. I am grateful to Sir John Elliott for his help and advice on innumerable occasions, and not least for informing me that, several years before, Gondomar also used this word in a letter to the Prince, though not in the charged atmosphere of 1622.

23 'from Spain, from there we expect the remedy', Coloma to Pedro de Sandoval, 8 Jan. 1623/29 Dec. 1622, AGS, Estado 8789, doc. 12.

24 Bristol to Charles, 4 Jan. 1623/25 Dec. 1622, PRO, SP94/25, fos 344–5. The letter is dated new style, as the earl was describing the New Year's festivities.

25 Gervas Huxley, *Endymion Porter: The Life of a Courtier, 1587–1649* (London, 1959), p. 67.

26 5 Jan. 1623, Bod., Tanner ms 73(ii), fo. 267.

27 'y se atisfaga de la rrealidad y seriedad con q[ue] se camina de parte de Su Mag[esta]d. Cat[olic]a en este neg[oci]o', Felipe to Bristol, 12/2 Dec. 1622, BNM, ms 8719, fo. 68v (for which see below, App. 2). The embassy in Madrid translated this as 'reality and sincerity', see Bod., Tanner ms 73(i), fos 263–264v, at 264. See also *Ven. Cal.*, xvii. no. 754, pp. 560–1; for Bristol, see *Tratados*, p. 191.

28 Bristol to Calvert, 4 Dec. 1622, PRO, SP94/25, fol. 317; the word 'reasonable' reappears on 20/10 Dec. in a letter to the King, fos 329v–330.

7. Wind, Metaphysics and the Court of Spain

1 Felipe was born in April 1605, and his sister María in August the following year. For an unflattering pen-portrait, see the report sent back to the ambassador of Genoa, Spain's close ally, in *Ambasciatori Genovesi*, p. 72; more generally, see Robert Stradling, *Philip IV and the Government of Spain 1621–1665* (Cambridge, 1988), and Eduardo Chamorro, *Felipe IV* (Barcelona, 1998).

2 To his French-speaking subjects in the Low Countries, he was the Emperor Charles, as in English.

3 For an outstanding history of the family, see Robert J.W. Evans, *The Making of the Habsburg Monarchy, 1550–1700: An Interpretation* (Oxford, 1979).

4 See G. Redworth and F. Checa, 'The Courts of Spain', ch. 1 (pp. 42–65) of *The Princely Courts of Europe. Ritual, Politics and Culture under the Ancien Régime 1500–1750* (London, 1999), ed. John Adamson. For a slightly later period, *A Palace for a King: The*

Buen Retiro and the Court of Philip IV by Jonathan Brown and John H. Elliott (London, 1980) remains unsurpassed.

5   NLS, ms Adv. 33.1.10, no. 23 a–c, with reply.

6   As he told his spiritual mother, Sor María, on his sister's death in 1646, María Jesús de Ágreda, *Correspondencia con Felipe IV: religión y razón de estado*, ed. Consolación Baranda (Madrid, 1991), pp. 95–6.

7   Bristol to Charles, 22 Feb. 1623, PRO, SP94/26, fos 38–40, at fo. 38.

8   Howell, *Epistolae*, p. 125.

9   Thomas Birch, *The Court and Times of James the First, illustrated by Authentic and Confidential Letters* (2 vols, London 1848), ii. 399 (24 May).

10 'si fuera el poder de Inglaterra omnipotencia no deseara con más ansia que lo deseo la amistad de aquella Corona con la del nuestro señor . . . no tengo entendido que aquélla sea tan formidable como v.s. la presupone, porque concediéndoles, como les concedo, gran poder en la mar no entiendo que lo tengan tan intrínseca y sustancialmente que puedan hacer conquistas reales', to Gondomar, 2 June 1625, *Memoriales y Cartas del Conde Duque de Olivares*, ed. John Elliott and José F. de la Peña (2 vols, Madrid, 1978 and 1980), ii. 114. I have translated freely; at p. 115 he mocks Gondomar with the '*sancta sanctorum* of your Great Britain'.

11 See ch. 6.

12 For a blatant piece of propaganda concerning the Rhenish 'usurpation', see BNM, ms 2354, fos 196–201v.

13 When Franz Christoph Khevenhüller, the Imperial ambassador, personally informed Spain of the reasons for the transfer of the electoral dignity, Felipe IV's chilling reply was that he doubted this would lead to 'peace in Germany and the security of the Empire', Felipe to the emperor, 29/19 June 1623, RBM, ms II–2220, no. 37, and also below, ch. 12, n. 11. I have consulted Khevenhüller's letterbook which, since 1974 has been in the OÖLA in Linz, as well as the originals in Vienna. For a largely reliable selection from his dispatches as ambassador in Madrid, see Franz Christoph Khevenhillers, *Annalium Ferdinandeorum* [i.e. Khevenhüller, *Annales Ferdinandei*] (Leipzig, 1721–26, 12 vols with 2 supplements), at vol. x. 79, though there the dispatch is dated five days later. For the ambassador's methodology, see Kurt Peball, 'Zur Quellenlage der "Annales Ferdinandei" des Grafen Franz Christoph Khevenhüller-Frankenburg', *Mitteilungen des Österreichischen Staatsarchivs* 9 (1956), pp. 1–22. I am indebted to Professor Leopold Auer of the HHStA in Vienna for providing me with a copy of this article.

14 To Sir James Croftes, Howell, *Epistolae*, p. 129.

15 *Testamento de Felipe III*, ed. Carlos Seco Serrano (Madrid, 1982), pp. 49, 55. His eldest child, Anne, queen of France, was excluded from succeeding to the Spanish throne. Intriguingly, his confessor makes a passing reference in his memoirs to a secret document – 'un papel cerrado' – which the dying king passed to his son, see F. Díaz-Plaja, *Historia de España en sus documentos. Siglo XVII* (Madrid, 1987), p. 76; also see Archivo Histórico Nacional (Madrid), Estado Libro 739, fos 3–9, a description of the king's death printed the following month.

16 AGS, Estado 8341, doc. 48, a 26-page report of a committee of theologians. The Jesuit on the committee thought there was no threat to the children. Another member said these were matters for the pope to decide. Amongst other items, this volume contains a selection of the musings of the committee of theologians which from 1613 to 1623 reported on the morality of the marriage as well as other similar material debated in the *consejo de estado*. This most important set of documents is among the many sources of information which were drawn to my attention by Professor Geoffrey Parker. I am profoundly grateful to him for sharing with me his compendious knowledge of the sources.

17 Felipe IV to Olivares, 5 Nov./26 Oct. 1622, BL, Add. ms 18,201 fo. 13–16v; for the reply, see also *Tratados*, pp. 48 and 192, note c, where it is pointed out that all the versions are essentially the same except for the fact that the English versions of Olivares's response omit the all-important passage stating that the marriage was not to happen, 'unless the Prince became a Catholic'. Gardiner, iv. pp. 391, 393, n. 1 deals with a quibble over dating.

18 *LJ*, p. 226. For Charles and Buckingham's detailed and entirely accurate English recollection of the version they were shown, see the memorandum jotted down in the Prince's own hand, PRO, SP94/25, fo. 271; copies of their recollected text are also to be found at fos 270, 273, 274, and esp. at fo. 269, and also see fos 279–81v. Unfortunately there is no certainty as to when or how they were allowed to glimpse this letter; whether it suggested to Charles that the marriage was a possibility so long as he granted toleration, or whether it indicated that a successful outcome was remote in the extreme, is a matter for conjecture.

19 'pongo en consideraçion al cons[ej]o se podria duda desto no reduçiéndose a n[uest]ra s[an]ta fe el prinçipe de gales, pues perseuerando en su religion aunq[ue] se diese la liuertad de conçiençia, les sera façil no cumplirlo', AGS, Estado 8341, doc. 57, royal apostil at fo. a.

20 'hasta ver si las cosas de Inglat[err]a se mejoran, o si ay otra forma de casar al Prin[cip]e de Gales donde pueda ser de menos daño a esta corona y a la c[rist]iandad', in the undated copies in MAE, ms 243, fos 67–71v, 72r–v, at 68v. This collection formed the documentary basis of Francisco de Jesús's account.

21 'este casamiento no se ha de effettuar á menos que ahí concedan libertad de conciencia, y aya seguridad de que se complira; mas por el peligro que puede auer de que, hablandoles en esto claro, so rompia la platica . . .', 2 Sept./23 Aug. 1620, transcribed by Gardiner in full, though I have preferred my own translation, in *Tratados*, pp. 321–2.

22 Anonymous letter writer cited in *Ven. Cal*, xvii. no. 741, p. 551.

23 Dec. 1621, *Ambasciatori Genovesi*, p. 94.

24 See Dieter Albrecht, *Die auswärtige Politik Maximilians von Bayern, 1618–1635* (Göttingen, 1962), p. 86.

25 The archduchesses were born in 1610 and 1611, respectively.

26 'Der Vorschlag mit Verwexlung der Heyraten', Khevenhüller to Prince von Eggenberg, 14/4 Mar. 1623, OÖLA, Khevenhüller Bestand, ms 11, fos 28v–29.

27 Khevenhüller to Olivares in 1625, OÖLA, Khevenhüller Bestand, ms 13, at p. 23. Gondomar's mission was cancelled on Charles's arrival in Madrid: see Alain Hugon, 'Au service du Roi Catholique: "honorables ambassadeurs" et "divins espions" face à la France. Représentation diplomatique et service secret dans les relations hispano-françaises de 1598 à 1635', doctoral thesis of the University of Caen, 1996, p. 176.

28 'gibt nit auf die puntillos sonder auf die substanz der negotien'; for full details, see Khevenhüller's letter to Eggenberg, 9 Jan. 1623/30 Dec. 1622, OÖLA, Khevenhüller Bestand, ms 11, fos 1v–2v.

29 Dieter Albrecht, *Maximilian I. von Bayern 1573–1651* (Munich, 1998), pp. 567–8. A secret investiture had taken place two years before. Among the countless marital solutions to the problems of the Palatinate was the suggestion that James's eldest grandson might marry one of the duke's nieces, as he then had no children of his own; see the Genoese ambassador's dispatch from Regensburg, ASG, Archivio Segreto, vol. 2543, no. 375, a–d, at a (17/7 Jan. 1623); cf. Cogswell, *Blessed Revolution*, p. 61.

30 J9 [11 March].

31 'se ha exasperado justamente', minutes of the Council of State's meeting of 26/16 Apr. 1623, AGS, Estado 2516, doc. 32 fos a–r, at j. The council members were presumably unaware that Olivares and King Felipe had already spoken to Khevenhüller about this

matter when they recommended that the least that should be done for James was to instruct the ambassadors in London and Vienna to float the possibility of an Austrian marriage for James's grandson, as there was 'no other way' (*por ningun otro camino*) to restore Frederick's family. See also Coloma to Gondomar, London, 7 Apr./28 Mar., Estado 8790, doc. 45, at c. *Pace* Pursell, 'The End of the Spanish Match'; believing that Olivares had been effectively overruled by the Council of State on the question of the 'Austrian alternative', Pursell states that 'Olivares did not find a way out' (at p. 703); cf. Gardiner, iv. 394–5, for further details of the favourite's independence of action, as well as below, ch. 10.

32   J10 [15 March].

33   For the silence about a Viennese match for Charles until the end of the visit, see F.H. Schubert, *Ludwig Camerarius 1573–1651* (Kallmünz, 1955), p. 193 and Albrecht, *Die auswärtige Politik Maximilians,* pp. 103, 109; and below, ch. 12, n. 11 and ch. 13, n. 24. Later, in August, Alvise Corner, the Venetian envoy in Madrid, reported that Khevenhüller had told him how Olivares was holding an Imperial marriage for Charles in reserve, as he put it, in case of need, *Ven. Cal.*, xviii. no. 114, p. 93.

34   For Charles's impatience at this time, see above, ch. 6, n. 23.

8. Dear Venturous Knights

1   Rushworth, *Historical Collections,* i. 5.

2   The agreement with the archduchess had been mooted for months and was finally signed in Newmarket on 19 Mar 1623, PRO, SP108/464; see Jürgen Kessel, *Spanien und die geistlichen Kurstaaten am Rhein während der Regierungszeit der Infantin Isabella (1621–1633)* (Frankfurt am Main, Bern and Las Vegas, 1979), p. 104 and Elmar Weiss, *Die Unterstützung Friedrichs V. von der Pfalz durch Jakob I. und Karl I. von England im Dreissigjährigen Krieg (1618–1632)* (Stuttgart, 1966), pp. 57–8.

3   Cogswell, *Blessed Revolution,* p. 61.

4   *LJ*, 1624, p. 221. Charles took with him no powers or instructions to discuss the Palatinate, see below, ch. 12, n. 27.

5   The phrase is the Venetian ambassador's, for which see above, ch. 5, n. 44, and *pace* Cogswell, who was under the impression that negotiations were still at the stage of 'a distant wedding date', *Blessed Revolution,* p. 37, which explains why he also wrote: 'A few months after the crisis over Heidelberg, Charles and Buckingham suddenly left for Madrid' (p. 59).

6   Clarendon, *Rebellion,* i. 14. For earlier discussion of this point, see above, ch. 1.

7   J6 [27 Feb. 1623]. The reference is to romances of chivalry, popular tales about knights errant who risked life and limb for love. See Glyn Redworth, '"¿Nuevo mundo u otro mundo?": conquistadores, cortesanos, libros de caballerías, y el reinado de Felipe el Breve de Inglaterra', *Actas del Primer Congreso Anglo-Hispano de 1992* (vol. iii, 'Historia'), ed. Ralph Penny and Richard Hitchcock (Madrid, 1993), pp. 113–25.

8   D'Ewes, *Diary,* p. 119.

9   Clarendon, *Rebellion,* i. 20.

10   Dudley Carleton to Sir Dudley Carleton, 27 Feb. 1623, PRO, SP14/138, fo. 99; Havran, *Caroline Courtier,* pp. 69, 74, says Cottington's marriage took place in the second week of February.

11   Cottington to James, 8 Apr., NLS, Advocates ms 33.1.10, vol. xxvii, no. 20, fos 53–54, at 53–54; the original reads 'whether wher'.

12   J5.

13 Bod., Rawlinson ms, D 793, fo. 73v. See also above, n. 10. Dr Jenny Wormald brought the significance of this poem to my attention and generally helped clarify my thoughts about early Stuart politics.

14 D'Ewes, *Diary*, p. 119.

15 A full ceremonial household was not far behind, however; see below, ch. 9, for the arrangements the Prince made before he left.

16 Coloma's letters are in RBM, ms II–2198, nos 47–9.

17 *Ven. Cal.*, xvii. no. 794, pp. 581–2.

18 D'Ewes, *Diary*, p. 121.

19 *Letters of John Holles 1587–1637*, ed. P.R. Seddon (Thoroton Society Record Series, vol. xxxv, 1983), p. 267.

20 Dudley Carleton to Sir Dudley Carleton, 27 Feb., PRO, SP14/138, fo. 99.

21 Secretary Calvert to Conway, 25 Feb., ibid., fo. 78v.

22 Ellis, *Original Letters*, iii. 138.

23 The expression is Martin Havran's, in *Caroline Courtier*, p. 70.

24 D'Ewes, *Diary*, p. 119.

25 Earl of Rutland to Buckingham, 16 Mar., Bod., Tanner ms 73(ii), fo. 289.

26 Coloma alerted King Felipe the next day, explaining he had no idea where they were going, RBM, ms II–2198, no. 47. The French court was a possibility.

27 Sir Henry Wooton, *Reliquiae Wottoniae* (London, 1651), p. 81; Chamberlain, *Letters*, ii. 480.

28 The junketing cost £57 13s. 5d.; see Buckingham's Expenses 1622–1628, BL, Add. ms 12,258, fo. 6v.

29 BL, Harl. ms 6297, at p. 84 ('The Life of Phineas Pette' being his autobiography).

30 Robert Carey, earl of Monmouth, *Memoirs of Robert Cary* (Edinburgh, 1808), p. 155.

31 Wooton, *Reliquiae*, p. 83; for the French ambassador, see J6.

32 See Bod., Tanner ms 73(ii), fo. 277.

33 Wooton, *Reliquiae*, p. 85.

34 J6.

35 Charles and Buckingham to James, Paris, 22 Feb. 1623, in Ellis, *Original Letters*, iii. 121–2.

36 Ralph Wingate also noted the scarcity of meat, see PRO, SP14/146, fo. 44v. The lack of victuals for the Prince's servants was gleefully recorded in an anti-Spanish ballad, see below, ch. 9, n. 41.

37 Wooton, *Reliquiae*, p. 88.

38 The following is based on Wynn's account contained in T. Hearne, *Historia vitae et regni Ricard II* (Oxford, 1729), App. iv, pp. 297–341.

39 Wynn, p. 323.

40 B7; see above n. 4, and for James's reply of 15 March, see J10.

41 Wynn, p. 327.

42 Bristol to James, 10 Mar. 1623, NLS, Advocates ms, 33.1.10, fos. 55–58v, at 51v.

43 Howell, *Epistolae*, p. 132.

44 Bristol to Sir Dudley Carleton, 20/10 March 1623, PRO, SP94/25, fos 4–5.

45 *Tratados*, p. 203.

46 See Juan Antonio de Vera y Figueroa, 'Fragmentos historicos de la vida de Don Gaspar de Guzman', conveniently extracted in *Tratados*, App. X, pp. 325–6; also Chamberlain, *Letters*, ii. 488 (5 April).

47 His written appointment took place the following Tuesday, 21 Mar., with the royal warrant citing that he had arranged for Charles 'to come here and put himself in my hands', RBM, II–2167, no. 12; the swearing in took place the following day, *Gaçeta*, p. 146.

48 Wooton, *Reliquiae*, p. 87.

49 I.e. a *coche encubierto* or *cerrado*, an enclosed carriage.

50   Howell, *Epistolae*, p. 132.

51   The letter is quoted in full in Townshend, *Life and Letters*, pp. 48–9, and Huxley, *Porter*, pp. 84–6 [PRO, SP14/139, fo. 81].

52   Ellis, *Original Letters*, iii. 137.

53   See Judith Richards, '"His nowe majestie" and the English Monarchy: The Kingship of Charles I before 1640', *Past and Present* 113 (1986), pp. 70–96.

54   Ellis, *Original Letters*, iii. no. 282, at p. 137.

55   Buckingham to James, 17 March, quoted in John Nichols, *The Progresses, Processions, and Magnificent Festivities of King James the First* (London, 1828), iv. 823.

56   *Gaçeta*, pp. 146–7. The royal decree had been an important part of Olivares's programme to make Spain more competitive and less snobbish. See also Cottington's letter to his wife, enclosed in one from Mead to Stuteville, London, 4 Apr., Ellis, *Original Letters*, iii. no. 284, pp. 141–4.

57   For 'embarrassment' over the arrival, see Diego Soto y Aguilar, *Jornada madrileña del príncipe de Gales: fiestas y toros y cañas en su honor* (Madrid, 1967), p. 31.

58   *Ven. Cal.*, xviii. no. 63, p. 47.

59   Howell, *Epistolae*, p. 134.

60   Redworth and Checa, 'The Kingdoms of Spain'. The ceremony of entry had its origins in the symbolic taking possession of the city, but, as with most ceremonies, it had lost its original meaning and was little more than a signal honour.

61   *Gaçeta*, p. 146, 'retirado detrás de golosía, por no haver hecho su entrada en público'.

62   He was enthusiastically and repetitively referred to as 'king of Scotland and Prince of Wales and Vualia [?Wales] and of Great Britain and England', Soto y Aguilar, *Jornada madrileña*, p. 16, n. 1. For James, see Akrigg, *Letters of King James*, 'Additional Letters', p. 525.

63   *Gaçeta*, p. 148, 'sin que falte cosa alguna'.

64   Ibid., pp. 147–8.

65   Soto y Aguilar, *Jornada madrileña*, pp. 32ff.

66   Charles and Buckingham to James, 16 Mar., in James O. Halliwell, *Letters of the Kings of England now first collected from the Originals* (2 vols, London, 1848), ii. 183.

67   Huxley, *Porter*, p. 85; *Gaçeta*, p. 149.

68   I.e. Felipe selected the 'Casa' or household but not the 'Cámera' or bedchamber, PRO, SP94/26, fos 119, 121, and *Gaçeta*, pp. 148–9.

69   J113.

70   See *La Corte de Carlos V*, ed. José Martínez Millán (5 vols, Madrid, 2000), iv. p. 13.

71   See Ellis, *Original Letters*, iii. 141–4.

72   Wynn, p. 332.

9. Cat and Mouse

1   Howell, *Epistolae*, p. 135.

2   Nichols, *Progresses*, p. 817.

3   BL, Harl. ms, 6987, fo. 119.

4   Roca, in *Tratados*, p. 326. For similar remarks by the king in Jan., see his apostil to AGS, Estado 2518, doc. 59, forthrightly reminding his advisers that the pope's licence and approval was not to be taken for granted.

5   B11 [27 Mar.].

6   Charles to Bristol, 21 Jan. 1626, letter no. xxxii, in Charles Petrie, *The Letters, Speeches and Proclamations of King Charles I* (London, 1935). Bristol's error was widely commented upon, amusing even the Spaniards, RAHM, ms K–38, fo. 58; see also, *Tratados*, p. 207.

7   Cogswell, *Blessed Revolution*, pp. 37–8.

8   'so weit suspendiert, dass man sider darvon nichts geredet noch tractiert hat', Kheven-hüller to Prince von Eggenberg, 12/2 Apr. 1623, OÖLA, Khevenhüller Bestand, ms 11, fo. 40v.

9   *Tratados*, p. 208.

10 *Gaçeta*, p. 151.

11 According to his Account Book, Charles gave the English fathers 40,000 *reales* in three instalments, with a *real* worth about 2.75 new pence, NLS, ms 1879, fos 17r–v.

12 *Gaçeta*, p. 151.

13 See Gil Gónzalez Dávila's Introduction (p. 1) in *Monarquía de España. Historia de la vida y hechos del inclito monarca, amado y santo D. Felipe Tercero* (Madrid, 1771), and cf. *Gaçeta*, p. 160. Professor Geoffrey Parker kindly drew this to my attention.

14 'y con ser los convidados de diferente professión y ley', *Gaçeta*, p. 150.

15 RBM, ms II–2167 no. 27, *parecer* of 4 April.

16 *Gaçeta*, p. 150. For a theological overview, including mention of Charles's desultory exchange of letters with Rome, see W.B. Patterson, *King James VI and I and the Reunion of Christendom* (Cambridge, 1997), pp. 323ff.

17 *Gaçeta*, p. 149.

18 See below, ch. 12.

19 *Tratados*, pp. 208–9.

20 PRO, SP14/139, fo. 46, nos 1 and 2; see also J7 and J8.

21 This may have been behind the complaints over the decision not to send Henry Burton, clerk of the closet first to Prince Henry and then to Charles, PRO, SP14/139 fos 191, 106. For D'Ewes, see *Diary*, p. 128.

22 J11.

23 Ellis, *Original Letters*, iii. 132–3.

24 Albert J. Loomie, *Spain and the Jacobean Catholics* (vol. ii for '1613–1624', being *Catholic Record Society*, 1978), App. III, 'The "Directions" of James I for Anglican Services in Spain' (Newmarket, 10 March), and Wynn, p. 328.

25 J14.

26 See Wynn, p. 319.

27 Howell, *Epistolae*, p. 140, and see Clarendon, *State Papers collected by Edward, Earl of Clarendon . . .* (Oxford, 1976), i. App. xviii–xix.

28 *Tratados*, p. 212, and *Gaçeta*, p. 165.

29 Wynn, p. 310, and J14.

30 PRO, SP14/139, fo. 46.1; fo. 46.2 contains the King's additions. See App. 4.

31 PRO, SP94/26, fo. 84.

32 London, 20 May, Owen Wynn to Sir John Wynn, National Library of Wales, ms 466E/1105. I owe knowledge of this reference to the generosity of Mr Simon Healy.

33 J13 [1 Apr.]

34 Charles to James, 22 Apr., BL, Harl. ms. 6987, fo. 77.

35 Buckingham to James, 25 Apr., in Ellis, *Original Letters*, iii. 146–8.

36 PRO, SP14/140, fo. 13.

37 PRO, SP14/139, fo. 16. Comprising three deep-red rubies around a central diamond, the Three Brothers began life at the fifteenth-century court of Burgundy. For James's jewels, see Roy Strong, *Lost Treasures of Britain* (London, 1990), pp. 84–6.

38 J11.

39 Wynn, p. 316.

40 PRO, SP14/146, fo. 44r.

41 BL, Tanner ms. 306 (ii.), fo. 258 ; also see above, ch. 8, n. 36.

42   RBM, ms II–2167, no. 31. This and other questions of protocol are also to be found in
     AGS, Estado 2516.
43   Huxley, *Porter*, p. 89 mistakenly dates this 7 Apr (o.s.).
44   *Gaçeta*, p. 152.
45   *Ven. Cal.*, xvii. no. 863, 638.
46   Bristol to Secretary Calvert, 8 Apr., NLS, ms Adv. 33.1.10, no. 32, fos 83r–86r, at fo. 85r.
47   Huxley, *Porter*, p. 89.
48   Cottington to James, 8 Apr., NLS, ms 27, no. 20 a–d, at a.
49   Howell, *Epistolae*, pp. 135–6, and *Gaçeta*, p. 156. An elaborated version is to be found in
     Puyuelo y Salinas, *Carlos de Inglaterra*, pp. 162–8.
50   *Gaçeta*, p. 154.
51   Howell, *Epistolae*, p. 135.

10. Dispute, Censures and Conclusions

1   For Archibald Armstrong, see D. Neal, *History of the Puritans* (London, 1822), ii. 122,
     Huxley, *Porter*, pp. 82, 95, 97 and esp. John Southworth, *Fools and Jesters at the English
     Court* (Stroud, 1998), pp. 140–51. As Professor Geoffrey Parker has pointed out to me,
     Archie finally went too far in 1637. He was banished from the court by Charles for mock-
     ing Archbishop Laud's intention to impose the Prayer Book on Scotland.
2   See Fernando Bouza, *Locos, enanos y hombres de placer en la corte de los Austrias* (Madrid,
     1991).
3   Howell, *Epistolae*, p. 136.
4   *Tratados*, p. 252.
5   *Gaçeta*, p. 157.
6   PRO, SP14/139, fo. 63 [Conway to Chamberlain].
7   Margaret D. Whinney and Oliver Miller, *English Art 1625–1714* (Oxford, 1957), p. 27.
8   PRO, SP14/139, fo. 98 [14 Mar.].
9   For the history of the secret diplomacy between Madrid and Rome in May–Apr., see the
     documentation contained in Luigi Arezio, *L'azione diplomatica del Vaticano nella ques-
     tione del matrimonio spagnuolo di Carlo Stuart, principe de Galles (Anno 1623) con molti
     e preziosi documenti* (Palermo, 1896). The importance of Arezio's findings is confirmed
     by the recent exemplary edition of Gregory XV's diplomatic correspondence, *Die
     Hauptinstruktionen Gregors XV. für die Nuntien und Gesandten an den europäischen
     Fürstenhöfen: 1621–1623*, ed. K. Jaitner (2 vols, Tübingen, 1997). S.R. Gardiner's accounts
     of this stage in the negotiations are redundant, for the reasons given by Arezio, pp. 37–8.
     As far as I am aware, the only works which made use of Arezio were Gordon Albion,
     Charles I and the Court of Rome, and Ludwig von Pastor, *The History of the Popes from
     the Close of the Middle Ages*, vol. xxvii, *Gregory XV and Urban VIII (1621–1644)*, trans.
     Ernest Graf (London, 1901–53); however, the former is useful only as background and
     the latter is highly garbled. Through his powers of historical intuition, Sir John Elliott,
     in *The Count-Duke of Olivares: The Statesman in an Age of Decline* (London, 1986),
     comes closest to divining Olivares's true role in the failure of the Spanish Match.
10   Howell, *Epistolae*, p. 133.
11   He reached Rome in June, *Gaçeta*, pp. 148, 162, which rules out the supposition in Gar-
     diner, Albion, etc. (following a remark by Arezio, *L'azione diplomatica*, p. 30) that it was
     his mission which would activate papal opposition to the marriage.
12   See *Hauptinstruktionen Gregors XV*, i. 'Einleitung', pp. 47–8.
13   Arezio, *L'azione diplomatica*, p. 69.
14   B9 [Buckingham and Charles to James, 10 Mar.].

15 See De la Fuente to Juan de Ciriza, 12/2 Apr., AGS, Estado 1869, fo. 26 (also reporting the dispatch of the first dispensation).

16 As with all other dates, I have converted this to old style. Accordingly, the actual date written in the documents is '12 Apr.'

17 The simplest overview is *Hauptinstruktionen Gregors XV*, i. 'Einleitung', pp. 30–40, esp. p. 34.

18 See Alburquerque (quoting Gage's reaction) to Felipe IV, Rome 5 Apr./26 Mar., AGS, Estado Libro 369, at fo. 394v.

19 'Le lettere di V.S. del primo d'Aprile [i.e. 22 Mar. o.s.] giuntemi hoggi col corriere espresso da lei speditomi intorno al negotio della dispensa, mi hanno apportato grandísimo dispiacere, che quanto più io mi studio, e mi fatico per seruire à S.M.^{tà}, et al S. Co. di Oliuares, tanto meno hò ventura di secondare il lor gusto', Ludovisi to De Massimi, Rome, 18/8 Apr., Arezio, *L'azione diplomatica*, pp. 77–8, at 78.

20 'di tirare alla lunga il negotio à compiacimento di Sua Maestà'; 'l'aggiunte lettere ostensibili, fatte sotto l'istessa data delli 12 [i.e 2 Apr. o.s.]', Arezio, *L'azione diplomatica*, p. 78.

21 8 Apr., NLS, ms 27, fo. 20a.

22 1 Apr., Howell, *Epistolae*, p. 279.

23 B9.

24 *Tratados*, pp. 213–14.

25 'pues viendo que he sido yo solo el ministro que deshizo el otro casamiento', Jan. 1630, BL Add. ms 24,909, fo. 154r. Francisco de Rioja's defence, though brief, was obviously written with Olivares's help, *Nicandro o Antidoto . . .* (Madrid, 1643?).

26 Arezio, *L'azione diplomatica*, pp. 76–7.

27 G. Redworth, 'Beyond Faith & Fatherland "The appeal of the Catholics of Ireland"', c. 1623', *Archivium Hibernicum* 52 (1998), pp. 3–23; *Hauptinstruktionen Gregors XV*, i. 962, n. 6. For confirmation of Gormanston's pivotal role, see the as yet unpublished work of Igor Pérez Tostado of the European University Institute, who is revolutionising our knowledge of the interest groups lobbying in Madrid and Rome.

28 Arezio, *L'azione diplomatica*, p. 74.

29 Cottington to James, 8 Apr., NLS, Advocates ms, 33.1.10, no. 20, fos 53–54.

30 B11 [27 Mar.].

31 Ludovisi to De Massimi, 19/9 Apr., Arezio, *L'azione diplomatica*, p. 80.

32 B9 [10 Mar.].

33 J12 [25 Mar.].

34 Cf. Albion, *Charles I and the Court of Rome*, p. 30.

35 J13 [1 Apr.].

36 See James's denials of 11 May, Akrigg, *Letters of King James*, no. 204, p. 412.

37 See below, App. 6.

38 The fleet was set up on 1 May; see below, ch. 11.

39 B12 [Charles and Buckingham to James, 27 Apr.]. Precisely one month before they had told James to 'lose no time in hastening the ships'; see B11.

40 For Charles to James [29 Apr.], see *Miscellaneous State Papers from 1501–1726*, ed. Philip Yorke, earl of Hardwicke (2 vols, London, 1778), i. 417–18. The King wrote,

> My dearest son,
> I do hereby promise, in the word of a king, that whatsoever ye my dearest son shall promise there in my name, I will punctually and faithfully perform, and so God bless you.
> Your loving father,
> *James R.*

See Akrigg, *Letters of King James*, no. 203, pp. 411–12.

41 MAE, ms 243, fos 113–28.

42 By the same token, the count would have to oppose those who dismissed the marriage out of hand. For an example, see Elliott, *Olivares*, p. 212; additionally, see Howell, *Epistolae*, p. 293.

43 MAE, ms 243, fos 137v–142r. This speech is also contained in *Tratados*, pp. 220–8; cf. Elliott, *Olivares*, pp. 209–10 (n.s. dating), who rightly says, 'This was a harder line than that taken by some of his colleagues'.

44 MAE, ms 243, fo. 100.

45 22/12 May, MAE, ms 243, fos 165–84; cf. *Tratados*, p. 229.

46 *Tratados*, pp. 233–5. A brief summary of its deliberations is to be found in BNM, ms 8719, fos 90v–93v.

47 For the meetings, see *Tratados*, pp. 216ff. For chronological accounts (albeit much simplified), see, with caution, Albion, *Charles I and the Court of Rome*, pp. 37–8 and Gardiner, v. 37–42.

48 *Tratados*, p. 229.

49 Ibid., p. 230.

50 Howell, *Epistolae*, p. 288.

51 15 June, Lord Keeper Williams to Buckingham, John Hackett, *Scrinia Reserata: A Memorial of . . . John Williams, D.D. . . . Lord Keeper of the Great Seal of England* (London, 1693), pp. 135–6; for further details, see Nichols, *Progresses*, p. 874.

52 See the copy of Charles's third submission included in the Council of State's rejection, dated 20/10 May, BNM, 8719, fos 110v–113.

53 *Tratados*, p. 230. The date is confirmed by Khevenhüller to Prince von Eggenberg, 24/14 May, OÖLA, Khevenhüller Bestand, ms 11, fo. 60.

54 *Tratados*, pp. 231–2. For a different emphasis, see Brennan Pursell, who suggests that, when Charles considered leaving Madrid, 'his hosts' pleas quickly convinced him to stay', 'The End of the Spanish Match', p. 711.

11. *Solely to his Own Courtesy*

1 Buckingham to James, 25 Apr., BL, Harl. ms 6987, at fo. 79r; also J19 and Havran, *Caroline Courtier*, p. 76 and NLS, ms 879, fos 20v, 21v.

2 Birch, *Court and Times of James*, ii. 409–12; for costs, see John Bowle, *Charles I: A Biography* (London, 1975), p. 75. Ms Bridget Clifford of the Tower Armouries kindly supplied this reference.

3 For an introduction to the art world of Madrid, see M.B. Burke and Peter Cherry, *Documents for the History of Collecting. Spanish Inventories 1: Collections of Paintings in Madrid, 1601–1755* (2 vols, Getty Museum and Turin, 1997), i. 109–87, esp. p. 131. A full-length examination of what Charles and his companions acquired and how has yet to be undertaken, but the magnificent work of Jonathan Brown and John Elliott (eds) in *La Almoneda del Siglo: relaciones artísticas entre España y Gran Bretaña, 1604–1655* (Madrid, 2002), along with the slightly revised English version, points the way.

4 Buckingham's Expenses 1622–1628, BL, Add. ms 12,528, fo. 8v.

5 NLS, ms 1879, fo. 17; for the conversion rate of one *real* for 2.75 new pence (or £1 for 36.03 *reales*), see fos 20, 32.

6 NLS, ms 1879, fo. 19v.

7 'muchas de las que avemos nombrado [i.e., pictures], estuvieron en grande riesgo quando estuvo aqui el Principe de Galés', Vicente Carducho, *Diálogos e la pintura: su*

defensa, orígen, esencia, definición, modos y diferencias, ed. Francisco Calvo Serraller (Madrid, 1970), p. 435.

8 *Gaçeta*, p. 173; cf. Burke and Cherry, *Collections of Paintings*, i. 181 and J. Miguel Morán Turina and Fernando Checa, *El coleccionismo en España: de la camera de maravillas a la gallería de pinturas* (Madrid, 1985), p. 302.

9 *Gaçeta*, p. 177.

10 NLS, ms 1879, fo. 30v (*pace Almoneda del Siglo*, p. 48).

11 NLS, ms 1879, fo. 35v.

12 Ibid., fo. 37v.

13 Ibid., fo. 38.

14 Carducho, *Diálogos*, pp. 422–3, 438, and *Almoneda del Siglo*, p. 48.

15 NLS, ms 1879, fo. 40.

16 Francisco Pacheco, *Arte de la pintura*, ed. Bonaventura Bassegoda i Hugas (Madrid, 1990), p. 205. Doubts have been aired on this identification owing to a misunderstanding of the term *de camino*, which most likely means 'quickly' rather than *en route*; for a full discussion, see José López-Rey, *Velázquez* (Cologne, 1996), i. 52 and 133, nn. 60, 61.

17 NLS, ms 1879, fo. 18v. The works in question are probably Antonio de Herrera y Tordesillas, *Historia general de los hechos de los castellanos en las islas i tierra firme de el mar oceano*; Juan Antonio de Vera y Zúñiga's *Epitome de la vida y hechos del invicto emperador Carlos*; and Luis Cabrera de Córdoba's *Felipe segundo rey de España*, Part 1 (1619). For the price of books in post-mortem inventories, see Trevor Dadson, *Libros, lectores y lecturas* (Madrid, 1998), App. 1 (pp. 513–15). For the argument with James, see 'Sarmiento de Acuña' (G. Redworth) in the *Oxford Dictionary of National Biography*.

18 NLS, ms 1879, fo. 25. They cost 8 and 4 *reales* respectively. For the identification with Alemán's *Guzman de Alfarache*, see John Rutherford, *Breve historia del pícaro preliterario* (Vigo, 2001), p. 70.

19 *Gaçeta*, pp. 155, 158.

20 Cf. María José del Río Barredo, *Madrid, Urbs Regia: la capital ceremonial de la monarquía católica* (Madrid, 2000), p. 153.

21 Francisco de Quevedo, *Obra Poética*, ed. José Manuel Blecua, ii (Madrid, 1970), no. 674, pp. 202–7.

22 'El auditorio le sigue/con aprobación risueña/y a remojar la palabra/se entraron en la taberna', ibid., no. 677, pp. 212–33. My translation is anachronistic in that beer was less popular at the time than wine or spirits.

23 See Huxley, *Porter*, pp. 98–9, and *Gaçeta*, p. 159.

24 See above, ch. 10.

25 Howell, *Epistolae*, p. 146. Buckingham repeated this story in the Lords in 1624.

26 *Tratados*, pp. 232–3.

27 MAE, ms 243, fos 170–178v.

28 Havran, *Caroline Courtier*, p. 74 ; cf. OÖLA; Khevenhüller Bestand, ms 11, fo. 65, says 8 June whereas *Gaçeta*, p. 158, gives the following day.

29 OÖLA, Khevenhüller Bestand, ms 11, fo. 61, and his *Parecer que dio en la ivnta el padre Ivan de Montemayor de la Compañia de Iesvs, acerca del casamiento de svs altezas* (Madrid, 1623). For an overview of the Jesuits' position, see Rodríguez-Moñino Soriano, *Razón de estado*, pp. 115ff.

30 *Tratados*, p. 242.

31 Charles to Felipe IV, in reply to the theologians' report of 23 May, BNM, ms 18,195, fos 37–41r. For the reply, see the ruminations of Francisco de Jesús, in his *Los papeles que por mandado del Rey nuestro señor ha hecho Fray Francisco de Jesús su predicador sobre el*

tratado del matrimonio que el principe de Gales pretende con la ... infante Maria (Madrid, 1623), section IV, pp. 30–1.

32 'por ser sus leyes y modo de governar diferente q[ue] lo de yngalaterra', AGS, Estado 2516, doc. 39 at b, being a draft of a report from the Council of State, 5 July/25 June.

33 'verò libero Catholicae Religionis exercitio . . .', see *Tratados*, App., Secret Articles, pp. 343–4.

34 Dated 23 May; see *State Papers collected by Edward, Earl of Clarendon* (Oxford, 1767), i., App. pp. xviii–xix.

35 See Albion, *Charles I and the Court of Rome*, p. 21.

36 Hackett, *Scrinia Reserata*, p. 136. The date of 17 June 1623 is impossible, but as new style it refers to 7 June.

12. Stricken Dead

1   J20 [14 July]; 'strucken' is the original spelling.

2   PRO, SP14/146, no. 76v; for Richmond, see Nichols, *Progresses*, p. 873.

3   BNM, ms 10,467, fos 7–8v. The ten ships were the *Prince Royal, St Andrew, Swiftsure, Defiant, Rainbow, Bonaventure, Seven Stars,* and the *Charles,* and the pinnaces, the *George* and the *Antelope,* in PRO, AO1 1698/61 and esp. E351/2261, being Sir William Russell's accounts for 1623 as Treasurer of the Marine. Rutland left court to join the fleet on 27 May, PRO, SP94/26, fo. 249v.

4   PRO, SP14/146, no. 103.

5   On the fleet's return with Charles in October it was said to have 315 pieces of ordnance, see Andrés de Almansa y Mendoza, *The Ioyfull Returne of the Most Illustrious Prince, Charles, prince of great Brittaine, from the court of Spaine. Tr. out of the Span* (London, 1623).

6   Gardiner, v. 589.

7   'The relation of Sir Balthazar Gerbier Kt.', BL, Add. ms 4181, fo. 17v (June 1648), his defence of the reputation of Buckingham and the kings he served; as for the visit to Madrid, it largely follows Buckingham's parliamentary account.

8   15 June; Hackett, *Scrinia Reserata*, pp. 126, 135–6. The second marquess's son, James, earl of Arran and future first duke of Hamilton, was one of the first to follow his kinsman, Charles. According to the King, he had been ready to leave by 27 Feb., possibly to serve Buckingham, his relative by marriage [J6].

9   Undated draft in Buckingham's hand, with interlineations, in BL, Add. ms 1583, fos 281–2.

10 *Tratados*, p. 245.

11 Khevenhüller to the emperor, 8 June/29 May 1623, OÖLA, Khevenhüller Bestand, ms 11, fols 62–4; for an overview, see Anton Gindely, *Beiträge zur Geschichte des dreissigjährigen Krieges. Auch den nachgelassenen Schriften Anton Gindely's herausgegeben von J. Hirn,* being *Archiv für österreichische Geschichte* 89 (1900), pp. 1–245, at p. 70.

12 Townshend, *Life and Letters*, pp. 59–61, and see Huxley, *Porter*, p. 102; also Olivares to Coloma, 17/7 July, AGS, Estado 8783, doc. 11.

13 *Tratados*, p. 246.

14 I.e. £1,250; *Gaçeta*, p. 165.

15 'como que yua a despedirse', Francisco de Jesús, *Los papeles que por mandado . . .*, section IV, p. 33; and *Tratados*, pp. 246–7.

16 B15 [Charles and Buckingham to James, 29 July].

17 Buckingham to Cottington, 8 July, Society of Antiquaries, London, ms 203, fo. 129.

18 *Gaçeta*, p. 165; Howell, *Epistolae*, p. 148; see also Bristol to James, 29 Aug., in Philip Yorke, earl of Hardwicke, *Miscellaneous State Papers* (London, 1778), pp. 476–8, at p. 476.

19 For the delay, see postscript to PRO, SP14/146, no. 74v.

20 Conway to Buckingham, 17 July, in Ellis, *Original Letters*, iii. no. ccxciv, pp. 158–9.

21 Williams to Charles, undated, Hackett, *Scrinia Reserata*, p. 141; Conway to Buckingham, 17 July, in Ellis, *Original Letters*, iii. 154.

22 Conway to Buckingham, 17 July, BL, Harl. ms 1580, fos 308–10v.

23 J21 [21 July].

24 Conway to Buckingham, 17 July, BL, Harl. ms 1580, fos 309–310v.

25 Hackett, *Scrinia Reserata*, p. 143.

26 J23 [31 July]. James had mentioned the same figure on 1 Apr. [J13].

27 'and this bearer will bring you the power to treat for the Palatinate and the matter of Holland', J21[21 July]. For James's further remarks on 31 July, see below, ch. 13, n. 18.

28 19 July, BNM, ms 10,467, fos 34r and 34v.

29 Ambassadors to the Infanta, London, 21 July, BNM ms 10,467, fos 38v–40.

30 23 July, Conway to Buckingham, Hardwicke, *State Papers*, i. 429–31, at p. 430. For the age until which the children would remain with the Princess of Wales, see App. 2.

31 Conway to Buckingham, 21 July, Hardwicke, *State Papers*, p. 431.

32 Hackett, *Scrinia Reserata*, p. 140.

33 See Gardiner, v. 97.

34 Townshend, *Life and Letters*, p. 61; cf. Howell, *Epistolae*, p. 146.

35 *Gaçeta*, p. 166.

36 Howell, *Epistolae*, p. 146 [19 Aug.].

37 See B15 [29 July], where news of the 'despatch of our business' was said to have arrived the previous day. Presumably this refers to the earlier conciliar decision to support the agreement rather than to news of the signing on the 20th.

38 The notarised original is to be found at AGS, Estado 2849, fo. 74ff.

39 B17 [20 Aug.]; *Tratados*, pp. 248–9.

40 See App. 6.

41 *Gaçeta*, p. 169; *Tratados*, p. 254.

42 Charles to James, Madrid, 29 Aug., BL, Harl. ms 6987, fos 159–160.

43 See Huxley, *Porter*, p. 109 and *Tratados*, p. 249.

44 See Howell, *Epistolae*, p. 138, and *Letters and Papers of the Verney Family*, ed. John Bruce (Camden Society, o.s. no. 56, 1853), pp. 112–13, confirming *Tratados*, pp. 249–50, which alleges the Prince's visit was becoming accident-prone. See also OÖLA, Khevenhüller Bestand, ms 11, fo. 110, and the undated report by the Genovese ambassador in ASG, Archivio Segreto vol. 2430, no. 246. For this and other poems, see Cogswell, *Blessed Revolution*, p. 46.

45 *Gaçeta*, pp. 172–5. See 'Jewelles to be sent to Spajne', BL, Add. ms 1583, fo. 274.

46 The gifts were returned in 1624. To have kept them might have given future suitors an excuse to claim that María was not free to marry.

47 *Tratados*, p. 253; Buckingham to 'My dear friend', 30 Aug., BL, Harl. ms 6987, fo. 166.

48 Secretarial note 26/16 Sept., Archivo Histórico Nacional, Madrid, Estado Libro 737, fo. 394r–v; see also *Tratados*, p. 254.

49 Inojosa to James, Bod., Tanner ms 82, at fos 207v–208v. Buckingham was also accused of profaning the palace with prostitutes, of doing 'obscene things' and using 'immodest gesticulations and wanton tricks with players in the presence of the Prince'. James had warned his boys to be discreet in their dancing and singing, J13.

50 Khevenhüller to the emperor, 12/2 Sept., OÖLA, Khevenhüller Bestand, ms 11, fos 108–11.

51 'so breche man mit Engelandt, wann er auch mit 100 Infanta Donna Maria verheyrathet währe', ibid. fol. 109; cf. Khevenhüller, *Annales Ferdinandei*, x. 96, where this is archaically rendered '100 Infantes de España', following the textual tradition of the Linz manuscript. As for the Elector Frederick's refusal to compromise, see Pursell, 'The End of the Spanish Match', p. 717.

52 Charles to James, BL, Harl. ms 6987, fos 159–60v, and Bristol to James, Hardwicke, *State Papers*, i. 476–8, at p. 476, both of 29 Aug.

53 Bristol's *Defence*, p. 50.

54 Dated El Escorial 12/2 Sept., copies of this and Charles's reply being in AGS, Estado 8781, docs 17 and 18, part of Ambassador Coloma's archive. See also below, ch. 13, n. 5.

55 Howell, *Epistolae*, p. 147. See App. 5.

56 For its importance as the prototype of the emperor's image, see Fernando Checa, *Carolus* (Madrid, 2000), p. 267, and in particular the essay by Miguel Falomir Faus, 'En busca de Apeles: decoro y verosimilitud en el retrato de Carlos V', pp. 157–79 (esp. pp. 169–72) in *Carlos V: retratos de famila*, ed. Fernando Checa, Miguel Falomir Faus and Javier Portús (Sociedad Estatal para la conmemoración de los centenarios de Felipe II y Carlos II, Madrid, 2000). Titian was ennobled for his work on this picture, which became the prototype of all subsequent studies of Charles.

57 Gregorio de Andrés, 'La despedida de Carlos Estuardo, príncipe de Gales, en el Escorial (1623) y la columna-trofeo que se levantó para perpetua memoria', *Anales del Instituto de Estudios Madrileños* 10 (1974), pp. 113–32.

13. Epilogue – The Codpiece Point?

1 Elliott, *Olivares*, p. 214.

2 *Gaçeta*, p. 175 (which for the departure largely follows the contemporary account by Andrés de Mendoza, published in Octobe 1623 and shortly after in an English version; see de Andrés, 'La despedida de Carolos Estuardo', pp. 125, 128).

3 Wynn, p. 339.

4 Glenn Murray, 'A Royal Visitor: The Prince of Wales and the Segovia Mint', in *Fleur de Coin* 17 (2000), pp. 4–7. The Friends of the Segovia Mint Association is working to reopen this monument.

5 'firme y constante resoluçion de cumplir todo lo que mi Padre y yo hemos tratado y acordado con v[uestr]a m[agestad] pero de hazer todo lo demas que sea menester para estrechar y ligar todo quanto sea possible la hermandad y sincera amistad', Segovia, 13/3 Sept., AGS, Estado 8781, doc. 18 at a–b.

6 For the letter, see below App. 3, which shows that Charles had revoked the proxy much earlier than previously thought.

7 *Tratados*, p. 258.

8 Howell, *Epistolae*, p. 148; this letter is impossibly dated 12 Aug.; if Howell had unthinkingly used new style, this would be 4 Sept. 1623. Alternatively, August might be a mistake for October, as Clarke himself says Bristol did not find out till the middle of September; see Clarke to Buckingham, 1 Oct., *Cabala sive scrinia sacra: Mysteries of State and Government in Letters* (London, 1654), pp. 306–7, being BL, Harl. ms 1580, fos 274–5 *et al.*, *Tratados*, p. 258, and cf. Gardiner, v. 120, n. 2.

9 Bristol to Charles, 21 Sept., Clarendon, *State Papers*, i. App. xix–xx.

10 See James to Bristol, 8 Oct. 1623, Akrigg, *Letters of King James*, no. 216, pp. 426–8, and Howell, *Epistolae*, p. 150. For the arrival on 12 Nov. of the final dispensation, see Heinrich

Lutz, *Kardinal Giovanni Francesco Guidi di Bagno: Politik und Religion im Zeitalter Richelieus und Urbans VIII* (Tübingen, 1971), p. 123.

11 Hackett, *Scrinia Reserata*, p. 163. For the legends about the letters, see esp. Lockyer, *Buckingham*, pp. 161–2. The stories probably arose because in a reply to Elizabeth Buckingham claimed that the marriage was broken on her account, cf. Cogswell, *Blessed Revolution*, p. 61, n. 13, and Gardiner, v. 118–19; for Buckingham to Elizabeth (undated), BL, Harl. ms 6987, fos 151–2. The story surrounding her letter quickly found its way back into the Spanish sources, *viz. Tratados*. Actually, Elizabeth was less belligerent than usual; she wrote on 6 September accepting James's demands that her husband adopt a slightly more conciliatory approach, adding she was worried for Charles's safe return, 'for I fear they will make their profit of his being there, before they let him go', Elizabeth to Conway, *The Letters of Elizabeth, Queen of Bohemia*, ed. L.M. Baker (London, 1953), pp. 66–7. Though he emphasises the importance of the fortuitous meeting with Elizabeth's secretary in Segovia in changing Charles's mind ('His mission appeared to have the desired effect'), Pursell's account of Frederick V's thinking at this time is most illuminating; see 'The End of the Spanish Match', p. 719.

12 *Ven. Cal.*, xviii. no. 152, p. 121; no. 149, pp. 119–20 (Sept.).

13 *LJ*, pp. 224–5, possibly being a distorted reference to the letter Williams was to burn, see ch. 11.

14 Howell, *Epistolae*, p. 149. Bristol blamed the failure of the match on the antipathy between Buckingham and Olivares. He begged Charles not to allow 'any personal distates' between the two favourites to stand in the way, Bristol to Charles, 24 Sept.,Clarendon, *State Papers*, i. App. pp. xx–xxi.

15 When Khevenhüller, the Imperial ambassador, had asked what support could be expected from Spain if hostilities broke out again, Felipe IV's response was genuinely lukewarm. See Felipe IV to his ambassador in Vienna, the count of Oñate, 29/19 June 1623, RBM, ms II–2220, no. 44.

16 Charles and Buckingham to James, 30 Aug., Halliwell, *Letters of the Kings of England*, ii. pp. 228–9.

17 James to Charles and Buckingham, 15 Mar., Akrigg, *Letters of King James*, no. 194, pp. 394–7. As Patterson put it, James considered that the match should 'contribute to a resolution of issues', *Reunion of Christendom*, p. 322.

18 J23 [31 July].

19 For the perils of the journey, see 'The Life of Phineas Pette', BL, Harl. ms 6297, p. 88.

20 Ellis, *Original Letters*, iii. 159–8.

21 D'Ewes, *Diary*, pp. 162–3.

22 Coloma to Felipe IV, 17/7 Oct., RBM, ms 2590, fo. 4 and *passim*.

23 *Tratados*, p. 245.

24 See Olivares to Cottington, 31 Oct. [n. s. or o.s.] 1623, BL, Add. ms 4155, fos 126–7, esp. 126r [with another English translation in Add. 36,446, fos 220–22v]. No direct mention was made of an Austrian marriage for Charles: it was not possible at this time, since his betrothal to the Infanta had been officially announced. The letter concentrates on the virtues of marrying 'the eldest son of the Palatine to the second daughter of the emperor, bringing him up in the court of his Caesarial Majesty whereby the restitution both of the States & the Electorate to that said son, might be the better & more satisfactorily disposed' [fo. 126r].

25 *Cabala sive scrinia sacra*, p. 246.

26 See *The Second Part of Vox Populi* (Goricum, 1624). The first instalment of *Vox Populi* had been published in 1620, when James's Hispanophilia caused its author to flee the country.

See also Roberta Anderson, '"Well disposed to the affairs of Spain?" James VI & I and the Propagandists', *Recusant History*, 25 (2001), pp. 613–35.

27 No precise date is mentioned; see Wren's memoirs, Bod., Rawlinson ms D 392, fo. 357.

28 For the omission of the specific references to the Palatinate in the final marriage treaty with France, see Weiss, *Die Unterstützung*, p. 77.

29 Accounts of the intervening months before a new parliament could be summoned make for unedifying reading, as do those concerning the prosecution of the war; although all take the desultory diplomatic exchanges with Spain more or less at face value: see Cogswell, *Blessed Revolution*, pp. 107–21, Gardiner, v. 119ff., and 153ff., and most usefully, Pursell, 'The End of the Spanish Match', pp. 720ff. A new study of the French marriage and its relationship to the slide into war is urgently required.

Appendix 1:   Gondomar to Buckingham, September 1622

BL, Harl. ms 1583, fos 349–350v (text 349r–v), described in *Catalogue of the Manuscripts in the Spanish Language in the British Library*, ed. Pascual de Gayangos (London, 1976, being a reprint of the 1875 edition), i. 706, no. 17.

My Lord, My good freind [*sic*], Mi buen
señor y amigo, que en françes no quiero
dezir nada, pero en Castellano y con toda
Verdad, digo que tengo grandissima embidia
a Don françisco Cotinton, pues llegara
a besar las manos del Marques de
Buckingham, personalmente, cossa que
yo me olgara tanto de poder hazer, Por
que me pareze que ha ya mil años
que sali de Inglaterra, donde He
rezibido tantas honrras, y tantas cortesias,

Mil cosas quisiera dezir a V[uestra] ex[celenci]a, que
escusso, por ser el portador desta, Don fran[cisc]o
Cotinton, que de todo dara particular cuenta
a V[uestra] ex[celenci]a de palabra, Solo digo que de
la parte de aca, la resolucion esta ya toma
da, y con muy gran Voluntad. de que
el Principe de Gales, monte sobre la
España, y busquen su remedio todos
los demas que lo pretendian, y tambien

(b)
se dessea, que se camine en ello, Por
la posta, pero las postas de España, No

puedo yo hazer, que anden mas a priessa
de su costumbre, pero en fin llegan, con Ver
dad y çerteza, y aunque soy chico postillon
pico fuerte, V[uestra] ex[celenci]a haga alla lo
mismo, con la Verdad y constancia que
hasta aqui, como yo lo he Visto, y fa
vorezcame, con escrivirme muy largo, y avi
sarme de todo lo que se ofrezca, que yo
hare lo mismo con todos,

A mi señora la condessa y a mi S[eñor]a
la marquessa,[1] bessamos las manos la
Condessa mi muger y yo, y suplicamos
a Nuestro señor guarde a V[uestra] ex[celenci]a
Muchos años, y con mucha felizidad.
En Madrid a 22 [12 o.s.] de setiembre. 1622

[Postscript in Gondomar's hand]
aqui la respuesta del C[on]de de
Olivares q[ue] es muy verdadero
servidor de V[uestra] ex[celenci]a y deseamos
trarlo con obras
   El C[on]de de gondomar

. . . My good lord and friend. I will say nothing in French but in Castilian and in all truth I say that I have the greatest envy of Francis Cottington, since he will get to kiss the hands of the marquess of Buckingham personally, something that I myself would so much like to be able to do, for it seems to me already a thousand years since I left England where I was the object of so many honours and courtesies.

I omit a thousand things that I should like to tell you, since the bearer of this letter is Francis Cottington, who will give Your Excellency a detailed account of it all by word of mouth. I will say only that, as far as we here are concerned, the decision has already been made, and with very great enthusiasm, that the Prince of Wales should mount Spain. All the others that tried must look somewhere else for their relief. Also, the wish here is that the matter should be dealt with post haste. But, as to the posts of Spain, I cannot make them move faster than is their wont, but in the end they do arrive with truth and certainty. Though I am no great postilion I spur hard and may Your Excellency do the same at your end with the same integrity and consistency that you have shown so far, as I myself can bear witness. Please favour me with a long letter and let me know whatever you may wish to be done, as I shall in the case of all concerned.

My wife the countess and I kiss the hand of my lady the countess and my lady the marchioness, and we pray to our Lord that he may grant Your Excellency long life and great happiness. Madrid, 22 [12 o.s.] September 1622.

Herewith the count of Olivares's reply, who is Your Excellency's very true servant and wishes to show the same by his deeds. The count of Gondomar.[2]

NOTES

1 Buckingham's mother and wife respectively.
2 A copy of the uncorrected transcription and translation of this letter appeared as an appendix to P. Sanz Camañes, *Diplomacia hispano-inglesa en el siglo XVII: razón de estado y relaciones de poder durante la Guerra de los Treinta años, 1618–1648* (Cuenca, 2002). There the letter is cited as being in a volume of manuscripts in the Royal Library in Madrid. That volume contains no such document and, as far as I am aware, no copy has been found in the Library.

Appendix 2:   The Religious Agreements of 3 December 1622 and 25 July 1623[1]

S.R. Gardiner was unable to find a copy of the religious articles which were passed to the earl of Bristol on 3 December 1622 and which were immediately assented to by James, his son, and his privy councillors at the start of January 1623. I have identified only one contemporary version of the articles in the original Spanish, i.e. BNM, ms 8719, fos 70v–74.

This is contained in a copy of the letter that was to be passed to the earl of Bristol. The articles are numbered up to article 17; thereafter the enumeration ceases, but the individual clauses remain clearly identifiable, and indeed they were referred to by number in a letter from Felipe IV to his ambassador in Rome dated 30/20 Dec. I have included that numeration in this edition of the text.[2]

The articles and the rest of the letter to Bristol were incorporated within a treatise comprising fos 55–119 which was drawn up at the end of May 1623 by don Diego de los Ríos Jerley or Xerley, as indicated at fos 63 and 119. The object of the treatise was to see whether there were any secular or strategic advantages to an alliance with Great Britain now that there was apparent agreement on religion. Though the compiler says he was instructed by Felipe IV in December 1622 to consider the so-called temporal issues while the court waited for news of the dispensation, Olivares was the intermediary. The favourite was gathering ideas for rejecting or countering the military or diplomatic demands which London would make when the temporal articles of friendship were considered.

Gardiner derived more or less the same text for the December 1622 articles from comments made by Francisco de Jesús.[3] In fact, the matter is simpler than he thought. The religious articles of December 1622 were, to all intents and purposes, identical with the formal part of the treaty of summer 1623. There are only two differences between the earlier and later agreements worthy of express note. One is circumstantial,[4] the other of substance. The substantive difference concerns the putative article 22 in the December 1622 text, and the article actually numbered 22 in the final agreement: in the version assented to by James at the start of January, it is agreed that all children of the marriage shall stay in their mother's care at least until the age of nine; the final version of the treaty in the summer stipulates that they shall remain at least until the age of ten. This substantive change must, however, be qualified on two grounds. First, in the autumn of 1622 James had pleaded not to have to agree publicly to any more than seven years, though privately he would assent to nine, or if necessary, ten. Since the clause would inevitably become public knowledge, he did not want 'to declare unto the world' that his grandchildren would be brought up till marriageable age 'in a religion which we profess not, nor is publicly confessed in our kingdom'.[5] Rome had already been agitating for the children to remain with their mother until they were twelve. Madrid compromised in the December articles, but still obliged James formally to assent to a higher age than he wished, and even more so by the time of the final version of the treaty. This leads to the second proviso, which is that in the final agreement of July 1623, the Prince of Wales bilaterally agreed with King Felipe that the children would anyway remain with their mother until the age of twelve, for which see additional article (v) (p. 183 below).

Regardless of the textual continuity, the effect of the two agreements was radically different. This is because in the summer the articles were to be interpreted in the light of the additional promises which James and Charles were required to make to the king of Spain. (Those promises essentially incorporated the demands made by the pope in April 1623, including those made at Olivares's request.) In the absence of these additional assurances, the January 1623 agreement guaranteed only the religious rights and freedoms of the Infanta and her household. Any benefits for the Catholic population were contained only in a private promise made by James in January 1623 not to persecute Catholics. In a separate letter he promised not to persecute Catholics and to allow them liberty of conscience, but only in private. (This letter was apparently not to be handed over till a dispensation had arrived from Rome.[6]) By July, the papal demands concerning the *bonum publicum* of all of James's Catholic subjects in each of his three kingdoms had been incorporated into the wider agreement. (Since the statutory repeal of all anti-Catholic legislation was required, it is a moot point whether the Catholics of London could be turned away from the 'public' church, which in the earlier agreement was intended only for the use of the Infanta's household.) With these additional promises, and quite apart from the humiliation of having to give prior guarantees that he would keep his word, James felt the new agreement had obliged him to grant his Roman Catholics 'an infinite liberty'.[7]

The text of the agreement sent to James in December 1622 and endorsed by him in January 1623 is given below in Spanish. The brief summary in English serves as a translation both of this agreement and of the full Latin version of the treaty as promulgated in July 1623 (with the alteration to the age of the children marked in clause 22); the additional five promises sworn by James and Charles are given only in English. The full Latin text is available in Edward Hyde, *State Papers Collected by Edward, Earl of Clarendon* (Oxford, 1767), i. App. xxv–xxx and in *Tratados*, pp. 327–44. An overview can be found in W.B. Patterson, *King James VI and I and the Reunion of Christendom* (Cambridge, 1997), pp. 329–30.

The Religious Conditions for the Marriage of December 1622[8]

Las Condiciones deste Matrimonio en Materia de Relijion
que se ajustaron, a 13 de decembre, de 1622 años.

Que este matrimonio se a de hacer Con dispensaçion de Su santidad
la qual, a de alcançar Su Magestad Catolica

1. Quel matrimonio se a de celebrar solamente una vez, y esta
en España y en Inglaterra, se rratifique, en la forma
fo. 71 siguiente.
2. Que por la mañana despues de auer dicho la Serenissima Infanta sus de=
boçiones en su capilla, el serenisimo Prinçipe Carlos y la Serenissima Infanta
se junten en la Capilla Rejia o en alguna sala de palaçio
como y donde pareciere mas conbeniente Y alli se lean todos los
poderes en cuya Virtud, se celebro el matrimonio en españa
y entrambos ratifiquen y aprueben el nombramiento hecho
en españa con toda la solemnidad y aplauso necessario a tal acto
sin que Interbenga en ello zeremonia ni cossa que Contradiga
a la rrelijion Catolica apostolica Romana.
3. Que la Serenísima Infanta, lleue consigo Criados y Familia con
beniente y neçesario para su serbiçio toda la qual familia y
las personas de ellas an de ser a eleçtion y nombramiento de
Su Magestad Catolica Con condiçion que no vassallos de Su
Magestad de la gran Bretaña sin su consentimiento y Voluntad.
4. Que la serenisima Infanta y sus criados y toda su familia
tendran usso liure y ejerçiçio puplico de la Relijion Catolica
en el modo y forma, que se dira adelante.

5. Que tenga oratorio y Capilla dezente, en su palaçio donde
se puedan zelebrar missa, como su Alteza quisiere y asi
mismo a de tener en londres y a dondequiera que estubie=
re, yglesia puplica y capaz junto a palaçio donde se çelebre
todos los ofiçios diuinos con su ziminterio y todo lo de
mas neçessario, para poder predican publicamente, y admi=
nistrar y zelebrar todos los sacramentos y enterras y
baptiçar y que el dicho oratorio Capilla y yglesia
fol. 71v se adornaran con la deçençia que pareçiere Conbeniente
a la dicha señora Ynfanta.
6. Que los criados y criadas de la dicha señora Ynfanta y criados
de Criados y sus hijos y descendientes y todos los fami=
liares que de qualquier manera, sirbieren a Su Alteza
puedan ser catolicos liure y publicamente.
7. Que los dichos criados y familiares de la dicha señora Ynfanta
puedan ser catolicos en la forma siguiente.
8. Que la señora Ynfanta tenga en palaçio su oratorio y una ca=
pilla tan capaz que los dichos criados y familiares de
Su Alteza puedan estar y entrar en ella, y que aya una puer=
ta publica y ordinaria para ellos y otra ynterior por la
qual la señora Ynfanta tenga entrada a dicha Capi=
lla, donde Su Alteza y los de mas en la forma que sea
nombrado, arriua puedan estar y asistir a los offiçios
diuinos.
9. Que el oratorio Capilla y Yglesia publica esten deçente=
mente, adornadas de altares y demas cossas neçesarias
para el Culto diuino que se a de zelebrar en ellas segun
el rito y zeremonias de la santa Yglesia Romana, y que
dichos criados y los demas arriua contenido podran liçita=
mente Yr a dicha Capilla Yglesia a todas oras como les pa
reçiere.
10. Que el cuydado y custodia de la dicha capilla y yglesia estara
a cargo de las personas que quisiere y ordinare la señora Yn=
fanta, y podra Su Alteza señalar guardas para que
fol. 72 no pueda entrar ninguno en ella a haçer cossa indeçente.
11. Que para administrar los sacramentos y serbir con dicha capilla y
Yglesia aura 24 sacerdotes y asistentes que an de serbir por
meses o semanas tantos de ellos como a la señora Ynfanta
pareçiere los quales ayan de nombrar Su Magestad Catolica y la dicha señora

Ynfanta con condiçion que no sean basallos de Su Magestad de la Gran
Bretaña y si lo fueren sea con su Voluntad y liçençia.

12. Que aya un ministro superior constituydo en orden y dignidad epis=
copal con autoridad neccessaria para en todos los cassos que suçedieren
en materia de religion y faltando el obispo pueda lo mesmo
su Vicario.

13. Que este Obispo y ministro superior pueda correjir enmendar
y castigar los catolicos que delinquieren y ejeçer toda jurisdiçion
eclesiastica sobre ellos y fuera desto pueda tanbien la dicha señora
Ynfanta, despedirlos de su serbiçio quando le pareçiere.

14. Que el dicho superior Constituydo en orden episcopal o el bicario podra
castigar a los criados y a los dimas [*sic*] arriua espressados y a los
eclesiasticos conforma a las penas y leyes eclesiasticas y les
podra tanbien la dicha señora Ynfanta despedir de su ser=
uiçio.

15. Que podra la señora Ynfanta y los criados arriua dichos alcancar
en Roma, dispensaçiones y Induljençias Jubileos y todas
las mas graçias Y cossa que pareçiera conbenientes para sus
conçiençias.

16. Que los criados y familiares en la forma dicha de la serenísma
Ynfanta, que fueren a Ynglaterra juraran fidelidad
a Su Magestad de la gran Bretaña, con condiçion que no aya clau=
fo.72v sula ni palaubra, contraria a la rrelijion y conçiençias de
los catolicos y si acasso fueren Vasallos de la dicha Magestad de la
gran Bretaña, aran el mesmo Juramento que los españoless
los unos y los otros en la forma siguiente:
yo fulano Juro y prometo fidelidad a la Magestad del serenissimo Rey de
la gran Bretaña, Jacobo y a los serenísimos Carlos principe de Wales
y Maria Infante de de las españas la qual obserbare, y guar=
dare, firme y fielmente, y si supiere que contra sus personas
Honrra y dignidad o contra sus estados, y bien comun de suss
Reynos se intenta o yntentare algo dare luego auisso de
ello al dicho señor Rey y principes o a los ministros que
para ello fueren constituydos.

17. Que las leyes que ay y obiere adelante, en Yngalterra, y suss
Reynos en Materia de relijion no se entenderan ni
xecutaran, con los dichos criados ni con los demas arriua espressados legos
los quales estaran esento de las dichas leyes y penas estableçidas contra
los transgresores y contra los eclesiasticos que de proçeder solamente

su superior eclesiastico Catolico, como es costumbre en la christiandad
y si la justiçia seglar prendiere a algun eclesiastico, sera solamente
para entregarle y rremitirle luego a su superior eclesiastico para
que proçeda contra el conforme a su Derecho

Demas de lo asentado arriua dijo, el embajador a voca que quando el
delito fuesse tal, que obligasse a prender algun ecclesiastico y que per
el mereçiese ser castigo, se enbiaria a españa con el proçeso que con=
tra el se hiçiese para que aca le castiguen

Y contra los eclesiasticos no pueda proçeder, ninguna justiçia seglar
sino que esten subjeto a la de sus superiores eclesiaticos como
fol. 73 es costumbre en la christiandad.

18. Que las leyes echas en Ynglaterra y sus Reynos Contra catolicos y las que
adelante se hiçieren no se entienda ni se execute con los hijos que na=
çieren deste matrimonio y Goçen libremente del derecho desta su=
çesion en los dichos Reynos y dominios de la Gran Bretaña.

19. Que las amas que dieren leche y criaren a los hijos de la serenísima Infan=
te, puedan ser catolicas y toque a Su Alteza el elejirlas o sean Yn=
glessas, o de la naçion que Su Alteza quissiere y pertenezcan a Su fa=
milia y goçen de los preuilejios de ella.

20. Que el Obispo las personas eclesiasticas, y Religiossas de la familia de
la señora Ynfanta, podran usan y tener el vestido y abito de su
dignidad y profesion Y relijion Conforme al estilo Romano.

21. Que para seguridad de que el dicho matrimonio no se disolbera, de ninguna
manera ni por ningunas Caussas, la Magestad del Rey de la gran
Bretaña y el serenissimo Principe Carlos su hijo dan, su pala=
bra Real soure su honrra, de que no disolberan y que si a Su
Magestad Catolica, se le ofreçiere otra alguna, otra mayor seguridad
que deçentemente, puedan dar la daran.

22. Que los hijos y las yjas que proçedienen deste matrimonio, se crien en poder
de la serenissima Infanta, por lo menos hasta edad, de nueve años
y goçen libremente, del derecho a la subcession a los dichos Reynos
de la gran Bretaña, como queda dicha.

23. Que si faltare por muerte o por ausençia o por qualquier otro casso o
azidente alguno de los criados o criadas que la serenissima Yn=
fante lleuare consigo de los nombrados por el Rey Catolico su
Hermano Toque a Su Magestad el nombrar otros en su lugar
y esto se entienda, de todos los criados y familiares en la
fol. 73v forma que arriua sea dicho.

24. Que para seguiridad de que se guardara y cumplira todo lo arriua dicho

la dicha Magestad de la gran Bretaña, y el serenissimo Principe Carlos su
Hijo lo confirmaran con juramento, y todos los consejeros de la dicha
Magestad lo confirmaran, y firmaran el dicho tratado, de mas de los
quales dichos señores Rey y prinçipe, daran su fe y palabra Real
de haçer todo lo possible, para que todas las cossas arriua dichas
se aseguren, y establezcan por el parlamento.
25. Que conforme a lo tratado y acordado de todo esto se a de dar quenta
a su santidad, para que se sirba, de aprouallo y dar su santa ben=
diçion y dispensa y para que el dicho matrimonio tenga efecto:
Y por quanto, Su santidad a rrespondido ultimamente a las dilijençias
y Ynstançias que por parte de Su Magestad Catolica se han echo
a Su Beatitud para que dispense, que todas las condiçiones arriua
dichas miran solo a la seguridad y conçiencia de la señora
Ynfanta, y de su familia y que para conçeder la dispensaçion
que se le pide se rrequieren otras cossas que miran a la Vtilidad
aumento, y algun gran bien de la Relijion Catolica aposto=
lica Romana, es menester que se le propongan algunas so=
bre que pueda, deliuerar si son tales que justifiquen, y merez=
can la dicha dispensaçion y en esta conformidad su Magestad ca=
tolica esta obligado en conçiençia y Reputaçion de mirar
que el Rey de la Gran bretaña haga y cumpla lo que
a prometido y lo que Conbiene Tocante la Relijion Catolica
que de mas de que sin esto no pudiera ni quisiera su santidad

fo. 74 Conçeder[9] la dispensaçion seria Vida de mucho desconsuelo para la señora
ynfante viuir a donde se persiguiese a los de su Relijion y porque el ca=
pitulado en publico tiene algunas dificultades y ynconbenientess
y ser justo que los bassallos Catolicos de Su Magestad de la gran Bretaña en=
tiendan que este bien y quietud les proçede de su natural benigni=
dad y clemençia y tengan mayor obligaçion de serle fieles llealess
bassallos el dicho señor Rey de la gran bretaña, y el serenisimo prin=
cipe de Walia su hijo se obligaran por sus cartas aparte, y daran su
fee y palaura Real de cumplir lo que muchas veçes an prome=
tido de palabra a los ministros de Su Magestad Catolica, que es que ningun
Catolico de sus Reynos sera perseguido ni molestado por Viuir en
la Relijion Catolica, apostolica Romana y ejerçiçio de todos
los sacramentos de ella Vsandolos sin escandalo que se entiende
de sus puertas a dentro, ni se les hara bejaçion alguna, con juramentos
ni otros pretestos Tocantes a la Relijion Catolica, y de que esto

se cumplira, y ejecutara, es buen Yndiçio lo qu el dicho señor Rey
de la Gran bretaña en contemplaçion desta union y parentesco
a hecho y ba haçiendo en benefiçio de los dichos catolicos como
lo pueden deçir los ministros de Su Magestad Catolica, y los mis=
mos Catolicos de Inglatera [*sic*], en Madrid a 13[3] de deciembre de 1622
años.

The Treaty of July 1623

1. Marriage to be authorised by papal dispensation.
2. Marriage to take place in Spain and the ceremonies taking place in England to contain nothing unacceptable to the Roman Church.
3. King of Spain to name the Infanta's household, though if any are James's subjects, only by permission.
4. Infanta and household to enjoy free public exercise of their religion.
5. There to be a chapel in the palace and in London a sufficiently large public church for all services and burials, or wherever she resides, with all vestments (*ecclesiam publicam et capacem*).
6. All those connected with the household to enjoy free exercise of their religion.
7. Infanta and household to receive regular Catholic instruction.
8. A public entrance, as well as a private door for the Infanta, to be provided into her chapel.
9. Chapel and public church to be fully equipped.
10. Those in charge of the chapel empowered to see decorum maintained.
11. Twenty-four clergy to be appointed by the king of Spain, though if any are James's subjects, only by permission.
12. A bishop shall be in charge.
13. The superior shall have ecclesiastical authority over all connected with the Infanta.
14. The superior shall be able to banish from the household.
15. The superior shall be able to grant all dispensations and jubilees.
16. Servants not to take an oath of fidelity against their Catholic conscience, but swear in form as given, to the King and to the public good.
17. No laws shall apply to the ecclesiastics and they will be under the authority of the superior.
18. No laws in England or elsewhere to apply to children of marriage, who may freely inherit.
19. Infanta may appoint Catholic wet-nurses.
20. Infanta's bishop to enjoy his full rights and dignity.

21. Charles and James to promise the Catholic King that the marriage will not be dissolved.
22. Children to remain with the mother at least to the age of ten.
23. All alterations caused through death or absence in the household to be the responsibility of the king of Spain.
24. All the above approved to receive parliamentary ratification.
25. All the above to receive papal ratification.

The oath referred to in clause 16 was as follows:

'Ego N. Juro et promitto fidelitatem Serenisimo Jacobo Magnae Britanniae Regi et Serenisimis Carolo Principi Walliae, et Mariae Hispaniarum Infanti, quam firmiter et fideliter observabo; et si quid contra personas honorem, et dignitatem regiam praefatorum Regis et Principum, statumve, et commune bonum Regnorum intentari cognovero, statim renuntiabo dictis Domino Regi et Principum, aut ministris ad id constitutis.'

I Name *swear and promise obedience to King James of Great Britain and to their highnesses Charles, Prince of Wales, and to María, Infanta of all Spain, which I will firmly and faithfully observe; and if I should learn of anything being planned contrary to the honour of their persons and the royal dignity of the aforesaid King and their highnesses, to their estate or to the common good of the kingdoms, I will immediately report it in person to the King and their highnesses, or to the ministers appointed for this purpose.*

In addition, James and Charles swore four oaths, with the Prince making an additional binding promise concerning the interpretation of article 22 above:

i.   no laws directly or indirectly to be employed against Roman Catholics in England, Scotland or Ireland.
ii. perpetual toleration to be permitted in private homes.
iii. nothing to be done, either directly or indirectly, to the Infanta against her religion.
iv. parliament to confirm everything and abrogate all existing penal laws within three years, and never to make new ones, as far as lies in our power (*quantum in nobis erit*).
v.   in addition, the Prince promises that the children of the marriage will remain with their mother till the age of twelve.

NOTES

1 The documents were drafted new style by the Spaniards. The articles passed to Bristol were dated 13 December 1622, and the exchange of promises by Charles and Felipe took place on 4 August 1623.

2 *Tratados*, pp. 323–4.

3 Ibid., p. 60ff. [see also *Hauptinstruktion en Gregors XV*, pp. 35–6]; to be precise, the text deduced by Gardiner is not the version that was given to Bristol, but most probably the version that was sent to Rome, as indeed Francisco de Jesús says. This is because in Gardiner's version the age until which the children are to remain with the Infanta is higher, which almost certainly reflects the fact that Bristol had indicated this was no problem and so it was incorporated in the copy produced for the pope. See below, nn. 4 and 5. Gardiner's text remains of value, as it incorporates the embellishments proposed by the papacy, which were subsequently discarded or moved to the additional oaths.

4 In the December document, there is an aside in clause 17 dealing with any offences committed by ecclesiastics in the Infanta's household. It mentions that the earl of Bristol has verbally agreed that serious offenders will not be dealt with by the bishop accompanying the Infanta, but will be sent to Spain for trial. It had already been agreed between the two sides that this was unlikely to occur and so was of no real consequence, and the aside did not reappear in the version of this text that was passed onto Rome nor in the final treaty; see *Tratados*, p. 335, note a.

5 Ibid., p. 338, note a, and p. 324.

6 See Gardiner, iv. 398–9.

7 See above, ch. 12, n. 20.

8 I have silently extended the abbreviations in this document, but respected wherever possible the original punctuation.

9 A simplified translation of this part of the text addressed to Bristol is as follows:

> If the pope grants the dispensation, it would be distressing for the Infanta to live in a country where Catholics are persecuted. It would be inconvenient to include the following clauses in the agreement, and also it is proper for James's Catholic vassals to understand that the following concessions stem from his clemency in order to make them even more loyal subjects. Therefore the King and the Prince of Wales will bind themselves in a separate letter by their royal promise, as often given to the Spanish king's ministers, to the effect that no Catholic in their kingdoms will be persecuted for following the Catholic religion or receiving all the sacraments quietly in their homes, nor will there be any persecution in the form of oaths or any other pretexts concerning the Catholic religion.

Appendix 3:   The Prince of Wales to the Earl of Bristol Revoking the Proxy, September 1623

Charles's holograph letter from Segovia halting his proxy is transcribed in the *Eighth Report of the Royal Commission on Historical Manuscripts*, Report and Appendix, Part 1, Section 1 (London, 1881), pp. 215b–216.[1] For a discussion of the letter's provenance, see Gardiner, v. 118–19. It was also quoted by Bristol in his *Defence*. It confirms that Charles had taken steps to revoke the proxy (and effectively break the match) earlier than previously thought.[2] As to Charles's claim that he had not discussed his scruples concerning whether an unconsummated marriage might be ended by a subsequent papal dispensation, he had, in fact, been furnished with an exhaustive reply. The Palatinate is not mentioned in either of the two versions of this letter given here.[3]

> Bristol. You may remember that a little before I came from St Lorenzo [the Escorial] I spake to you concerning a fear I had that the Infanta might be forced to go into a monastery after she is betrothed; which you know she may do with a dispensation. Though at that time I was loath to press it (because I thought it fit at the time of my parting, to eschew distastes or disputes as much as I could) yet since considering that if I should be betrothed before that doubt be removed and that upon ill-grounded suspicions or any other cause whatsoever they should take this way to break the marriage, the King my father, & all the world might justly condemn me for a rash-headed fool, not to foresee & prevent this in time: Wherefore I thought it necessary by this letter to command you not to deliver my proxy to the king of Spain until I may have sufficient security both from him and the Infanta that after I am betrothed a monastery may not rob me of my wife, & after ye have gotten this security send with all possible speed to me, that if I find it is sufficient (as I hope I shall), I may send you order by the delivering of my proxy to dispatch the marriage. So not doubting but that ye will punctually observe this command, I rest your loving friend,
>
> CHARLES P.

James O. Halliwell, *Letters of the Kings of England now first collected from the Originals* (2 vols, London, 1848), ii. 229, printed a copy of the following shorter version of this letter, now to be found in BL, Add. ms 2232, fo. 18v. Halliwell erroneously suggested this copy was in the Prince's hand. The letter is dated 9 October but Halliwell dated it to November 1623, presumably confusing date and month. It is headed 'from the seaside'. The date is puzzling even as 9 October o.s. or n.s., since Charles had embarked on 18 September and arrived back in England on 5 October. I assume the shorter version of the above letter was sent from Santander just as the Prince was safely departing, in case the original letter entrusted to Clarke had not yet been handed over to Bristol.

BL, Add. ms 2232, fo. 18v.

The Princes l[ett]re from the seaside nono: octob[e]r.[4]

Bristoll you know that I told you I feared when
I came away that the Infanta might goe to a
Monastery after I was contracted by vertue of
a dispensacion graunted from Rome, and soe the
marriage might be broken, and they K[ing] my father
and all the world, might condemne mee and accompt
me a rash headed foole not to have p[re]vented it,
And therefore doe not dispose of my Proxie untill
you heare more from mee, for such a Monastery
may robb[5] mee of my wieffe, soe not doubtinge but
you will observe p[ar]ticularly this I leave you.

NOTES

1 A modernised version taken from the *Historical Manuscripts Commission* is to be found in Sir Charles Petrie, *Letters, Speeches, and Proclamations of King Charles I* (London, 1935).
2 This letter was unnoticed by Cogswell, *Blessed Revolution*, pp. 107–8.
3 See *Tratados*, p. 242.
4 9 Oct. n.s. is 29 Sept. but Charles set sail on 18 Sept.
5 Halliwell reads 'pill'.

Appendix 4:   Charles's Entourage in Spain

Of those gentlemen who went out to Madrid, it is difficult to be certain who actually attended on the Prince in Madrid and for what length of time.[1] For instance, towards the end of May it was reported that 'most of the Prince's train have not seen the Prince's face as yet'.[2] This was largely due to the fact that the normal excesses of courtly life were of necessity curtailed since Charles had to make do with two rooms in the palace. For a variety of reasons, the official lists drawn up for the household (first by Charles and then revised by James) are not indications of who actually served. Sir Richard Wynn's name, for example, does not appear on the Prince's original list and is crossed out on the King's.[3] Those who did set sail did not necessarily reach their destination. Both Dr Maw and Lord Compton seem never to have got further than Burgos, and at Charles's request several of his servants, including Lord Vaughan and Sir Richard Wynn, left Madrid shortly after arriving.

To add to the confusion, when his servants first landed Charles ordered various members of his household to turn back there and then. This order he countermanded more than once, creating both confusion and disobedience.[4] Those who did make it found themselves lodged outside the city in a house rented from the duke of Monteleón for 2,295 *reales* and 18 *maravedís* or slightly over £63 a month.[5] Howell says they whiled away the hours playing cards and Wynn's brother in London heard a rumour

> that all the letters to private men that come by post, are continually suppressed and burnt, because there should be no intelligence given of what they do intend to do in the Spanish business . . . They are kept in a house of the Duke de Mount de Lyons out of Madrid, all the Prince's company by themselves, & must not much stir abroad . . .[6]

Under these conditions it is not surprising that Lord Carey left Madrid after a month, arriving back at court on 26 May.[7] The Prince feared 'the heat of the year coming fast on' would prove too much for his elderly courtier, who had been sent by Elizabeth I earlier in his career to explain to James that she was not responsible for his mother's death. In addition, various important figures visited the capital without seeming to hold office under the Prince, such as Buckingham's brother-in-law, the earl of Denbigh, as well as the earl of Carlisle (whose path crossed with some of Charles's servants as he was making his way home and as they were just arriving in Spain).[8] When Charles departed the Spanish court, Lord Kensington (Henry Rich, who the following year became the earl of Holland) acted as captain of the Prince's Guard.[9]

Buckingham had his own retinue. It included Sir George Goring, who left the Prince's court in mid-July,[10] and perhaps the Favourite's young nephew by marriage, James Hamilton, earl of Arran, who may have served his kinsman rather than the Prince. Arran appears to have been one of the very first to follow Charles to Madrid and seems to have remained there throughout the visit, as a Lord 'Hamiltor' departed from Madrid with the Prince.[11] The notorious convert to Catholicism and son of an Anglican archbishop, Tobie Mathew, also visited Charles in Madrid without ever have been formally attendant on the Prince.

Below is Sir Richard Wynn's record of the names and offices of the gentlemen who set out for Spain in the *Adventurer*.[12] Some of the offices mentioned were in the King's household (e.g. Carey as chamberlain); others were in Charles's household (e.g. Cottington as secretary). The importance of this list is that it reminds us how King and Prince felt able to alter the normally rigorous rules governing the composition of a princely household as and when they felt necessary.

Officers:

Master of the Horse	Viscount Andover (Thomas Howard)
Master of the Wardrobe	Lord Compton (Spencer Compton, son of earl of Northampton)
Chamberlain	Lord Carey (Robert Carey, Lord Carey of Leppington, later first earl of Monmouth)
Comptroller	Lord Vaughan (John Vaughan)
Secretary	Sir Francis Cottington
Gentleman of the Bedchamber	Sir Robert Carr[13]

Gentlemen of the Privy Chamber:

Sir William Howard
Sir Edmund Verney
Sir William Crofts

Sir Richard Wynn

Mr Ralph Clare

Mr John Sandinells

Mr Charles Glemham

Mr Francis Carew

Gentlemen Ushers of the Presence:

Mr [Peter] Newton

Mr Younge[14]

Mr Tirwhitt

Wynn mentions that there were also:

5 grooms of the bedchamber

3 pages

2 chaplains [i.e. Dr Leonard Maw and Dr Mathew Wren]

NOTES

1   With the support of the National Library of Scotland, I am editing the Prince's accounts for 1623 (ms 1879). This will provide a fuller but still incomplete list of his entourage.

2   London, 20 May, Owen Wynn to Sir John Wynn, National Library of Wales, ms 466E/1105.

3   PRO, SP14/139, nos 46.1 and 46.2.

4   *Letters and Papers of the Verney Family* and Wynn, *passim*; also Carey, *Memoirs*, pp. 156–7.

5   NLS, ms 1879, fo. 31.

6   See above, n. 2.

7   PRO, SP94/26, fo. 249v.

8   Howell, *Epistolae*, pp. 285–8 [13 Aug.]. On 27 Feb. James had written: 'Noblemen you will have enough, and too many. Carlisle and Mountjoy already gone, Andover goes presently, and Rochford by land, Compton goes by sea, and I think Percy and Arran and Denbigh go by land' [J6].

9   See App. 5. For his captaincy, also see PRO, SP94/26, fo. 226.

10 NLS, ms 1879, fo. 27v.

11 *Gaçeta*, p. 171, where the following may also be among the English nobles who were with Charles when he left: conde de Enden (Denbigh?), conde de Arundel (Thomas Howard?), conde de Garlet (Carlisle?). A list 'of all my lords servants that are to attend him this Jorney' almost certainly refers to Buckingham's household, but the 40 servants mentioned do not include any great gentlemen, nor is there even a reference to Sir George Goring: see PRO 94/26, fo. 204.

12 Wynn, p. 299.

13 Endymion Porter should presumably be included as a gentleman of the bedchamber. 'Antonio' Porter and 'Tomás Crey' (?) were singled out as being of the Prince's chamber when farewell gifts were distributed.

14 Marked in the manuscript, 'Querie'.

Appendix 5:   The Farewell Inscription of *La columna del adiós*

Charles and Felipe said their goodbyes in the broad plain that lies below the Escorial. At the point midway between the Escorial and the small town of Guadarrama, just beyond the medieval hunting lodge of El Campillo, a monument was erected to mark the precise spot of the Prince's departure. It was set up within a matter of weeks if not days.[1] The orotund inscription was said to have been the work of the Jesuit, Hernando Chirinos de Salazar, one of King Felipe's preachers. That he was also confessor to the count of Olivares may explain why the duke of Buckingham's name was excluded, but despite the antipathy between the two favourites, this omission was unwarranted, as the earl of Bristol observed in December 1623. At some stage the column split into two. It was re-erected in simplified form in 1965 and is now known as *La columna del adiós.*

Hic ubi fausta sors tulit ad praerupti montis radices,
in late patenti Campillo, solemni Regum venatione nobili
sed insolentis rei eventu longe nobiliori.

Philippus Quartus Hispaniarum Indiarumque Rex catholicus,
et Carolus serenissimus Walliae Princeps pactis cum Maria
serenissima infanta nuptiis, ad quas (i fama per orbem) in Hesperiam[2]
propererat, dexteras dederunt et in amplexus peramantes ruentes,
pacis et amicitiae aeterna foedera pepigerunt.

O magnum et invictum regum par sine pari!
Nullus mehercule Hercules contra duos.
Ipsi potius contra omnes (perfidia fredente et invidia)
duo Alcidae solo saloque insuperabiles.

Siste Fama, non plus ultra[3]

Viderunt, suspexerunt, stupuerunt duo Austriacae sobolis
incrementa maxima, Carolus et Ferdinandus serenissimi infantes,
Gaspar Olivariorum excellens Comes, a belli statusque consiliis,
sacri cubiculi ac regii stabuli praefectus;

Didacus Carpentis Marchio, cui fas per sacratioris aulae limen.
Ex Britannis, Ioannes Comes Bristolius, orator extra ordinem;
Guilielmus Castonius legatus ex munere;
Baro Kensingtonius praetorianae militiae Britannicae princeps.

   Posteritati sacrum.

Here is where kind fate led, to the foothills of the sheer mountain, in *El Campillo*,
that stretches out and already is distinguished as the venerable hunting place of
kings, but much more so because of the conclusion of a remarkable event.

Philip the Fourth, Catholic king of all the Spains and of the Indies, and his
highness Charles, Prince of Wales, having arranged a marriage with her highness the Infanta María for which he had hastened south to these lands (go,
Fame, around the world), they offered their right hands and, rushing into very
loving embraces, pledged eternal treaties of peace and friendship.

O great and unconquered pair of kings without equal! By Jove, no Hercules
could stand against the two of them. Rather, they themselves stand against all,
with Treachery and Envy gnashing their teeth, two descendants of Alceus,[4]
unbeatable by land or sea.

   Stop here, Fame, there is nothing more than this.

They saw, they admired, they were stupefied – the two greatest progeny of the
House of Austria, Charles and Ferdinand, their highnesses the Infantes. Gas-
paro the most excellent count of Olivares, of the Councils of War and State, of
the sacred bedchamber and master of the horse.

Also the marques of Carpio, who also is permitted to cross the threshold of the
most holy palace. From Britain, John, the earl of Bristol, ambassador extraordinary; William Aston, resident envoy; and Lord Kensington, captain of the
British royal guard.

   Dedicated to those who come after.

NOTES

1 The sole modern source of information is the very full article by Gregorio de Andrés, 'La despedida de Carlos Estuardo, príncipe de Gales, en el Escorial (1623) y la columna-trofeo que se levantó para perpetua memoria', *Anales del Instituto de Estudios Madrileños*, 10 (1974), pp. 113–32. Don Gregorio was responsible for the column's partial restoration. I am grateful to Mr Richard Boyle of San Lorenzo de El Escorial for arranging the generous permission of the owners of El Campillo to visit the monument.
2 More precisely, the lands of the western Mediterranean, but meaning Spain and Italy.
3 This otherwise inexplicable reference is to the motto of the Emperor Karl V, Felipe's great-grandfather.
4 A heroic forebear of Hercules.

Appendix 6: The Exchange of Letters between James and the Infanta, April and August 1623

James's letter is interesting for two reasons: first for its reminder that Charles's infatuation with the Infanta was behind the journey to Madrid, and second because the King refers to her as his daughter, which is in line with the view that he too had fallen into the trap of believing that a marriage was all but agreed. The Infanta's reply is so formulaic that, even if it cannot be taken as proof of her reluctance to marry a Protestant, it is indicative of the rigidity with which the Spanish royal family normally conducted its affairs.

James to the Infanta, Theobalds, 27 Apr. 1623, PRO 94/26, fol. 195

Madame la renommée de vos vertus a non
seulement attiré [acquirré *crossed out*] comme un aymant mon
tres cher Filz de vous venir voir de loing, mais [m'a *interlineated*]
aussi rempli d'un ardent desir d'avoir l'heur de vostre
presence, et iouir de pouvoir embrasser une belle
Princesse en qualité de ma Fille, consolation nompareille

   Vostre tres affectionné Pere

Madame, the fame of your virtues has not only drawn like a magnet my very dear son to come from afar to look upon you, but it has also filled me with a burning desire to enjoy your presence and take delight in being able to embrace a beautiful princess as my own daughter, an unequalled consolation.

   Your very affectionate Father

Infanta María to James, 30 Aug. (or 20th, if o.s.),[1] BL, Harl. ms 6987, fol. 161

Señor

asido para mi de mucha estimacion la carta de
v[uestra] m[agestad] me significa su voluntad y a

ficion y aunque en anbas cossas pago a v[uestra] m[agestad]
en igual grado quedo reconocida dello y
con desseo de tener ocassiones en que satisfaçer
en quanto en mi fuere a tan gran deuda
correspondiendo tan bien en esto al gusto del
Rey mi Señor y mi hermano que tanto ama y
estima a v[uestra] m[agestad] y a sus cossas n[uest]ro Señor guar
de a v[uestra] m[agestad] como desseo de Madrid a 30 de
agosto 1623.

> de v[uestra] m[agestad] aficionadissimo
> Maria

At fol. 163, there is a contemporary translation which I have modernised as follows:

Sir

I was very glad to receive the letter your majesty hath been pleased to send me, by which your majesty showeth a good will and affection to me; and although in both these things I do correspond with equal degree and measure, yet I do acknowledge the favour, and with a desire to have some occasion to satisfy (as far as is in my power) to so great an obligation, being also answerable to this, the good pleasure of the king my lord and brother, who loveth and esteems your majesty so highly, as also all that belongeth to your majesty. God save your majesty as I desire. Madrid, 30 August 1623.

> *Your majesty's most affectionate*
> *Maria*

NOTES
  1   See the reference to a letter from the Infanta in B19 [1 Sept.].

Index